Ambition, Federalism, and Legislative Politics in Brazil

Ambition theory suggests that scholars can understand a good deal about politics by exploring politicians' career goals. In the United States, an enormous literature explains congressional politics by assuming that politicians primarily desire to win reelection. In contrast, although Brazil's institutions appear to encourage incumbency, politicians do not seek to build a career within the legislature. Instead, political ambition focuses on – and Brazilian political careers are constructed at – the subnational level. Even while serving in the legislature, Brazilian legislators act strategically to further their future extralegislative careers by serving as "ambassadors" of subnational governments. Brazil's federal institutions also affect politicians' electoral prospects and career goals, heightening the importance of subnational interests in the lower chamber of the national legislature. Together, ambition and federalism help explain important dynamics of executive-legislative relations in Brazil. This book's rational-choice institutionalist perspective contributes to the literature on the importance of federalism and subnational politics to understanding national-level politics around the world.

David Samuels teaches in the Department of Political Science at the University of Minnesota. He has been a visiting scholar at the Centro de Estudos da Cultura Contemporânea and at the Fundação Getúlio Vargas, both in São Paulo, Brazil. He received his Ph.D. at the University of California, San Diego, in 1998.

Ambition, Federalism, and Legislative Politics in Brazil

DAVID SAMUELS

University of Minnesota

CAMBRIDGE
UNIVERSITY PRESS

CAMBRIDGE UNIVERSITY PRESS
Cambridge, New York, Melbourne, Madrid, Cape Town, Singapore, São Paulo

Cambridge University Press
The Edinburgh Building, Cambridge CB2 2RU, UK

Published in the United States of America by Cambridge University Press, New York

www.cambridge.org
Information on this title: www.cambridge.org/9780521816717

First published 2003
This digitally printed first paperback version 2006

A catalogue record for this publication is available from the British Library

Library of Congress Cataloguing in Publication data

Samuels, David, 1967–
Ambassadors of the state : federalism, ambition, and congressional politics in Brazil /
David Samuels.
    p.   cm.
Includes bibliographical references and index.
ISBN 0-521-81671-8 (hb)
1. Federal government – Brazil – History – 20th century.   2. Legislators –
Brazil – Attitudes.   3. Ambition.   4. Legislative power – Brazil.   5. Politics,
Practical – Brazil.   6. Rational choice theory.   7. Brazil – Politics and
government – 20th century.   I. Title.
JL2420.S8 S26   2002
320.981 – dc21   2002024684

ISBN-13 978-0-521-81671-7 hardback
ISBN-10 0-521-81671-8 hardback

ISBN-13 978-0-521-03062-5 paperback
ISBN-10 0-521-03062-5 paperback

For ESB

Contents

List of Tables and Figures

FIGURES

Abbreviations and Acronyms

NEWSPAPERS

FSP: *Folha de São Paulo*
GM: *Gazeta Mercantil*
JB: *Journal do Brasil*
NYT: *New York Times*
OESP: *O Estado de São Paulo*

POLITICAL PARTIES*

ARENA: *Aliança Renovador Nacional* (National Renovating Alliance)
PAN: *Partido da Ação Nacional* (Party of National Action)
PCdoB: *Partido Comunista do Brasil* (Communist Party of Brazil)
PDC: *Partido da Democracia Cristão* (Christian Democratic Party)
PDS: *Partido Democrático Social* (Social Democratic Party)
PDT: *Partido Democrático Trabalhista* (Democratic Labor Party)
PFL: *Partido da Frente Liberal* (Party of the Liberal Front)
PL: *Partido Liberal* (Liberal Party)
MDB/PMDB: *Partido do Movimento Democrático Brasileiro* (Party of the Brazilian Democratic Movement); known as the MDB before a party-law reform in 1979
PP: *Partido Popular* (Popular Party)
PPR: *Partido Progressista Renovador* (Party of Progressive Renewal)
PPS: *Partido Popular Socialista* (ex-*Partido Comunista Brasileiro*) (Popular Socialist Party)
PRN: *Partido da Reconstrução Nacional* (Party of National Reconstruction)
PSB: *Partido Socialista Brasileiro* (Brazilian Socialist Party)

* *Note:* See Mainwaring (1999) for descriptions of most of these parties.

PSD: *Partido Social Democrático* (Social Democratic Party)
PSDB: *Partido da Social Democracia Brasileira* (Party of Brazilian Social Democracy)
PSL: *Partido do Solidarismo Libertador* (Party of Liberating Solidarity)
PST: *Partido Social Trabalhista* (Social Labor Party)
PSTU: *Partido Socialista dos Trabalhadores Unificados* (Unified Socialist Workers' Party)
PT: *Partido dos Trabalhadores* (Workers' Party)
PTB: *Partido Trabalhista Brasileiro* (Brazilian Labor Party)
PV: *Partido Verde* (Green Party)
UDN: *União Democrática Nacional* (National Democratic Union)

OTHER

BNDES: *Banco National de Desenvolvimento Econômico e Social* (National Economic and Social Development Bank)
CMO: *Comissão Mista do Orçamento* (Joint Budget Committee)
COFINS: *Contribuição para o Financiamento de Seguridade Social* (Contribution for Financing Social Security)
CONFAZ: *Conselho de Política Fazendária* (Council on State Finance Policy)
CPMF: *Contribuição Provisória sobre Movimentação Financeira* (Provisionary Contribution on Financial Transactions)
DIAP: *Departamento Intersindical de Assessoria Parlamentar* (Inter-Union Legislative Research Department)
FGV: Fundação Getúlio Vargas (Getúlio Vargas Foundation)
FPE: *Fundo de Participação dos Estados* (State Participation Fund)
FPM: *Fundo de Participação dos Municípios* (Municipal Participation Fund)
FRL: Fiscal Responsibility Law
FSE: *Fundo Social de Emergência* (Social Emergency Fund)
GDP: Gross Domestic Product
ICMS: *Imposto sobre Circulação de Mercadorias e Serviços* (Tax on Circulation of Merchandise and Services)
IMF: International Monetary Fund
IPI: *Imposto sobre Produtos Industrializados* (Tax on Industrialized Products)
IR: *Imposto de Renda* (Personal Income Tax)
MC: Member of Congress
NGO: Nongovernmental Organization
PIS: *Contribuição para o Programa de Integração Social* (Contribution for the Social Integration Program)
TRE: *Tribunal Regional Eleitoral* (Regional Electoral Tribunal)
TSE: *Tribunal Superior Eleitoral* (Superior Electoral Tribunal)

Acknowledgments

This book began as my doctoral dissertation in political science at the University of California at San Diego (UCSD). I thank the members of my committee, Professors Paul Drake, Matt Shugart, and Stephan Haggard, for reading and contributing to the development of each chapter. I particularly thank Professor Gary Cox, who patiently and carefully waded through draft after draft, offering priceless – and efficient – advice from start to finish. Every graduate student should be so fortunate. I also thank other UCSD faculty who took the time to read parts of my dissertation and offer comments: Gary Shiffman, Sam Kernell, and Victor Magagna.

I also benefited – directly and indirectly – from comments from and conversations with many friends and colleagues at UCSD, the University of Minnesota, and elsewhere, including Barry Ames, Scott Basinger, Octávio Amorim Neto, John Carey, Scott Desposato, Lisa Disch, James Druckman, Kent Eaton, John Freeman, Christopher da Cunha Bueno Garman, Ed Gibson, Mark Jones, Peter Kingstone, Mona Lyne, Scott Morgenstern, Al Montero, Tim Power, Marc Rosenblum, Phil Shively, Kathryn Sikkink, Gordon Silverstein, Steve Smith, Rich Snyder, and Frank Sorauf. I am also eternally grateful to Scott Mainwaring for his advice and encouragement.

For funding support I thank the National Science Foundation (Doctoral Dissertation Improvement Grant Number 963-1784), the UCSD Center for Iberian and Latin American Studies, the UCSD Friends of the International Center, the Benjamin E. Lippincott endowment in the Department of Political Science at the University of Minnesota, and the University of Minnesota McKnight-Land Grant Professorship endowment.

Parts of this book are revisions of published material. Parts of Chapter 5 appeared in the October 2000 issue of *Comparative Politics* and in the February 2000 issue of *The Journal of Politics*, and a version of Chapter 7 appeared in Scott Morgenstern and Benito Nacif (editors), *Legislatures and Democracy in Latin America* (Cambridge University Press).

This book would contain far more errors of fact and interpretation if it were not for my friends and colleagues in Brazil. My first thanks goes to Deputy Jacques Wagner (PT-BA) and to companheiro Athos Pereira, who introduced me to the intricacies of Brazilian politics before I cloistered myself in the ivory tower. In Brasília, Antônio Octávio Cintra, Lincoln Cardoso, Rosi Gomes, and Professor David Fleischer answered countless questions, helped arrange interviews, and gave my tired feet a place to rest.

I would also like to thank the many Brazilian colleagues who have discussed and debated their country's politics with me, and without whom I would not have learned quite as much as I hope I have: George Avelino, Socorro Braga, Argelina Figueiredo, Eduardo Kugelmas, Fernando Limongi, Marcos Mendes, Bernardo Mueller, Jairo Nicolau, Carlos Pereira, Lúcio Rennó, Brasílio Sallum Jr., Fabiano Santos, Rogério Schmitt, and Lourdes Sola. In addition to José Luciano dos Mattos Dias of Goés Consultores, several of the previously mentioned individuals also generously provided data that aided my work.

In São Paulo, I am grateful to the people at Centro de Estudos da Cultura Contemporânea for granting me an academic home for the 1996–97 year, and to the Fundação Getúlio Vargas/Escola de Administração de Empresas de São Paulo for providing an affiliation during 2001–02. A special thanks goes to Ricardo Sennes, Andrea Bueno Buoro, Cecília Cavalheiro, and Lídia Rebouças for all their help, and I am particularly indebted to Cláudio Couto for all the favors he has done for me, for providing such great insight into Brazilian politics, and for pointing out where the best mandiocas fritas, pizza, and Brahma chopp can be found in São Paulo. Finally, I must give credit where credit is most due: this book would not exist if not for the brilliant work of Fernando Abrucio, whose M.A. thesis (and later book), _Os Barões da Federação_, set that first light bulb off in my head. Without his book, I might still be floundering about, looking for a dissertation topic. With Fernando, I look forward to years of continued collaboration (and Corinthians games).

Introduction

Virtually all legislative theory rests upon the assumption that politicians are driven by the desire to win repeated reelection. Indeed, because it is so often taken at face value, John Carey recently noted that the reelection assumption "has reached near axiomatic status" (1994, 127) among political scientists. It is important to understand that this assumption implies not only that legislators direct their energies toward ensuring repeated reelection, but that they usually succeed in their efforts. All else equal, we expect little legislative turnover in systems where the reelection assumption holds.

At first glance, Brazil appears to be a case that confirms this assumption's validity. As in the United States, Brazilian incumbents do not require national party leaders' approval to run for reelection. Moreover, Brazil's electoral laws actually *encourage* incumbency. Incumbents do not have to battle to win renomination, because a "birthright candidate" (*candidato nato*) law automatically places their names on the next election's ballot (until 2002). Given this institutional backdrop as well as the idea's intuitive plausibility, several scholars have employed the reelection assumption to explain important aspects of Brazilian – and comparative – politics (e.g., Ames 1987, 1995a; Geddes 1994).[1]

Yet upon closer examination Brazil turns out to be a particularly perplexing case. Although its electoral laws encourage incumbency, in contrast to the United States (where turnover in the House is less than 10 percent with each election) turnover in the Brazilian Chamber of Deputies has consistently exceeded 50 percent.[2] A turnover rate this high appears to contradict the fundamental expectation of the reelection assumption – low turnover – and

---

[1] Other comparativists who have employed the reelection assumption include Cain, Ferejohn, and Fiorina (1987); Ramseyer and Rosenbluth (1993); and Epstein et al. (1997).

[2] In democratic elections. About two-third run with each election, and of those, about two-third win. I explain why *both* the rates of running and winning are both important to the reelection assumption in Chapter 2.

as a result such an assumption may not make much sense when applied to Brazil.[3]

In fact, in this book I argue that while Brazilian deputies can run for reelection and are even institutionally encouraged to do so, they confound political scientists' expectations and do not aim to build careers within the Chamber of Deputies, nor are they primarily interested in rising through the ranks of a national party. Instead, incumbent deputies exhibit a particular form of "progressive" political ambition: following a relatively short stint in the Chamber, they seek to continue their career outside the Chamber, particularly in state and/or municipal politics.

Scholars have employed the reelection assumption to explain the development of legislative institutions, the process of policy choice, and of course legislators' efforts to advance their own careers. Indeed, because scholars have applied the reelection assumption to Brazil, we already have a set of predictions about legislative behavior in that country that can be tested against competing hypotheses. For example, the reelection assumption generates the prediction that legislators seek access to "pork-barrel" goods in order to secure reelection. In contrast, a different motivational assumption might suggest that deputies engage in pork-barreling precisely to *leave* the legislature, in order to improve their chances of winning an extralegislative position.

The validity and thus utility of a methodologically individualist assumption depends on both its descriptive and predictive accuracy. The purpose of this book is not only to show that the reelection assumption has been incorrectly applied to Brazil – and by implication potentially elsewhere – but also to provide rational choice approaches in comparative politics with more solid theoretical support. By showing how a more nuanced understanding of political ambition can enhance our ability to explain electoral and policy processes and institutional dynamics in Brazil, this book should also encourage research on the consequences of different political career structures in comparative politics.[4]

Doing so requires a more sophisticated understanding of political ambition than we currently possess. Most countries do not restrict reelection, yet scholars have yet to explore the consequences of political ambition in a country like Brazil, where reelection is allowed or even encouraged but may

---

[3] Ames (e.g., 2001, 141–2) agrees that Brazilian deputies do not seek long-term legislative careers, but his analysis of pork-barreling, for example, (see Ames 1995a or 2001, 93–7) explores deputies' efforts to win reelection. See my analysis in chapters 6 and 7.

[4] Schlesinger (1966) pioneered research into the sources and consequences of political ambition. Black (1972) and Rohde (1979) formalized the approach in terms of utility maximization. All three focused on political offices in the United States. Likewise, Schlesinger (1991) demonstrated how the theory of ambition can be used to explain the nature of political parties in the United States.

not be legislators' primary goal.[5] As a result, political scientists are poorly equipped to provide theoretical insight about legislators' decisions, legislative politics and process, and executive-legislative relations in many political systems. Careful exploration of the structure and consequences of political ambition in comparative perspective will begin to fill this gap and encourage further development of rational-choice analyses in political science.

THE PROJECT: LINKING AMBITION AND FEDERALISM IN BRAZIL

Ambition shapes political behavior, but politicians do not operate in an institutional vacuum. Political institutions structure actors' behavior by shaping their self-perception, relative power, and strategies. To understand why the reelection assumption inadequately describes and explains Brazilian politics (and why it might also not apply elsewhere), I focus not only on the "micro" politics of legislators' ambitions but also take into account how Brazil's institutions shape the "political opportunity structure" (Schelsinger 1966, 11).[6] This requires a careful look at the institutions of federalism, which shape political ambition and strengthen state-based interests in Brazilian national politics.

Scholars have yet to fully focus on how federalism affects legislative behavior in Brazil and thus how federalism affects national-level political dynamics. In Brazil, federalism "matters" because its historical development and institutional configuration shape politicians' career strategies. These constraints and incentives in turn affect how politicians act while serving in the national legislature. In short, federalism shapes political ambition, and the consequences of ambition drive broader political processes.[7]

We can begin to understand the link between federalism and ambition in Brazil by considering the most basic tenet of ambition theory, that ambitious politicians pay close attention to the interests of those who may affect their career prospects. In this way, ambitious legislators may ignore their current vote bases in an attempt to appease potential future supporters (Schlesinger 1966, 5). This need to appeal to future supporters helps explain the link between federalism, ambition, and congressional politics in Brazil.

For example, we do not typically think that *state*-based pressures particularly motivate U.S. House members. Institutional contrasts between Brazil

---

[5] Carey's (1996) important work explored the consequences of limiting or prohibiting reelection.

[6] My research thus falls under the rubric of "rational choice institutionalism," with a strong dose of "historical instiutionalism." See Tsebelis (1990).

[7] Numerous scholars, especially Victor Nunes Leal (1975), have shown how state-level actors influenced local politics (and vice versa), but few scholars have emphasized how state-based politics can also influence national politics. The best treatment of this subject is Abrucio (1998).

and the United States shed some light on why this is the case. In the United States, Representatives are seated in one of 435 single-member districts. Apportioning districts generates real-world political battles, but at base House districts spring from mapmakers' imaginations: they have no institutional existence of their own and do not conform to the boundaries of any other government institution (except in states with only one representative). Consequently, House members represent, institutionally, nothing more and nothing less than their district. Simplifying for the sake of argument, this means that they represent the interests that exist and organize pressure, or come to organize pressure, within their district.[8]

In contrast, members of the Brazilian Chamber of Deputies are nominated and elected in at-large multimember constituencies that conform to state boundaries. This injects the nature of representation in the Chamber with an institutional dynamic found more commonly in upper chambers of federal systems, where senators are often elected in districts that conform to state or provincial boundaries. Furthermore, unlike in the United States, in Brazil state-level party leaders play an important role in determining the nominations for federal deputy. Thus, while many if not most successful Brazilian politicians depend on local municipal-level networks to start a political career, a politician who seeks election to the Chamber of Deputies enters a state-level game, and a politician who wins election as deputy does not simply represent an institutionally disembodied U.S.-style district. He or she represents a state. Thus, all deputies represent the interests that exist and organize pressure within their states.

State-based political pressures affect deputies' behavior in three ways. First, many deputies actively seek political positions in state government – before, during, and after serving in the Chamber. Given this desire, while serving as legislators deputies act to promote their own careers by currying favor with state-government officials and by cultivating political clienteles who will help them *leave* the Chamber for a state-level position. In this way, as I will explain in the chapters that follow, political ambition tends to favor state-based political interests and actors in Congress.

Second, although Brazil's use of an open-list proportional representation electoral system infuses legislative elections with a high degree of individualism (Ames 1995a, 2001), a focus on the electoral system draws attention away from the important ways in which state-level factors drive congressional elections. For example, the gubernatorial race influences the congressional campaign in each state to a much greater extent than the presidential race. All politics is not local or individualized in Brazil, nor is it highly

---

[8] Especially in the pre–Civil War era, state-level pressure did influence U.S. House members (and Senators, of course) to a greater degree. Among other factors, the decline of state-level pressure was a function of the decline of state party machines and of their control over nomination, and the advent of the Australian ballot and of party primaries.

nationalized: deputies' electoral success depends on their insertion into and connections with *state-level* political networks.

Third, in important ways federalism constructs the nature of legislative representation in Brazil. Whatever the direction of their career ambitions, and whatever the nature of their vote bases, deputies face intense pressure to "represent" their state in the Chamber after they win election. For most incumbents (i.e., except those who can rely entirely on "votes of opinion"), state-level actors and dynamics affect their future careers. Incumbent governors in particular possess tremendous powers to affect the contours of politics within their state (Abrucio 1998). Governors may also dominate many of the state's municipalities, which in turn means that "municipal" pressures on deputies may derive from state-level pressures. The importance of state governors over incumbent federal deputies also means that the president often deals directly with governors, not deputies, when doling out politically valuable pork-barrel resources in exchange for support within the legislature. Given the importance of state politics, which I will describe in more detail, deputies willingly respond to pressures from their state's government while they are in the Chamber. This holds even for opposition-party deputies, who fear being painted as "against" the people of their state. Thus, state-level politics plays a key – if sometimes unseen – role in national politics.

ON THE PATH – DEPENDENCE OF FEDERALISM IN BRAZILIAN POLITICS

The claim that federalism shapes the nature of political ambition and that this consequently shapes Brazilian national politics is essentially an argument for the path-dependent consequences of Brazilian federalism. While its social and political origins lie in Brazil's colonial (pre-1822) and imperial (1822–89) periods, federalism truly emerged in Brazil in 1889, after the military overthrew a hereditary monarchy. The republican constitution promulgated in 1891 copied a good deal from the U.S. constitution and codified a presidential, federal system of government. The subsequent period has come to be known as the "Politics of the Governors," because state governors for all intents and purposes dictated the flow of national politics as well as controlled politics within their states.

This period still casts a shadow over Brazilian politics. Despite two lengthy authoritarian and centralizing periods (the second of which only ended in 1985), on many measures Brazil remains one of the most highly decentralized federations in the world. Its degree of political and fiscal decentralization exceeds all other Latin American countries, and rivals or exceeds better-known federal systems such as the United States, Canada, and Germany. Since the "Politics of the Governors" period, territorial and largely nonprogrammatic cleavages have driven Brazilian politics (when competition was allowed, of course). By territorial cleavages I mean that states (e.g., as opposed to regions)

comprise the most salient arenas of political competition. Politicians compete to lead state-level parties, and compete for the votes of their state's
residents. Politicians could of course compete for votes according to many
other nonspatial political cleavages, such as race, religion, ideology, lan-
guage, or class, but throughout Brazilian history they have not for the most
part. Despite tremendous socioeconomic transformations and a number of
regime changes over the last century, state-based politics still greatly influences Brazilian national politics.

Although scholars have paid significant attention to certain continuities
in Brazilian history since the end of the "Politics of the Governors" era in
1930 (e.g., the strength of the national executive branch and the tenacity of
the local economic and political elite) we know relatively little about how
federalism may have limited centralization during either Getúlio Vargas'
Estado Novo regime (1930–45) or the 1964–85 military regime.[9] Still, scholars of contemporary Brazil increasingly recognize that federalism merits serious theoretical and empirical investigation. The most important recent works
are Frances Hagopian's *Traditional Politics and Regime Change in Brazil*
(1996), which explores the interaction between the centralizing direction
of the 1964–85 military regime and the state-based organization of Brazil's
traditional political elite, and Fernando Abrucio's *Os Barões da Federação*
(The Barons of the Federation) (1998), which explains the power of state
governors to influence contemporary Brazilian national politics. Other analysts, including Abranches (1993), Ames (2001), Camargo (1993), Lima Jr.
(1997), Mainwaring (1999), Montero (2000), Selcher (1998), and Souza
(1994, 1996) have also brought federalism to the fore. The main purpose
of this book is to build on this research by linking the recognized importance of Brazilian federalism to an understanding of how ambition shapes
Brazilian congressional politics and executive-legislative relations. Indeed, I
claim that the link between ambition and federalism is a necessary ingredient
to explaining important aspects of policy and process in Brazil.

ON THE IMPORTANCE OF UNDERSTANDING AMBITION
IN COMPARATIVE POLITICS

Brazil teaches us that close attention to the structure and consequences of
political careers can provide substantial analytical leverage into a wealth of
questions of interest to political scientists – leverage that existing theories
of legislative behavior cannot provide. In this way, my findings point toward
a more comprehensive understanding of the impact of political ambition in
comparative politics. Presently, the reelection assumption serves as the key
element in nearly all legislative theory. It has been used to explain important

[9] On these historical periods, see Medeiros (1986), Abrucio (1998) Chapter 2, Lima Jr. (1983),
   Camargo (1993), Love (1993), Campello de Souza (1994), and especially Pandolfi (1999).

aspects of democratic politics in the United States and elsewhere, including the evolution of legislative norms and institutions (e.g., Polsby 1968, Epstein et al. 1997); why legislators' take certain policy positions on any number of policy issues (e.g., Arnold 1990); how legislators decide to divvy up "pork-barrel" goods (e.g., Weingast 1979; Bickers and Stein 1994; Ames 1995b); and the emergence of legislative parties (e.g., Schlesinger 1991; Rohde 1991; Cox and McCubbins 1993).

A broader approach to the study of political ambition will reveal variations in legislator goals, which in turn will allow for construction of better-specified comparative rational-choice institutionalist theories on issues such as those mentioned previously. For example, in many countries where re-election is allowed but where turnover is relatively high, including several other Latin American systems (see e.g., Morgenstern 2002), we still lack a way to understand the *consequences* of different political career structures. By placing the Brazilian experience in comparative perspective, this book contributes to these important lines of research.

Furthermore, this book highlights the potentially critical role that subnational actors and institutions play in shaping legislators' career strategies, and thus in shaping national politics. In recent years comparativists have increasingly focused on the impact of federalism on party systems (e.g., Ordeshook 1996; Jones 1997); fiscal resource distribution (e.g., Rodden 1998, Oates 1999); economic growth (e.g., Weingast 1995); economic reform programs (e.g., Gibson 1997); decentralization and intergovernmental relations (e.g., Willis et al. 1998; Solnick 1999; Treisman 1999); and democratic transitions and consolidation broadly considered (Stepan 1997).

When scholars talk about how federalism affects national policy, they typically focus on how subnational governments articulate their interests in the *upper* chamber of the legislature. This book develops a new way to understand the impact of federalism, by showing how members of a *lower* chamber act to reinforce federalism. By showing how federalism affects the career goals, electoral strategies, and legislative behavior of Brazilian federal deputies, this book expands our understanding of the way in which federalism may affect both policy and process in comparative perspective.

Finally, my exploration of the consequences of political ambition in contemporary Brazil can also inform emerging work on the evolution of the incentive structure in the contemporary U.S. House. As I will argue, the structure of political careers in contemporary Brazil resembles in important ways the political career ladder in the early nineteenth-century United States, before the emergence of the "textbook" post-World War II House (Price 1971, 1975, 1977; Kernell n.d.(a), n.d.(b), 1977). For scholars of the U.S. Congress, the question is now "how did we get here, from there?" Given that Brazil is also "there" in a way, exploring the Brazilian case has the potential to teach us something quite interesting about the dynamics of the early U.S. Congress.

In sum, by positing and testing alternative hypotheses regarding the consequences of political ambition, this book not only provides significant insight into the Brazilian case but also contributes to the development of legislative theory in comparative politics and broadens our understanding of how federalism can influence national politics in cross-national perspective.

OUTLINE OF THE BOOK

This book is organized into three sections. Section 1 focuses on the first way in which subnational politics affects national politics in Brazil – through deputies' own career ambitions. In Chapter 1 I present a general framework for analyzing the structure of political careers. Then I build upon my basic hypothesis that political ambition in Brazil focuses on the state and local level. Using data from Brazilian legislative elections from 1945–98,[10] in Chapter 2 I present evidence that Brazilian politicians rarely build political careers within the Chamber of Deputies. In addition, I explain the absence of seniority norms in the Chamber as both a cause and a consequence of the low demand for a long-term career in the Chamber – the opposite of the argument that scholars have made for the presence of seniority norms in the U.S. House.

In chapters 3 and 4 I provide additional empirical evidence that deputies do not desire a career in the Chamber and that their ambitions are primarily directed at subnational government. Chapter 3 explores what I call "Congressional Hot Seats," wherein a large number of just-elected deputies take leaves of absence or resign their congressional seats in order to take a position *outside* the Chamber. Similarly, Chapter 4 shows that following a relatively brief stint in Congress, Brazilian deputies typically continue their political careers in state and/or municipal government. In sum, the chapters in Section 1 provide theoretical and empirical support for an alternative to the reelection assumption that highlights the importance of subnational politics for members of the Brazilian Chamber of Deputies.

Section 2 brings in the second way in which subnational politics drives national politics in Brazil, adding an institutional layer to the logic of political ambition in Section 1. Chapter 5 demonstrates how federalism shapes politicians' electoral strategies, and how this consequently affects executive-legislative relations. I focus on a concept I call the "gubernatorial coattails effect." In the United States, scholars have long known about the potential importance of presidential coattail effects, which can affect the distribution of seats in the legislature and thus affect the party system more generally (McCormick 1982). When an electorally powerful presidential candidate helps elect members of his party, his subsequent task of constructing a stable

---

[10] In Chapter 2 I explain why I include the period from 1964–85, when a military government controlled Brazilian politics.

legislative coalition is made easier. In Chapter 5, I assess the dynamics of presidential elections in Brazil, and argue that presidential coattails are generally weak. As a result, the president cannot use his personal electoral popularity as a tool to influence Congress. In contrast, "gubernatorial coattails" are quite long – in each state. That is, the race for governor shapes congressional candidates' campaigns. Consequently, gubernatorial coattails explain why state governors influence their state's congressional delegation, and thus how federalism directly impacts executive-legislative relations in Brazil.

Sections 1 and 2 help explain how federalism affects both the nature of political ambition and electoral politics in Brazil. The two components of this framework – federalism and ambition – also generate numerous hypotheses about legislative behavior and processes. In Section 3, I demonstrate the utility of this framework by exploring the implications of federalism and ambition for the real-world dynamics of congressional politics in Brazil.

Chapter 6 challenges the findings of scholars who claim that Brazilian deputies seek access to "pork-barrel" goods in order to win reelection. My argument about the nature of deputies' ambitions suggests that deputies' pork-barreling efforts, through submission of amendments to the yearly budget, ought to provide a highly *uncertain* political return even to those deputies interested in maintaining their seats. I test the relationship between pork and reelection success and find no significant relationship.

Chapter 7 addresses the question that Chapter 6 leaves unanswered: "If access to budgetary pork does not help win reelection, why do Brazilian deputies seek pork?" I argue that deputies seek to strengthen subnational interests (particularly state interests) in the budget process in an attempt to appease those who will influence their future careers and to lay the ground for a run for subnational political office. That is, in contrast to what the reelection assumption predicts, deputies do not seek pork in an attempt to *stay* in Congress; rather, they seek pork to continue their political careers *outside* Congress.

In Chapter 8 I explain the process of fiscal decentralization in Brazil that occurred from 1975 through 1994. I argue that while pressures from states and municipalities are necessary to explain fiscal decentralization, without adding in deputies' careerist motives any explanation would be insufficient. In Chapter 9 I explore the changes in intergovernmental relations under President Cardoso, 1995–2002. Although some have interpreted Cardoso's economic reforms as the beginning of a new period of recentralization, I argue that although the central government did bring much-needed coordination to Brazil's federation, Cardoso's reforms did not alter the president's reliance on state governors to drum up legislative support or the state-based nature of elections and political representation in Brazil. This continuity has important implications for the ability of future presidents to maintain or build upon Cardoso's reforms. The conclusion summarizes my findings and discusses their contribution to the literature.

SECTION I

Chapter 1

Ambition Theory and Political Careers in Brazil

"A politician's behavior is a response to his office goals."
—Joseph Schlesinger

INTRODUCTION

Ambition theory suggests that if politicians' behavior can be traced either wholly or partly to their office goals, then scholars can understand politicians' behavior by exploring their political careers. Given this hypothesis, a substantial number of scholars have explored the impact of political ambition in the United States.[11] Research focuses on the House of Representatives, where scholars typically assume that politicians are "single-minded seekers of reelection" (Mayhew 1974, 17).[12] Fewer scholars have explored political careers outside the United States,[13] but the growth within comparative politics of the study of institutions and the roles politicians play within those institutions suggests that scholars ought to seek to uncover how politicians' career incentives influence their legislative, partisan, and electoral behavior.

In this chapter I begin to explore the political careers of members of the Brazilian legislature. While numerous studies of Brazilian legislators' *background* characteristics exist (e.g., Leeds 1965; Verner 1975; Fleischer

---

[11] The literature stemming from Schlesinger, Mayhew, Fiorina and others is vast. For examples, see Schlesinger (1991); Black (1972); Levine and Hyde (1977); Kernell (1977); Rohde (1979); Brady et al. (1997); Bianco and Stewart (1996); Buckley (n.d.); Gilmour and Rothstein (1996); Katz and Sala (1996).

[12] As Mayhew and other acknowledge, this is an artificial assumption. Nevertheless, I agree with Arnold (1990, 5n), who wrote that "Some legislators may make trade-offs among their goals, incurring small electoral costs in the course of achieving some other important goal. [However,] incorporating such realism into my theoretical model would make it vastly more complicated without any obvious gain in explanatory power."

[13] But see for example Smith (1979); Hayama (1992); Atkinson and Docherty (1992); Carey (1996); Epstein et al. (1997); Patzelt (1998); F. Santos (1999).

1976; Nunes 1978; A. Santos 1995), and some scholars have suggested that Brazilian politicians do not focus their career energies on the Chamber of Deputies (e.g., Packenham 1990 [1970]; Fleischer 1981; Figueiredo and Limongi 1996; F. Santos 1998), this book is the first to provide an empirical and theoretical treatment of incumbent deputies' career goals. I concur that Brazilian politicians do not focus their energies on building a career within the Chamber of Deputies, and in this chapter and the next three chapters I demonstrate that political ambition in Brazil begins and ends at the subnational level. Service in the Chamber serves merely as a springboard to higher office, at a lower level of government.

In this chapter I first discuss the study of political careers generally. I then ask two questions: what is the structure of political careers in Brazil; and why does Brazil have this political career structure? To answer the first question I explore the benefits, costs, and probabilities of winning several offices in Brazil. The sum of this information describes the "opportunity structure" (Schlesinger 1966, 11) Brazilian politicians face. To answer the second question, I highlight how federalism has historically shaped this opportunity structure in Brazil.

ON THE STUDY OF POLITICAL CAREERS

The Political "Opportunity Structure"

To discover what drives political ambition, we must first explore a country's political "opportunity structure." Three factors shape the political opportunity structure: the relative benefits of each office, the relative costs of seeking and/or holding each office, and the probability of winning each office given the decision to seek it (Black 1972; Rohde 1979).[14] Each factor is sensitive to a number of other variables. For example, the relative probabilities of reaching each office depends on the number of candidates, the number of offices at stake, as well as individual attributes of each candidate. I describe these factors in the following text.

The concept of an "opportunity structure" is simple, useful, and sufficiently broad for comparative research. However, most research on political ambition has focused on the United States (e.g., Schlesinger 1966, 1991; Black 1972; Rohde 1979; Brady, Buckley, and Rivers 1999), and this literature usually concentrates on the origins and consequences of careerism in the U.S. House of Representatives. What little comparative work that exists tends to focus either on careers within (and controlled by) national-level parties (e.g., see Smith 1979 on Mexico and Carey 1996 on Costa Rica), or on national-level legislative careers that are highly influenced by national-party

---

[14] Rohde (1979) argues that whether politicians are risk averse or risk taking also affects the opportunity structure, but for simplicity's sake I do not discuss this issue.

control (e.g., Epstein et al. 1997 on Japan; Cain, Ferejohn, and Fiorina 1987 on the United Kingdom; Hibbing 1998).

By focusing on national party and/or legislative careers, this literature thus largely ignores the possibility that *subnational* positions could hold significant attractions to career-minded politicians, including those who have already reached the national legislature, and ignores the possibility that subnational politicians may be more important to incumbent legislators' future careers than national party leaders. This was the case in the early nineteenth-century United States (e.g., Young 1966; Price 1975; Kernell 1977), and certainly remains a possibility in federal systems (where positions in state government may be important), in systems where municipal mayors hold great power and prestige, or in countries where a seat in the legislature appears to hold few long-term attractions. As I will show, the Brazilian case points to the importance of looking beyond national parties and national legislatures when mapping a country's "political opportunity structure."

Motivational Assumptions and the Political Career Ladder

Before I turn to the Brazilian political opportunity structure, it is important to state the assumptions behind ambition theory. I adopt a straightforward rational-choice approach and assume that politicians are instrumentally rational: they will, when making career decisions, examine the alternatives, evaluate these options in terms of the probability of their leading to victory or defeat (with the value of victory depending on the costs and benefits associated with the office), and choose the alternative that yields the greatest expected value (Black 1972, 146). We can formalize this relationship simply as:

$$U_i(\text{Running for Office o}) = P_{io}B_{io} - C_{io}$$

That is, the utility to individual "i" of seeking office "o" equals the probability of "i" attaining office "o" times the benefit to "i" of attaining office "o," minus the cost to "i" of running for office "o" (ibid.). Thus, an individual will run for an office only if the expected benefits of holding that office times the probability of obtaining that office exceed the costs of running for that office.[15] While the values of the variables in this simplified "calculus of ambition" are in reality endogenous and interrelated, for any country we can assume that the value of B_o is determined exogenously, at least in the short term. Moreover, by using real-world examples and comparisons across countries we may gain some insight into the ways in which politicians view

---

[15] The theory implies that a politician will run for the office with the highest PB-C, if that PB-C is greater than the utility of holding no office (U_{io}). We could call this the politician's "reversionary utility," whatever benefit the politician obtains from going to the private sector, for example.

the relative costs, benefits, and probabilities attached to various political offices.

I further assume that politicians hold "progressive" ambition. That is, given that $\{B_1, \ldots, B_n\}$ is the set of expected benefits of each office in the political system,[16] if $B_n \geq \cdots \geq B_1$ for all politicians, then it follows that a politician would always take a more attractive office if it were offered without cost or risk (Rohde 1979, 3). Finally, I assume that political careers – whether within or outside of legislatures – are *hierarchical*: a set of office benefits makes certain *organized* or sequenced career paths possible. The analyst must thus discern the "rungs" on the career ladder by describing the costs, benefits, and probabilities of seeking various political offices and then explaining the hierarchy of career paths that emerge, moving from the lower-rung offices to the top-of-the-ladder offices. In short, ambition theory guides research into political careers by focusing research on the relative costs, benefits, and probabilities politicians associate with different political jobs.

THE POLITICAL CAREER LADDER IN BRAZIL

Before attempting to answer the question "What is the structure of political careers in Brazil," we should know something about what offices an ambitious Brazilian politician might seek. Brazil is a presidential, federal system that resembles the United States in its basic institutional structure. However, far fewer positions are elective in Brazil than in the United States. In Brazil, the set of elective positions includes president and vice-president (1 each), governor and vice-governor (27 total), senator (83 total), federal deputy (513 total), state deputy (state assemblies are all unicameral, 1,069 total), municipal mayor and vice-mayor (5,500 approximately total), and city council member (75,000 approximately total). No judges, sheriffs, county clerks, school board members, or water district managers are elected in Brazil.

On the other hand, as was the case throughout much of U.S. history and is still the case in many countries, many important political positions in Brazil are appointed, such as minister of state, judge, head of a state-level executive-branch department, or countless other national-, state-, or municipal-level positions. One recent estimate gave the president the power to make 19,600 political appointments (L. Santos 1996, 224) (as compared to about 4,000 in the United States today), and governors also have the power to hire and fire hundreds or even thousands of people (depending on the size of the state).

Given this set of political offices, where in Brazil could a politician attempt to carve out a piece of "turf?" When assessing a potential job opportunity, an ambitious politician would ask three questions: (1) What's it worth to

---

[16] Here $\{1, \ldots, n\}$ is the set of political offices and B_0 is the average value politicians attach to office "o."

me?; (2) What are my chances?; and (3) What's it going to cost me? In an attempt to place political jobs in Brazil in hierarchical order, in this section I consider the answers to these questions.

What's it Worth to Me?

Here I describe the office benefits associated with five sought-after political offices in Brazil: federal deputy, national minister, state governor, state secretary, and municipal mayor.[17] In general, the benefits of office include pay and other perquisites, the size of the budget the office controls, the ability to influence policy, the patronage opportunities attached to the office, the length of the term, the reelection and advancement potential, and so forth. As a first cut to putting these positions in hierarchical order, I also present interview excerpts that illustrate how Brazilian politicians rank these positions. Interviews provide a window into how politicians view offices' relative values.[18] If politicians typically said a congressional career had the highest political value, this would point the empirical research in one direction. On the other hand, if they placed a congressional seat lower on the career ladder, research would head in a different direction.

The Value of a Seat in the Chamber of Deputies. Brazil's 513 federal deputies have considerable political prestige as representatives of districts that conform to state boundaries. Deputies serve four-year terms, with no restriction on reelection. They receive good pay (currently about $8,000 per month), free housing in Brasilia, four free air tickets to their home district every month, rights to hire several staff members at no personal expense, franking privileges, and many other perks. Deputies have the right to submit pork-barrel amendments to the yearly budget, they can participate in attempts to acquire additional funds for their states and regions, they sometimes nominate associates for positions in the federal bureaucracy, and they may be able to participate in important policy negotiations between the executive and the legislative branches.

All of these activities might bring significant benefits to the people in a deputy's district, and could focus media attention on the deputy. Thus, although the position of federal deputy may not concentrate *extraordinary*

---

[17] In Brazil, we can separate political offices according to their governmental level: national, state, and municipal. I counted twenty-three types of national-level positions that deputies have held, fifteen types of state-level positions, and three types of municipal-level positions. See Appendix 1 for a complete list of all positions.

[18] I conducted seventy-nine unstructured interviews with elected officials and high-level bureaucrats. Appendix 2 provides information on each interview. For a variety of reasons interviews with politicians suffer potential problems of bias, reliability, and validity and thus cannot be treated as data that one can readily quantify. They do, however, provide essential complementary information to the empirical data about deputies' actual career choices.

powers in the hands of an individual, the office potentially holds significant political attraction. Yet despite these potential attractions, Brazilian politicians consistently pointed to the relative political inefficacy of a Chamber seat.[19] For example, in response to a question as to why so many deputies opt to leave the Chamber for other jobs even *during* their term, deputies responded:

"Being a deputy is exhausting, a lot of work, and provides absolutely no results."[20]

"The political return for being in the executive is very, very large. For being in the legislature, it's very small."[21]

"When you're in the executive, you can measure the effects of what you do. In the legislature, this is difficult."[22]

"It's difficult to obtain recognition for legislative work … your name disappears from public view. The legislature is like political exile – it's a job, but everyone spends their time here thinking 'how is it that I can move on from here?'"[23]

One ex-deputy even claimed that serving as federal deputy in Brasilia *harmed* his political career, because it drew him far away from his electoral bases. He stated that

I perceived that if I didn't return [to state politics] to take care of my people, I would not last long in politics. I might have been able to win a second term, but by the end of my second term in Brasilia I would have been so far removed from things here that I would have been finished.[24]

In sum, although the position of federal deputy appears to offer some attractions, interviewed politicians consistently belittle the relative value of the office.

The Value of a National Portfolio. In 1997, 21 national civilian ministries existed in Brazil (Brasil. MARE 1996). From time to time, ministries are created (e.g., Culture and Science and Technology in 1985) or extinguished (e.g., Administration in 1989) (FGV n.d.). Ministers receive the same salary as a federal deputy, but the real attractions of the job are the perks, the pork, and the power of the pen. Ministers command an entire department of the national government, and are often chosen because of their leadership qualities in relation to Congress. Consequently, they receive a great deal of national media attention, and senators and deputies constantly seek them out.

---

[19] To precisely assess deputies' career ambitions, we would ideally survey all deputies during each legislature about their career goals. This proved unfeasible due to time and resource constraints, so I rely on interviews and inferences from deputies' observed behavior.
[20] Interview with Adhemar de Barros Filho.   [21] Interview with José A. Pinotti.
[22] Interview with Marcelo Caracas Linhares.   [23] Interview with Lúcio Alcântara.
[24] Interview with César Souza.

Ministries' political attractiveness vary: the Ministry of the *Casa Civil*, or Chief of Staff, has enormous political power but no budget and no direct control over hiring and firing, while the Finance Minister has a small budget but guides the national economy. This gives the Finance Minister considerable influence beyond the halls of Congress. Although ministries' attractiveness may vary, national ministries appear to offer considerably more political benefits than a seat in Congress because of their significant power and prestige.

The Value of a Governorship. Brazil's 27 governors serve four-year terms, with one consecutive or unlimited nonconsecutive reelection allowed. Armed with ample resources and mostly unhindered by oversight, governors in Brazil possess the power to influence federal deputies' electoral bases and career opportunities. This gives governors, and the states they rule, a voice in Congress (Abrucio 1998). Gubernatorial influence derives from control over state-government pork-barrel funds and over thousands of jobs in state bureaucracies. Governors also coordinate many large-ticket investments that involve federal-government funds, and they may control or influence many nominations to *federal* government posts in their state, in the second and third echelons of the federal bureaucracy. Notably, while few deputies expressed much interest in staying in the legislature, politicians typically expressed views like the one belonging to this ex-deputy:

The legislature was, for me, an accidental journey. I never felt like 'a legislator,' I never fully realized my potential there. Resources [for your career] come much more from the state government than from the federal government, and when I went to collect the return on my investment, I ran for vice-governor, not for deputy.[25]

Control over valuable political resources gives governors power over deputies' careers: if the deputy opposes the governor, either at the state or the national level, the governor can exclude him or her from the distribution of "credit," or refuse his requests to land his cronies plum jobs. Brazil's electoral system exacerbates deputies' vulnerability to gubernatorial influence. Given Brazil's at-large, statewide electoral constituencies, although some deputies concentrate their electoral bases in a few contiguous municipalities (Ames 1995a), deputies can and do seek out votes in any corner of their state. However, this is a double-edged sword. Even if a deputy has a concentrated vote pattern (which might seem more electorally secure than a dispersed vote pattern) he cannot afford to waffle in his support of the governor, because the governor can "sponsor" a competing candidate, for example by letting the newcomer take credit for a project, in just a part of the deputy's bailiwick.

In addition, governors hold power over municipal mayors, whom candidates for federal deputy rely upon to bring out the vote. Despite their

[25] Interview with Ivo Wanderlinde.

recent gains in fiscal resources, the vast majority of Brazilian municipalities remain tremendously poor. Although mayors can seek funds in Brasilia,
governors control the distribution of resources for many municipal public
works projects. Political criteria often determine this distribution; thus, mayors seek to remain on good terms with the governor. Consequently, a deputy
must also remain on good terms with the governor, for the governor might
punish the deputy by cutting off "his" municipalities from state-government
programs. The mayors in the "punished" municipalities would then turn to
a different deputy, one presumably on better terms with the governor.

Few checks and balances exist at the state level to contain governors'
political machinations. State legislatures make little effort to oversee state-
government spending (Azevedo and Reis 1994). Instead, state deputies
scramble to enter the governor's party coalition, knowing that if they fail
to do so, they will be cut off from the resources they need to advance their
careers (Abrucio 1998). Governors can also nominate their cronies to the
one organ that might oversee state government, the *Tribunal de Contas do
Estado*. The state legislature must approve these nominations, but governors typically "buy" support for their nominees easily, assuring himself that
his actions will never be scrutinized (ibid.). Finally, scant public accountability exists at the state level. In comparison to municipal or national government, the public cares relatively little about what state governments do
(Balbachevsky 1992).

In short, control over sizable budgets, the power to hire and fire, an electoral system that leaves deputies' electoral bases vulnerable, and little accountability provide Brazilian governors with an arsenal of carrots and sticks
they can employ against politicians in their state. This gives them influence
over federal deputies, which in turn gives them the power that national party
leaders have in other countries: influence within Congress. In sum, a governorship offers more benefits than a seat in the Chamber (or the Senate), but
it remains unclear whether it ranks higher than a ministry.

The Value of a State Portfolio. Every state in Brazil has a secretariat modeled on the national ministry. Salaries of state secretaries are lower than
that of a federal deputy,[26] but the office's attractions, like those of the national ministries, are political, not financial: prestige, pork, and the pen. State
secretaries run entire state-government departments. In some states, these departments have larger budgets and more power to hire and fire than some
national ministries. Because they are constantly on the road inaugurating

---

[26] In São Paulo, Brazil's wealthiest state, the base salary of a high-end state official was about
R$5,800/month in August of 1997, at the time equal to about U.S.$5,800/month. A few
state officials, such as lawyers for state-government corporations, earn much more, but
these positions are not typically held by career politicians (*OESP* 4/17/96, p. 6).

state-government public works projects, state secretaries also receive substantial media attention. The prestige and power of these offices lift state secretaries into a position as much-feared candidates for (re)election as federal deputy or even governor.[27]

Politicians typically pointed to the attractiveness of a state secretary position. The example one ex–state secretary provided is worth quoting at length:

A politician prefers an executive-branch position to being in the legislature, because it gives him a better chance to lay the ground for his next election. As a secretary you increase your exposure to the public. Take the Secretary for Sports and Tourism. You'd think that this secretariat is not that politically valuable, but it really is, even though its budget is small, because all over the state, there are sports clubs that the state sponsors . . . politicians have a lot of success with these groups, because the government builds little stadiums, puts in soccer fields, sponsors sports tournaments. The Secretary is always there. Imagine, if the Secretary of Sports pays for your team's jerseys, or sponsors your team's tournament. Most people can't afford this stuff by themselves, so they're grateful. It's much easier this way, being in the executive, than being in Congress, where you're mixed in with a pile of others, with more competition for attention. Every congressman's complaint is that he has problems getting media attention. Few deputies appear in the media.[28]

Other deputies who had served as state secretaries echoed this statement. One stated that,

When I was a state secretary, I was more effective. I felt more useful to my state than I do holding a seat in Congress. The exercise of an activity within one's state ends up being more gratifying in both the sense of working for the public benefit and working for your own benefit, because you're closer to the people, closer to the problems of your voters.[29]

Given the powers and prestige associated with state secretariat positions, and what politicians say about those positions, we have reason to believe that a state secretariat offers substantially greater benefits than a seat in the Chamber of Deputies.

The Value of a Municipal Mayoralty. The smallest unit of government in Brazil is the municipality, akin to the county in the United States. Brazil has

---

[27] Deputies may use the position of state secretary to boost their personal vote base and then subsequently run for deputy again, but this does not imply that the deputy is particularly interested in a *career* in the Chamber. In fact, the opposite is true: the seat in the Chamber is the "fall-back" position. Many deputies win reelection several times, only to leave during each term for a "better" position outside the Chamber, in their home state. They exhibit congressional careerism in one sense, but in the more important sense they do not. See Chapter 4 for more details on this phenomenon.

[28] Interview with Luiz Gonzaga Belluzo.　　　[29] Interview with João Henrique.

over 5,500 municipalities, ranging in size from tiny hamlets of a few hundred souls to the city of São Paulo, with a population of nearly 10 million. Mayors serve four-year terms, and can run for one consecutive or as many nonconsecutive terms as they please. Like the other positions, while a mayor may make a good salary, political power is what makes the position attractive: in every municipality, the mayor is the local political "boss," the person the people turn to with requests. Across Brazil, city councils are weak; the population looks instead to the mayor to solve local problems.[30]

The political attractiveness of a mayoralty depends on the size of the municipality: in larger and wealthier municipalities, the mayor controls a good number of political appointments and a sizable budget, and has the final word on the division of the spoils. Moreover, like state secretaries, the mayor gets considerable media attention and political credit for implementing public works programs within the municipality. Sixty-five percent of Brazil's municipalities have fewer than 10,000 voters, but 119 municipalities have over 100,000 (TSE 1996). Half this number of votes will elect a federal deputy in any state. Thus, a successful mayor from a larger municipality can reasonably expect to count on considerable local support if he were to seek a different political post when his term expires.

A position as municipal mayor in one of these larger municipalities offers more political prestige and power than does a seat in Congress. As one deputy stated,

In a Chamber of 513, a deputy can't stand out. It's rare, very rare. Many deputies don't feel that they have any power. Whereas a mayor, even of a medium-sized city, he's the boss. He is the power, he has the power of the pen. In the Chamber, nobody has the power of the pen. It's impossible for the average deputy to feel that he has any power.[31]

Another explained why mayors have a much more political impact than deputies. I quote from an exchange with an ex-deputy who had recently run for mayor in his hometown:

Deputy: A deputy suffers a tremendous erosion of electoral support back in his home bases, particularly in larger cities, because he is not the one who attends to the population directly in terms of implementing public works projects. If you spend a lot of time as a deputy, your image becomes one of somebody who hasn't done anything for the city.
Author: Even though you may have access to the budget, through the yearly amendments?
Deputy: Yes, this still might mean a loss of support because the mayor is the one who is going to *implement* the amendment and take credit for it. So, many deputies run for mayor for this reason. It's important for a politician to be a candidate for mayor.

---

[30] On municipal institutions, see Couto and Abrucio (1995) and Andrade, ed. (1998).
[31] Interview with Alberto Goldman.

Especially in the larger cities, where he can show that he has some influence, that he's accomplished important things.[32]

Another politician summed up this perspective by affirming that

From the point of view of a political career, a mayoralty represents a real advance. Many deputies say . . . that winning the race for mayor of his principal city is the most important thing that could happen to him. It represents the crowning achievement of his career, his highest aspiration.[34]

Summary. Thus far I have only explored the benefits of each office: national minister appears most desirable, and governor also seems quite attractive. Without analysis of the costs and probabilities of attaining each of these positions, we cannot discern where these two positions fall on the hierarchy of political positions in Brazil. However, positions in the executive branch of *subnational* governments, such as governor, state secretary, or mayor of one of Brazil's many larger municipalities, do appear to provide greater political payoffs than does a position as federal deputy. One politician encapsulated his colleagues' views and affirmed that

There's a strong tendency for a person in the legislature to have interest in a position in the executive. Either as governor or mayor of a good-sized city. These are more able to establish their presence politically, to stand out more. Governors and mayors have the power, like the president, to set their own budget and distribute resources, which of course brings benefits to the executive. Executive positions provide more status, and consequently more political projection.[34]

Given only deputies' comments about the benefits of office, a seat in Congress appears to hold but a middling position.

What are My Chances?

The calculus of ambition remains incomplete without an exploration of the probabilities a politician might associate with obtaining each office. For example, while a ministry might be most attractive, it also might be nearly impossible to obtain. Thus, the estimated probability of reaching an office will affect a politician's expected utility from attempting to reach that office.

Certainly, the hardest office to achieve would be national minister, because fewer than a dozen of these positions open up in any given legislature to career-minded politicians (see Chapter 3). Moreover, career politicians do not typically fill all ministries.[35] They typically fill only the "politicized" ministries, such as Transportation (which controls the road-building budget),

---

[32] Interview with Airton Sandoval.   [33] Interview with Antônio Carlos Pojo do Rêgo.
[34] Interview with Onofre Quinan.
[35] For example, in August 1997 eight of the twenty-one ministries were held by people without long-term political careers. These were Finance (Pedro Malan), Communications

Agriculture (which controls subsidies and investments in that policy area), and Labor (which controls a great number of political jobs). Overall, as a result of the relative scarcity of ministerial positions, only about 1 percent of elected deputies reach the ministry.

Politicians have a slightly better chance of reaching the statehouse, because Brazil has only twenty-six states plus a federal district that elects a governor. On the other hand, each state also has a vice-governorship, and each governor also controls a secretariat. The probability of attaining a position in the secretariat is significantly higher than that of governor (e.g., about one in ten sitting deputies obtains a secretariat during his or her term – see Chapter 3). Likewise, although Brazil has over 5,500 municipalities, only about 100 of these are worthy political prizes for a politician who has reached the Chamber of Deputies. Given that a mayoral race is a plurality race,[36] a politician's chance of winning compared to winning a race for deputy would be relatively low.

In sum, of the five positions I analyze here, deputies probably estimate that their chances of obtaining the position of minister as the most difficult, followed by governor and vice-governor, followed by mayor, state secretary, and then deputy.

How Much Does it Cost?

Finally, let us estimate the costs associated with seeking each office. I estimate costs in monetary terms, although we could certainly associate other costs with running, such as opportunity costs, or stress-induced health problems. I generate this estimate by comparing the relative costs of running for several offices in Brazil and the United States. In doing so, we can infer what an average politician is willing to spend to reach that office – and consequently also gain an idea of how valuable politicians consider each office.

The monetary costs of obtaining a national ministry are no higher than that of obtaining a Chamber seat, because deputies are nominated from within the Chamber. Winning gubernatorial candidates, on average, declared about U.S.$2.5 million in donations in 1994.[37] And, as Table 1.1 shows, in

(Sérgio Motta), Administration and State Reform (Luís Carlos Bresser Pereira), Culture (Francisco Weffort), Education (Paulo Renato Souza), Sports (Pelé), Foreign Relations (Luís Felipe Lampréia), and Health (an interim minister). While Motta, Weffort, Bresser Pereira, and Souza had all previously held powerful positions, their careers are not typically political: Motta was Fernando Henrique Cardoso's campaign finance manager, Weffort is best known for his works as a professor, Bresser Pereira is a well-known economist and banker, and Souza has made a career as an educator. Lampréia is a career diplomat, and Pelé requires no explanation.
[36] Or majority runoff if the city has over 250,000 people.
[37] Brazilian campaign finance law requires declaration of contributions, not expenditures, so I assume that the former equals the latter (candidates must declare contributions to their own campaigns). See Samuels (2001a, 2001b, 2001c). I was unable to find data on the average cost of running for governor in the United States.

TABLE 1.1 *Campaign Expenditures for Brazil and the United States*

Position	Brazil 1994	United States 1986
Senate	377,000	3,200,000
Lower Chamber	94,000	397,000
State Legislature	34,000	62,000

Sources: Gierzynski and Breaux (1993, 521); Federal Elections Commission (1998); Samuels (2001a, 2001b).

Brazil, using declared campaign donations, winning candidates for federal deputy raise about 2.75 times more money than do winning state deputy candidates, and winning senate candidates declare about four times more than winning federal deputy candidates. In the United States, using the declared campaign expenditures, winning House candidates in 1986 declared 6.4 times as much as a winning state legislature candidate, while winning senate candidates declared expenditures fifty times larger than state legislative candidates.[38] (In 1994, the one Brazilian Real was worth approximately one U.S. dollar.)

Little information exists regarding the costs of mayoral races in Brazil or the United States, but for Brazil we can compare the relative costs of a campaign for governor of São Paulo state with that for mayor of São Paulo city. The winning gubernatorial candidate in São Paulo in 1994 spent at least U.S.$10 million, and the winner of the 1996 mayoral race also spent at least U.S.$10 million (*Veja* 9/11/96, p. 8–15). Although lack of information impedes generalizing, this finding at least implies that mayoral races in the larger cities may generally be quite expensive, much more so on average than a race for deputy.

The U.S. and Brazilian campaign finance figures are not directly comparable – the Brazilian figures are donations, while the U.S. figures are expenditures – but even if donations do not accurately reflect expenditures in Brazil, we have no reason to suppose that the ratio of expenditures between offices differs from the ratio of donations between offices. That is, the true cost of a seat in the national legislature in Brazil is most likely about three times the cost of a seat in a state legislature. This is the crucial figure: the *relative* cost that candidates attribute to each office in each country permit inferences about how politicians apprise the expected utility associated with each office. The numbers thus suggest that U.S. politicians value a House seat much more than a seat in a state legislature relative to their Brazilian counterparts.

[38] I use 1986 figures for the United States because that is the year I found information on state legislative elections. In 1986, senate candidates declared donations of U.S.$3.1 million, and congressional candidates declared donations of U.S.$397,000, so the difference is not that great (FEC 1998).

In sum, in Brazil the most expensive race is that for governor. Appointed positions are of course the "cheapest," although typically a politician has to spend a great deal of money to reach the level at which he or she would be considered a significant "player" to be considered for appointment. Depending on the size of the city, the second-most expensive race is probably mayor, although senate races in the larger states are probably more expensive than many mayoral races. Finally, while running for federal deputy costs most than running for state deputy, a comparison of campaign spending ratios across offices in the United States implies that Brazilian politicians estimate that a seat in the Chamber generates a lower relative expected utility than a U.S. politician estimates for a seat in the House, compared to other positions in each political system.

WHICH WAY IS UP?

Given the information provided, a picture of the hierarchy of political positions in Brazil emerges. Politicians clearly value the position of governor more than state secretary, state secretary more than state deputy, senator more than federal deputy, and minister more than federal deputy. Deputies also report that the benefits of a state secretariat or of serving as mayor are greater than of being federal deputy. Indeed, not one deputy interviewed stated that the benefits for being in the Chamber exceeded those for being in the state or municipal executive.

As for costs, running for federal deputy appears expensive, but it costs less than running for any other elective office except state deputy (excluding the possibility that deputies run for mayor of tiny towns), and in any case many politicians may run for federal deputy simply to place themselves among the available candidates for an appointed position in either the national or state level executive branch. Finally, although the probability of winning a seat in the legislature is certainly higher than winning a race for executive office at any level of government, it remains unclear whether the balance of costs and benefits of *repeatedly* winning a seat in the Chamber outweigh the costs and benefits of seeking office *outside* the Chamber.

The sum of the benefits, costs, and probabilities points to the conclusion that a Chamber seat is but a middling position on the Brazilian career ladder. In subsequent chapters, I provide a wealth of empirical support for this claim. Before presenting this data, in the next section I provide an argument as to *why* Brazil has this hierarchy of offices, by describing both macro- and micro-level structures that generate incentives for politicians to desire a position in state or municipal government over a career in the Chamber.

WHY DOES BRAZIL HAVE THIS CAREER STRUCTURE?

The answer to this question requires a two-level "New Institutionalist" approach. New Institutionalism suggests both that political institutions shape political outcomes, because they shape actors' strategies, and that historical "path-dependent" factors shape institutions.[39] Schlesinger (1966; 1991) employed a similar logic to explain political ambition: at a macro level, historical factors shape the opportunity structure, and on a micro level, the opportunity structure systematically molds individual politicians' behavior. This suggests that to understand the structure of political careers we must explore politicians' immediate environment (which may be most important for actual career decisions) as well as how historical factors affect politicians' calculations.

At the macro level, the evolution of federalism in Brazil has shaped the political opportunity structure, creating incentives for individual politicians to concentrate their career goals at the state level – and more recently the municipal level – instead of the national level. In turn, at the micro level, politicians' ambitious office-seeking behavior helps keep a seat in the Chamber at a relatively low value.

Federalism and the Political Opportunity Structure in Brazil

Since 1889, a series of regime changes has rocked Brazilian politics, swinging the country from decentralized to more centralized political systems. Most Brazilian and Brazilianist scholars have focused largely on the centralized side of this coin. However, some scholars have recently begun to investigate the political consequences of federalism in Brazil (e.g., Medeiros 1986; Camargo 1993; Hagopian 1996; Abrucio and Samuels 1997; Abrucio 1998). My argument depends on, and hopefully invigorates, the strength of this flip side of the interpretive coin of Brazilian history. I argue that despite several periods of political centralization, federalism and subnational politics are the key factors that have shaped and continue to shape the political opportunity structure.[40]

Federalism and Empire? From independence in 1822 until 1889, Brazil was ruled as an officially unitary, hereditary monarchy. The Emperor centralized great political power in his hands, as he could nominate and dismiss provincial "presidents" (state governors) at will, nominate and dismiss cabinet members, and call elections to the national parliament (suffrage was highly restricted).

The first signs of opposition to this centralization emerged in the 1870s, when the Republican Party called for "unity through decentralization" (Carvalho 1993, 66). Political elites outside of Rio de Janeiro (then Brazil's capital) chafed under the central power and argued that, with the growth

---

[39] Thelen (1999) explains well the various facets of the New Institutionalism.
[40] This is not the place to delve into the various historiographical debates surrounding either the periods I explore or the reasons for the transition from one to the next. I merely hope to establish that Brazil has historically been and continues to be a comparatively highly federalized polity.

of the coffee economy in São Paulo and elsewhere, political and economic power no longer coincided. Carvalho (1993, 73) concludes that "there have been since Colonial days ... important centrifugal forces," and that toward the end of the nineteenth century these forces invigorated the arguments for political decentralization (see also R. Graham 1990, 267–8).

Federalism under the "Old Republic." The monarchy was overthrown in 1889 and replaced with a republican form of government. Scholars agree that the dominant political characteristic of this 1889–1930 "Old Republic" was the so-called "Politics of the Governors," because of the rapid emergence of a dramatically decentralized federal system in which the governors of the most powerful states (generally, Minas Gerais and São Paulo) dominated the country's politics. The Old Republic's federal constitution granted extensive powers to states, such as the ability to impose "export" and "import" taxes on *interstate* trade within Brazil. States could recruit troops in times of peace (prohibited by the Mexican constitution of 1917 and the Argentine constitution of 1860), and many created what were essentially independent armies (Dallari 1977). Brazilian states could also write their own civil, commercial, and penal codes (again unlike Mexico and Argentina), and had exclusive domain over subsoil mineral rights. Finally, Brazilian states could negotiate loans on the international market independently of central-government authority (Love 1993, 186–7). In sum, in stark contrast to the other emergent *de jure* federalisms in Latin America at the time, Brazilian federalism granted extensive *de facto* power to states.[41]

Because less than 6 percent of the population could vote up through the 1930s, politics during the Old Republic became an intraelite game, dominated by rural landholders, and divided according to *state* boundaries. No national political parties emerged; instead, most states had only one party, which existed only in that state, and which generally acted cohesively (Campello de Souza 1987; Fausto 1987). A small elite dominated all aspects of politics within each state, and controlled political competition from above. During the Old Republic, the incumbent state government regulated elections, which meant that state power brokers had the power to annul or verify electoral results, not federal legal authorities (Nunes Leal 1975, 226). Clearly, even if we cannot precisely pinpoint the origins of Brazil's political opportunity structure in the Old Republic, this period certainly consolidated the strength of federalism.

1930–45: Federalism under Vargas? Getúlio Vargas, a former governor of the state of Rio Grande do Sul, led the overthrow of the Old Republic in 1930.[42] While historians have focused on Vargas' personal dominance

---

[41] Of course, due to their profound poverty, most states could scarcely enjoy these powers, and depended on resources from São Paulo to survive.

[42] For a very brief introduction to the forces behind the 1930 revolution, see Skidmore (1967, pp. 3–12). A more extensive treatment is Fausto (1987).

of politics or on the growth of the central government during the 1930–45 period,[43] we must also note that Vargas ultimately failed to shift the basis of Brazilian politics away from state-based intraelite competition. For example, Love (1993, 208) notes that the 1934 constitution limited states' powers relative to the Old Republic, but states continued to serve as electoral districts, which "inevitably signified the reappearance of state-based political parties. In this way politics seemed to be tending toward the norm of the Old Republic."

Yet in 1937 Vargas engineered a *coup d'etat* and declared himself dictator, beginning a short but important period (until 1945) known as the "New State" (*Estado Novo*). He revoked the 1934 constitution, promulgated a new one, and proclaimed the end of federalism: Brazil became a *de jure* unitary state, with the states now called "administrative units." Vargas abolished all state parties and directly nominated state "interventors," who replaced the elected state governors. In a well-known demonstration of his intention to destroy federalism, Vargas publicly burned each state's flag.

Yet this project was more rhetoric than reality. The "ex-states" continued to administer much of the government apparatus: state tax receipts from 1938–45 were 56 percent of national tax receipts, while in Mexico at the same time (a *de jure* federal state), state tax receipts were only 17 percent of national tax receipts (Love 1993, 210).[44] Love writes that during the *Estado Novo*, "states conserved important powers and continued to innovate, above all in terms of social policy. And ironically, fiscal federalism continued" (1993, 180). In short, a great deal of continuity characterized the Vargas era, despite the growth of the central government and formal political centralization. When Vargas left the scene in 1945, decentralization and federalism still characterized many aspects of Brazilian politics.

1945–64: Federalism and the Democratic Experiment. Following Vargas' ouster in 1945, Brazil began its first experience with mass democracy. During this period, states and state governors regained powers they had lost, and state politics once again became the locus of politicians' career ambitions. Because governors were directly elected and because the governor controlled politically valuable resources, Abrucio (1998, 56) writes that "much more than the parties, the state executives organized deputies' electoral life...the governor, as a rule, commanded the state's political life. Deputies depended on him." Moreover, in terms of legislative politics, from 1945–64 "a new politics of the governors surged forth, and the state delegations in the Chamber of Deputies had sufficient power to bargain for more resources from the Treasury for their clients" (ibid.). Thus, despite Vargas' efforts from 1930–45 to centralize and nationalize politics and his creation of ostensibly "national"

---

[43] See for example, Skidmore (1967), Wirth (1970), Sola (1987), Levine (1970).
[44] Love further notes that the federal government's portion of tax receipts actually *declined* from 1938–45 relative to 1930–7 (ibid.).

parties in 1945, political elites retained their state-based political allegiances throughout his reign and into Brazil's first democratic period (Camargo 1993; Campello de Souza 1994).

1964–85: Federalism and Military Rule. Like Vargas, the military commanders who took power in 1964 also failed to dramatically transform the nature of Brazilian federalism because they also failed to transform the Brazilian political elite's organizational structure, based on state politics (Hagopian 1996; Abrucio and Samuels 1997). Soon after the coup, military leaders realized that governors' strength could undermine their plans for political centralization. Consequently they attempted to reduce governors' and state political elites' power. Although the military allowed legislative elections to continue (in an effort to maintain a semblance of popular legitimacy), they eliminated direct elections for governor, and instead nominated state governors themselves. However, this policy backfired: traditional elites resisted military meddling in their affairs, and military-nominated governors failed to unite them behind the regime's project. This weakened the regime's political base of support among its ostensible allies.

This emerging tension between the military and its civilian political allies, as well as overblown economic expectations, led to electoral disaster in 1974, when the military-sanctioned opposition party gained significantly in congressional races. Subsequently, the military faction favoring redemocratization and a gradual transfer of power to the regime's civilian allies won the upper hand, and military President Geisel and his allies began to return power to state governors and reintegrate state-based traditional elites, who remained formally allied to the regime and who of course did not want to lose power to the opposition (Ames 1987; Hagopian 1996).

Because the military chose this strategy, no new *national* political elite emerged, and political elites in all states successfully resisted central-government imposition of state executives, preserving their traditional organizational structure, based on state politics. Contrary to their early centralizing plans, by returning power to states during the *abertura*, the military would strengthen federalism and aid the rise of state governors as the transition advanced (Abrucio and Samuels 1997).

1985–Present: A "New Politics of the Governors?" Federalism in contemporary Brazil is not the same federalism of a century ago. Today, the central government is vastly more powerful, municipalities possess much greater political and fiscal autonomy, and, unlike during the "Old Republic," no one state or small group of states dominates the federation. Still, despite a century of dramatic political, social, and economic transformations, the institutions of Brazilian federalism remain quite strong. To this day state governors wield extraordinary power, and states control a good deal of total government revenue – more so than in most federations (see Chapter 8).

State-based political disputes also continue to play a key role in *national* electoral politics (see Chapter 5). In short, federalism in Brazil continues to divide the political elite along territorial lines. Following redemocratization, although some presidents have been stronger than others, federalism has been reinvigorated to such a degree that state interests in congress, fortified by gubernatorial strength, have blocked or delayed presidential reform initiatives in important areas (Abrucio 1998; Mainwaring and Samuels 1999; Montero 2000).

Summary: Federalism and the Opportunity Structure. On a macro level, the historical development of Brazilian federalism has shaped and continues to shape the political opportunity structure. State borders and the quest to control or at least participate in the machinery of state government have defined political competition since the Old Republic. Instead of demolishing state-based political ties, periods of authoritarianism merely "froze" them (Hagopian 1996). Moreover, neither Vargas nor the 1964–85 military leaders encouraged the emergence of a new, truly national political elite that could win large numbers of votes across the country and over time. As a result, when electoral competition began after periods of dictatorship, political elites concentrated on winning power at the state level, not the national level. (In Chapter 3 I explain how the political evolution of municipalities has altered the opportunity structure).

The flip side of the persistence of state borders for defining political competition in Brazil is the relative absence of strong *national* political cleavages, whether class-based, ethnic, religious, or linguistic, or otherwise ideological.[45] The absence of such national cleavages has meant that state-based elites have lacked strong incentives to form strong national party organizations. That is to say, although parties may be cohesive on the floor of the legislature (Figueiredo and Limongi 2000a), this cohesiveness does not result from deputies' recognition of a nationally shared electoral fate, à la Cox (1987) or Cox and McCubbins (1993) or from some form of top-down imposition, as in pre-1999 Venezuela's parties (Coppedge 1994; Crisp 1999) or the pre-2000 PRI in Mexico (Weldon 1997).

The way that federalism shapes the opportunity structure in Brazil resembles that found in the nineteenth-century United States, where politicians concentrated on obtaining office in state and/or local government (Young 1966; Kernell 1977). Of course, the opportunity structure in the United States has evolved so that state and local positions no longer hold the same attractions, but this has not occurred in Brazil, despite several regime changes and dramatic socioeconomic developments. We cannot attribute the rise of the congressional career in the United States to the increase in the importance of

---

[45] However, Soares (1973) (among others) has argued that *regional* cleavages have been strong throughout Brazil's history.

the national government relative to subnational governments, because this happened in Brazil as well. The key in the United States appears to be the emergence of *nationalized* electoral competition over the purpose of federal government. Thus the key to why the opportunity structure in Brazil has not changed so that congressional careers are relatively more important lies both in the persistence of federalism as a defining political cleavage and in the lack of clear *nationalized* political-partisan cleavages.

UNSTABLE REGIMES + PERSISTENT FEDERALISM = STABLE PREFERENCES?

The macrohistorical story tells one side of the careerism coin. Historical factors have shaped the Brazilian opportunity structure, and given this picture, we have good reason to believe that politicians would value subnational positions highly, and less reason to believe they would value a career in a national party or in the national legislature.

It might be unreasonable to believe that the average Brazilian politician thinks about career strategy given only his or her knowledge about broad historical patterns. Instead, we might more plausibly assume that a politician's immediate environment directly impacts his or her decisions. I argued previously that federal deputy appears to be a middle-ranking position on the Brazilian career ladder. Let us assume for the moment that I am right. What does the persistence of strong federalism throughout a century of regime changes in Brazil mean to an individual politician's immediate environment?

At the micro level, we can suppose a mechanism that keeps the benefits of being a deputy relatively low, having to do with the interaction of the strength of federalism, the length of Chamber careers, the institutionalization of the Chamber, and the relative benefits of a seat in the Chamber compared to other positions. If I could describe such a mechanism, we would know not just that Brazilian politicians *have* certain preferences about the relative importance of a Chamber seat, but we would know something about *why* they have them.

Numerous scholars have argued that if legislative careerism exists, then we should also see an "institutionalized" legislature, with an internal hierarchy of offices (e.g., a committee system) and nondiscretionary norms for distributing those offices (e.g., a seniority system) (Polsby 1968; Polsby, Gallagher, and Rundquist 1969; Price 1971, 1975, 1977; Epstein et al. 1997). Logically then, if a hierarchy of legislative offices accessed through seniority exists then the value of a legislative career will tend to increase. This implies that the nature of political careers and the structure of legislative institutions are mutually reinforcing. Figure 1.1 illustrates this line of reasoning. I dichotomize legislative careerism into either "High" or "Low" for simplicity's sake:

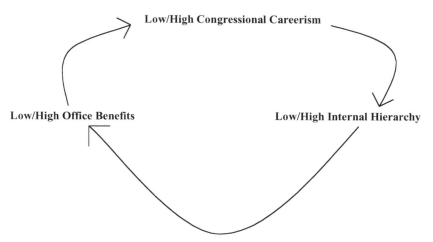

FIGURE 1.1 The Impact of Low or High Congressional Careerism on Legislative Organization.

If careerism dominates in a legislative body, individually rational politicians will want to regularize their career advancement by institutionalizing a hierarchy of positions one could climb as one accumulates experience, and by attempting to increase the relative benefits of holding office (Epstein et al. 1997). Likewise, when politicians establish a hierarchy and increase the relative value of holding legislative office, they will also have greater incentives to develop a congressional career. Mayhew (1974) posited the most famous example of this dynamic when he claimed that members of the U.S. House designed the internal rules of the legislature to suit their reelection goals perfectly. This situation is an equilibrium: career goals generate the internal legislative structure, and that structure then serves to maintain careerism.

On the other hand, when legislative careerism is absent, politicians have few incentives to amass power in the legislature over time or to institutionalize norms that would encourage legislative careerism, such as a seniority system. With no guarantee that repeated reelection will result in a steady increase in political power, relatively few politicians will want to build a congressional career. Thus, both "High" and "Low" legislative careerism and "High" and "Low" levels of internal hierarchy and office benefits are equally mutually reinforcing, and both are equilibria.

This hypothesis supposes that the length of careers within a legislative body, a legislature's internal organization, and the benefits of a legislative seat covary together, spiraling "up" or even "down," or holding in a steady state. Thus, to move from a legislature filled with politicians uninterested in a legislative career to one resembling the modern U.S. House, some exogenous force would have to enter the equation, as numerous scholars have argued for the emergence of the modern U.S. House (e.g., Price 1971, 1975, 1977).

On the other hand, we would be puzzled to see, for example, situations where legislative careerism is high, and legislative institutionalization and office benefits are low, or vice versa.[46]

If I am correct that Brazilian deputies have few incentives to make a career in the Chamber, this argument implies that we should observe an undeveloped hierarchy of offices within the legislative body, and no clear norms for distributing those offices. To support the claim that Brazil is "stuck" in the "Low" cycle described by Figure 1.1, we must gather empirical data on political careers, the internal distribution of power in the legislature, and so forth. In the next three chapters I present data from 1945 to the present confirming that the structure of political careers in Brazil has changed relatively little over a long period of time, except for an increase in municipal-directed careerism. To show that federalism continues to shape the political opportunity structure, I explore not only the length of congressional careers, but also what Brazilian deputies do during and after their congressional terms. Because analysts have not undertaken this task, existing theories of Brazilian legislative politics remain incomplete.

CONCLUSION

In any political system, ambitious politicians seek to climb a career ladder. Where offices are located on the ladder depends on the relative costs, benefits, and probabilities of attaining each office – the "political opportunity structure." I described the political opportunity structure in Brazil, which provided tentative support for my hypothesis that Brazilian politicians do not value a career in the Chamber of Deputies relatively highly, but instead focus their career energies on positions in subnational government. I also posited some of the macrostructural features maintaining this situation. I argued that there is a fundamental relationship between political careerism and the structure of legislative institutions. The crucial behavioral implication of this argument is that when politicians do not seek to build a long-term career in a legislative body, they lack incentives to develop an internal hierarchy of positions and nondiscretionary norms for distributing those positions. In turn, this very incentive structure discourages politicians from developing a legislative career. In subsequent chapters I investigate this phenomenon in depth.

---

[46] This logic supposes that individual politicians, and not party leaders, make the decisions about whether to run for reelection or not. A party-centric nomination dynamic might change this.

Chapter 2

In the Absence of Congressional Careerism: Short Stints, Flat Hierarchies, and Low Payoffs in the Chamber of Deputies

INTRODUCTION

In Chapter 1 I hypothesized that Brazilian politicians do not seek to build careers in the Chamber of Deputies. Instead, they view a Chamber seat as a potential stepping-stone to a more powerful office, typically at the executive level in state and/or municipal administration. I also tried to explain why this career path exists by noting that legislative careerism is associated with the institutionalization of a hierarchy of positions, and of norms regulating access to such positions, within a legislature. When politicians desire long-term careers in a legislative body, they will create a hierarchy of positions and nondiscretionary access norms. In the absence of legislative careerism, neither hierarchy nor such norms should exist.

In this chapter I provide evidence to support this hypothesis. First, I present quantitative evidence of the rates at which Brazilian deputies seek and win reelection. I gathered data from all legislative elections held from 1945–98, including the "controlled" elections during the dictatorship,[47] and show that legislative turnover is fairly high and that legislative careerism is extremely rare in Brazil. I also show that the relatively stronger, more prominent legislators tend to run for positions outside the Chamber, while weaker deputies are more likely to run for reelection. This is not only additional evidence of a low incentive to develop a career in the Chamber, but also helps explain the high turnover rate.

Second, to explore the relationship between careerism and legislative organization, I examine whether or not we see a hierarchy of positions and universalistic norms allowing access to those positions in the Chamber of

[47] Democratic elections were held for the first time in Brazil in 1945. Although the military controlled the executive branch and purged dozens of members of Congress during its 1964–85 rule, it only briefly shut Congress down, and continued to hold regularly scheduled elections as part of its quest for "legitimacy." Controlled legislative elections were held in 1966, 1970, 1974, and 1978.

Deputies.[48] I find no established hierarchy of legislative offices, an insignificant role for committees, and no seniority system, all of which ought to be associated with the absence of careerism. In sum, this chapter provides evidence that explains the absence of legislative careerism in the Brazilian Chamber of Deputies.

THE ABSENCE OF CAREERISM: RUNNING AND WINNING REELECTION

The most obvious indicators of legislative careerism are the rates at which members run for and win reelection. Both indicators are important for demonstrating that politicians do or do not desire a long-term career in a legislative body. The rate of running for office is of obvious importance, but the rate of winning also has theoretical relevance. Following the logic that permeates the story of the "incumbency advantage" in the United States, if most legislators desire a long-term career in the same institution, they will create institutions that will help them achieve that goal. Conversely, if reelection is not the most prized objective, then politicians will fail to create institutions that protect their positions. Thus, the rate of winning reelection also can tell us much about the degree to which legislative careerism dominates politicians' career objectives.

Seeking Reelection

Table 2.1 presents the average percentage of deputies who sought reelection in each election year from 1945 to 1998, beginning with the first chance for reelection in 1950 (controlled elections are italicized).[49] In democratic elections, the average percentage of deputies seeking reelection is 73.8 percent.[50]

One might consider this rate "high" rather than "low," but this number hides important dynamics that tend to overestimate deputies' preferences for reelection and thus for a career in the Chamber. First, many deputies either take a leave of absence to serve in municipal, state, or national government during the term, or actually resign during the middle of the term to take a position as municipal mayor (see Chapter 3). Deputies who win election to

---

[48] The three indicators (careerism, hierarchy, norms) are derived from Polsby's (1968) three conditions for the "institutionalization" of a legislature: boundedness, complexity, and universalistic norms. I use more specific terms, but the reasoning is similar.

[49] This calculation excludes *suplentes*. For details on how I calculated reelection rates, see Appendix 2.1 of Samuels (1998).

[50] The apparent increase in the number running for reelection may be temporary, or may be a result of the law that allows mayors and governors to run for reelection. This demands further study, but in any case changes in career structures typically occur over decades and the changes in legislative organization tend to follow the changes in legislative career structures.

TABLE 2.1 *Percentage of Deputies Seeking Reelection*

Year	Percentage
1950	66.0
1954	68.6
1958	75.4
1962	74.8
1966	80.5
1970	61.9
1974	81.8
1978	82.1
1982	74.9
1986	64.1
1990	70.1
1994	78.7
1998	80.2

Source: Author's compilation.

the Chamber but who then take a leave of absence are obviously not primarily concerned with building a career *as a deputy* – even if they win repeated reelection! Any notion of careerism in Brazil must take into account the large numbers of deputies who take leaves of absences but who nevertheless run for reelection.

Second, because deputies who become mayors are not technically eligible for reelection, we cannot include them in the calculation of the denominator for the total number of deputies eligible for reelection. For example, in the 1995–8 legislature, thirty-two deputies won election as mayor and resigned. This deflated by 6.2 percent the total number of deputies eligible for reelection, which of course serves to inflate the apparent percentage of deputies desiring reelection. In the end, both the numerator and the denominator that result in a percentage of deputies running for reelection obscure important facts about the direction of political careers in Brazil: by including those deputies who run for reelection but who use the position in the Chamber as merely a fall-back position and excluding deputies who won election as mayor, the apparent proportion of deputies who "desire" reelection increases by over 15 percent.

Do the Best Candidates Run for Reelection?

Another indicator that the rate of running for reelection hides important dynamics about the nature of political ambition in Brazil is that the more experienced and more effective deputies – that is those who are considered the best legislators *per se* – are more likely to seek to leave the Chamber

TABLE 2.2 *Political Experience of Deputies Running for Reelection vs. for Other Positions*

	1991–94 Legislature		1995–98 Legislature	
Previous Position Held	% Running for Reelection	% Running for Other	% Running for Reelection	% Running for Other
Ex-Governor or Senator	3.2%	6.7%	3.2%	11.9%
Ex-State Secretary	28.2%	32.0%	29.2%	32.9%
Ex-Mayor	14.9%	24.0%	19.4%	31.3%

Source: Author's compilation.

and seek another position. Consequently, the incumbents who do run for reelection are relatively weaker candidates.[51]

The incumbents who choose not to run for reelection are more experienced and are considered more prominent. Table 2.2 shows that deputies who choose to run for positions outside the Chamber are more experienced politicians to begin with: they are more likely to have held important political offices at the state and/or municipal level *prior* to their election to the Chamber. Thus, the deputies who choose to leave the Chamber at the end of a term are more likely to be those with already well-established political careers at the beginning of a term.

In addition, deputies who run for reelection tend not to be considered the best legislators in the traditional sense. Every year, a nonpartisan watchdog group publishes a list of Brazil's "Congressional Elite" (Departamento Intersindical de Assessoria Parlamentar [DIAP] 1994, 1998). This designation categorizes deputies by their capacity to sway others' opinions, articulate positions, and negotiate agreements, and for their technical capacity and specialization in specific policy areas. Unfortunately for the development of legislative professionalism, these elite tend not to dally long in the Chamber. Instead, they typically move on after one or two terms. For example, in both 1994 and 1998, DIAP designated 28 percent of those who ran for statewide office among the congressional "elite," while only 15 percent of those who decided to run for reelection were managed to obtain "elite" status. In brief, the political "heavyweights" in the Chamber typically choose not to run for reelection, but to seek positions outside the Chamber.

Winning Reelection

When considering the direction of political ambition, we must also recognize that while the rate of running for reelection is important, it is not the

---

[51] This and the following three paragraphs are based on Samuels (2000b).

TABLE 2.3 *Percentage of Deputies Winning Reelection*

Year	% Win, All	% Win 2nd Term	% Win 3rd Term	% Win 4th Term	% Win 5th or > Term
1950	50.0	50.0	—	—	—
1954	69.2	66.4	75.0	—	—
1958	62.7	57.6	71.2	65.8	—
1962	73.4	68.9	71.7	87.1	88.9
1966	72.9	70.0	73.3	85.7	75.9
1970	75.4	76.5	70.7	83.3	76.5
1974	80.7	78.4	70.5	77.4	81.0
1978	71.8	71.6	73.1	68.8	72.4
1982	71.4	72.3	69.1	77.3	67.9
1986	60.6	62.9	60.3	53.3	56.3
1990	54.5	51.7	57.8	65.4	58.3
1994	61.5	56.1	70.3	75.0	78.3
1998	69.4	65.7	74.0	77.1	71.4

Source: Author's compilation.

only indicator of the extent of congressional careerism. As Mayhew (1974), Fiorina (1977), and others have argued, if politicians primarily desire repeated reelection, then we expect to see them act to create an "incumbency advantage" for themselves by either enhancing the prestige of their office or by setting up barriers against strong competition. When the reelection incentive is strong, we therefore also expect the rate of running *and* winning reelection to be very high. Do Brazilian deputies act to protect their positions, to increase their incumbency advantage? Let us begin by looking at the simplest measure, the rates of winning reelection.

Table 2.3, column two, relates the average percentage of deputies who win reelection, given that they run, in every election since 1945. The average winning rate for democratic periods is 63.6 percent, with significant increases observed during the dictatorship to 75.3 percent.[52]

The 63.6 percent figure casts some doubt on scholars' claims that Brazilian deputies use access to particularistic resources to their advantage (e.g., Ames 1995a, 2001; Mainwaring 1999). Is this claim thus false? Several possibilities exist: (1) the aggregate rate disguises an incumbency advantage that deputies accumulate over time, as Ames (1987, 112–14) suggests; (2) deputies use particularistic goods to lay the ground for a job *outside* the Chamber; or (3) deputies are in fact poor pork-barrellers who have limited success either

---

[52] This calculation also excludes *suplentes*. As for the rise during the dictatorship, the military expelled a total of 146 deputies (mostly in 1964, right after the coup) from office and stripped thousands of others of their political rights during its reign, limiting but not prohibiting political competition. Consequently, deputies who wanted to keep their seats during this period had an easier time of it.

holding onto their seats or laying the ground for a different position.[53] Here, I address the first possibility. In the last section of this chapter and in other chapters I address the second and third.

Table 2.3, columns three through six breaks down deputies' probability of reelection success by the number of terms held. For example, column three provides the percentage of deputies who run and win a second consecutive term, column four a third term, etc. If an incumbency advantage exists in the Brazilian Congress, we should see the probability of winning reelection increase as deputies accumulate experience. However, given the figures in Table 2.3, no clear incumbency advantage exists. In some years the rate of success goes up after winning a second term (e.g., 1994), in other years it declines (e.g., 1986), and in other years in increases and then decreases again (1990, 1998). (In Chapter 6 I confirm that the number of terms served is not statistically related to deputies' probability of winning reelection.)

The Chamber of Deputies: An Amateurs' Forum?

From the data provided in the preceding text, we know that turnover is fairly high in the Chamber of Deputies. In Polsby's terms, the legislature's "boundedness" is very low. Table 2.4 details Brazilian deputies' limited congressional experience by relating the percentage of deputies in each legislature according to the number of terms previously served.

On average, at the start of each new legislature about 80 percent of all deputies are either newcomers or have served only one prior term. This is a clear indicator that very few deputies build long-term careers within the Chamber. Thus, while the inhabitants of the Chamber typically possess a good deal of *political* experience, on average they have little experience *as national legislators*.

Seeking and Winning in Comparative Perspective

How does this turnover rate compare with other countries? Some comparative referents help place these numbers in perspective. In the United States, the "model" of congressional careerism, an average of 91.3 percent of Representatives ran for reelection between 1960 and 1992, and of those, 92.8 percent won (Abramson et al. 1995, 259). In Japan, where politicians are also considered to demonstrate parliamentary careerism, an average of 92 percent of deputies from 1958 to 1990 ran and 81 percent of those won (Hayama 1992). Compared to these systems where legislative careerism flourishes, Brazilian deputies seek and win reelection at relatively low rates.

---

[53] No significant differences in terms of rates of running or winning reelection exist across Brazil's regions. See Samuels (1998), Chapter 2.

TABLE 2.4 *Percentage of Deputies with a Given Number of Terms Served at the Start of Each Legislature*

Year	% Freshmen	% Sophomores	% with 2 Terms Served	% with 3 Terms Served	% with 4 Terms Served
1945	100.0	—	—	—	—
1950	69.4	30.6	—	—	—
1954	57.4	27.9	14.7	—	—
1958	54.6	23.3	14.4	7.7	—
1962	57.5	22.7	9.3	6.6	3.9
1966	50.6	27.4	10.8	5.9	5.4
1970	52.6	25.2	13.2	4.8	4.2
1974	50.0	26.9	11.8	6.6	4.7
1978	52.1	24.0	13.6	5.2	5.0
1982	55.1	24.0	9.8	7.1	4.0
1986	64.1	20.5	8.4	3.3	3.7
1990	65.2	21.3	7.4	3.4	2.8
1994	58.3	25.9	8.8	3.5	3.5
1998	49.1	24.9	14.6	6.2	5.1
Average	55.5	24.3	10.8	5.3	4.2

Source: Author's compilation.

How does Brazil compare to other countries in Latin America? In both Costa Rica and Mexico, the entire legislature turns over with each election, but the comparison with Brazil is invalid because running for reelection is prohibited in each country. We therefore have no way to know whether Mexican or Costa Rican politicians desire reelection or not. In any case, in contrast to Brazil, political careers have long been made in the main national parties in both countries (Carey 1996; Smith 1979), although this may be changing in Mexico as the party system evolves.

Other countries, such as Uruguay and Argentina (Morgenstern 2002; Jones 2002) also exhibit higher turnover than Brazil. However, the comparison with Brazil is problematic given differences in party and electoral institutions. In both countries party leaders decide who gets to run again and who doesn't, eliminating the possibility that incumbents can freely choose their career path (as in the United States and Brazil). Moreover, even if renominated, party leaders may place a candidate much further down on a (closed) list than previously, which would seriously damage the incumbent's reelection chances. Thus, the reasons for high turnover in Argentina and Uruguay are different from those in Brazil. Party influence and overall party results are the main factors in Argentina and Uruguay, while in Brazil the turnover rate is a function of *individual* career choices and *individual* electoral performance.

The only other Latin American country for which we have data and for which the comparison is somewhat valid is Chile. There, national party leaders play a greater role in the nomination process than in Brazil, which makes the comparison problematic. However, the electoral institutions are somewhat similar. Just like Brazil, Chile uses a form of open-list proportional representation (albeit with much smaller district magnitudes). Thus, in both Chile and Brazil whether a candidate wins or loses is at least partly a function of his or her individual electoral performance.

Carey (2002) reports that turnover is higher in Brazil than in Chile. This suggests either that (like the U.S. House) the Chilean Chamber of Deputies provides greater attractions for career-minded Chilean politicians compared to Brazil, or that a position in the legislature is relatively high on Chile's political career ladder because there are far fewer attractive political positions *outside* the legislature. Both of these may be true.

In most political systems, national political parties exert significant control over nomination to legislative office. Thus, internal party politics may account for much of the cross-national variance in legislative turnover. It is critical to remember that Brazilian national parties exert almost no influence over whether candidates do or do not run for reelection. Consequently, one cannot directly compare cross-national turnover rates without taking this into account. Like the United States, Brazil's institutions appear to *encourage* legislative incumbency, because until 2002 candidates could not be denied a spot on the ballot and individual candidates make the decision to run or not. Yet despite these institutions, the data in this section confirm that legislative turnover is relatively high and thus that very few deputies develop long-term careers in the Chamber. In the next section I begin to explore what the literature on the Brazilian Congress suggests about the consequences of this relatively high turnover rate.

CAREER INCENTIVES AND THE INTERNAL STRUCTURE OF THE BRAZILIAN CHAMBER OF DEPUTIES

With each election, about half of the membership of the Brazilian Chamber of Deputies turns over. In Chapter 1 I posited that in the absence of long congressional careers, individual legislators have few incentives to create a hierarchy of positions within the legislature, and few incentives also to institutionalize nondiscretionary norms governing access to those positions. In contrast, other legislatures that possess relatively stable membership ought to develop both hierarchy and nondiscretionary norms (Epstein et al. 1997).

Thus, the raw turnover rates are not the only indicator of the absence of incentives to develop a career in the Chamber. Equally important are the actions that deputies choose to take or not to take while in office. The literature on the internal organization of the Chamber of Deputies uniformly suggests that, as I hypothesized in Chapter 1, a relatively flat internal hierarchy of positions exists and that no universalistic access norms exist. This provides additional evidence of deputies' low desire to build a career in the Chamber, and begins to reveal how the structure of political careers in Brazil affects legislative politics.

Spreading Power Near and Thin

The Brazilian Chamber of Deputies currently has 513 seats. Few positions vested with considerable institutional power exist within the Chamber, either within parties or within the Chamber's committee or internal leadership structure. This is not to say that *no* hierarchy of positions exists, only that the average deputy has little opportunity either to climb a career ladder or to build up his own institutional "fiefdom" within the legislature.

The hierarchy of positions in the Brazilian Chamber has really only two rungs: top and bottom. A deputy who pushes his or her way to the top reaches a position of influence: most agenda-setting and decision-making powers are concentrated among party leaders and in the hands of the members of the *Mesa Diretora*, a kind of legislative board of directors, over which the Chamber President (akin to Speaker) presides. However, only about two dozen top-rung positions exist. Given this, Figueiredo and Limongi (1996, 25) have concluded that "there exist few positions of power that would help establish a congressional career" in the Chamber.

Positions on the *Mesa Diretora* are highly coveted. Among other responsibilities, the Chamber President presides over plenary sessions, deals regularly with the President of Brazil, sets the legislative agenda, and frequently appears on the nightly news. Other positions on the *Mesa* involve substituting for the Chamber President when he is unavailable to preside; allocating office space to deputies and parties; hiring and firing the Chamber's internal staff; and controlling the Chamber's internal purse strings. However, access is extremely limited: only seven positions on the *Mesa* exist. Moreover, a deputy cannot even hope to maintain the position for an entire legislature, because deputies select new *Mesa* members every two years, and reelection is prohibited (Câmara dos Deputados 1994, Art. 5).[54]

[54] Article 8 of the Chamber's internal rules determines that the distribution of the seven positions on the *Mesa* shall be according to the proportional size of party or bloc delegations. Thus the largest gets the presidency, the second largest the 1st Vice-Presidency, and so forth. However, because of deputies' frequent party changing, party sizes change frequently. Consequently, at the start of each legislature, the leaders of the largest parties meet to determine the division of the spoils. These negotiations sometimes involve deals with Senate leadership. For example the 1995–8 legislature, when the PFL and PMDB switched presidencies of the two houses at the mid-point of the legislature. In any case, Article 8 provides a loophole for upstarts who feel party leaders have grabbed excessive control of the power positions: paragraph 4 of Article 8 allows any deputy to run for a position on the *Mesa*. In 1997, one such upstart

Party leaders also have significant power. They meet with the Chamber President to establish the legislative agenda, have extra office space and staff, and can cast votes for their whole delegations under certain conditions in the plenary. Positions of "vice-leader" exist, but these positions have little if any power (Novaes 1994).[55] Parties sometimes keep their leaders for the entire legislature, but others change every two years (or even every year), impeding one deputy from consolidating his or her rule (Figueiredo and Limongi 1996, 24). The number of party leaders is limited to the number of parties, so relatively few party leadership positions exist at any point in time.

If a deputy fails to reach one of these two positions, unlike in the United States, for example, he or she cannot hope to specialize in a policy area and build up a legislative "niche" in a committee. The primary reason for this is that although after the 1987–8 Constitutional Assembly the legislative branch took back some of the power it had lost under the authoritarian regime (Fleischer 1990; Shugart and Carey 1992), the executive branch still dominates policy making by controlling the overall agenda and maintaining most of the initiative and technical capacity for submitting legislation (Bernardes 1996; Figueiredo and Limongi 2000a).

Another reason is that in the Chamber, committees have a "secondary and imprecise role" (Figueiredo and Limongi 1996, 25), precisely because most deputies are simply not interested in developing a niche over the long term. As such, deputies have limited the power of committee presidents (chairs): the internal rules (Article 39 of the *Regimento Interno*) of the Chamber require new committee chairs every year. This limits the value of a committee presidency for a career-minded deputy.

Another indicator of deputies' disinterest in developing legislative capacity is that they rarely remain in the same committee for the full legislature (Figueiredo and Limongi 1996; F. Santos 1999; Pereira and Mueller 2000). One scholar has concluded that "Because no incentive exists in the Chamber for deputies to invest in specialization, there is also no reason for them to remain in one committee, given that they have no guarantee of rising through a committee hierarchy" and reaping electoral benefits from such dedication (Bernardes 1996, 93).

If a deputy fails to reach the top rung of the Chamber's leadership, he or she is left with everyone else at the bottom rung. At the bottom, so many deputies fall into virtual anonymity that a specific term describes backbenchers: *baixo clero*, literally meaning a member of the "lower orders" of

(Wilson Campos) nearly defeated the "agreed-upon" candidate, Michel Temer. Candidates for Chamber President go to ridiculous lengths to win over the required majority of 257 deputies, distributing pencils, ties, desk organizers, and other "gifts," and making "campaign promises" about salary increases, staff increases, and piling on additional perks.

[55] Some states also organize "state delegation coordinators," typically an emissary of the governor.

the clergy.[56] Members of the *baixo clero* get no respect, no glory, and no attention. While the "Cardinals" of the Congress grab the spotlight, the *baixo clero* scramble to have their speeches "taken as read" into the Brazilian Congressional Record so that local radio stations back home can report that the deputy "gave" a speech on the plenary floor. In short, a hierarchy of positions does exist in the Chamber, but the vast majority of deputies never get off the bottom rung. Few positions in the Chamber allow an average deputy to build up power or construct a "niche."

The Absence of Universalistic Access Norms

Even given that the number of powerful positions is limited, we might suppose that deputies could develop some kind of universalistic norm for reaching the top rung. For example, deputies could create a system that would benefit more senior members, as in the United States (e.g., Polsby 1968; Price 1977; Katz and Sala 1996), or Japan (Epstein et al. 1997). However, no such "seniority system" has evolved in Brazil, because the incentives to develop such a norm are nonexistent: deputies do not desire a long-term career in the Chamber, so they are uninterested in increasing the value of a seat over time.

To be elected chair of a committee, seniority is unimportant. The distribution of posts is not institutionalized according to level of experience, and from 1989–96, freshmen presided over 43.3 percent of Chamber committees (111 total) (Bernardes 1996, 89). Novaes also reports that "the designation of committee chairs is rarely tied to questions of technical capacity," (1994, 134) and instead involves personalistic wheeling and dealing. Less experienced deputies can not only obtain committee presidencies, but "older deputies do not even covet those positions" (Figueiredo and Limongi 1994, 19) because the place of committees within the hierarchy of power in the Chamber is ill defined. In sum, unlike in the United States, the distribution of power in the committee system is not institutionalized according to experience.

To become a party leader or reach the *Mesa*, experience does apparently matter more, but still, no institutionalized access norm exists (Figueiredo and Limongi 1996, 23–4). For example, a *suplente* – a candidate who does not even finish high enough on the list to win a seat outright but who takes office by virtue of a higher-placing candidate resigning or taking a leave of absence to take another position – was elected 2nd Vice-President of the *Mesa* for the 1993–4 term (Novaes 1994, 119n). And in the 1995–8 legislature, a man who had served as *suplente* twice but who won his seat outright for

---

[56] The party leaders and members of the *Mesa* are sometimes referred to as the "College of Cardinals," a term also used to describe congressional leaders in the United States, particularly of the Budget Committee.

the first time only in 1994 served as Chamber President.[57] These men were elected to the *Mesa* because of their personal prestige, not because of their extensive experience *within* the Chamber.

Unlike what one sees in countries with established congressional careerism, in the Brazilian Chamber of Deputies one can observe a relatively flat hierarchy of positions and no institutionalized nondiscretionary norms for accessing those posts. This comparison reinforces the hypothesis that a desire for a long-term career in the Chamber does not primarily drive deputies' political ambitions. We have now traveled two "segments" along the line of reasoning I outlined in Chapter 1. To reach the end of the line, in the next section I question whether a seat in the Chamber provides significant political return.

A SEAT IN THE CHAMBER: LOW OFFICE BENEFITS

The findings in this chapter would be puzzling if we believed that Brazilian deputies are primarily interested in reelection. Although some scholars have questioned the reelection assumption (e.g., Packenham 1990 [1970]; Fleischer 1981; Avelino Filho 1994; Figueiredo and Limongi 1996), other scholars have explicitly or implicitly assumed that Brazilian deputies do desire reelection, and have claimed that a seat provides politically valuable goods. For example, both Ames (1987, 112) and Geddes (1994, 12) assumed that Brazilian deputies do care about reelection as well as presented hypotheses and deduced conclusions from this assumption. Ames and Nixon (1993) acknowledged that assuming reelection in Brazil might be improper, but then Ames (1995a, 2001) implied that deputies seek pork to construct secure electoral bailiwicks. Mainwaring (1995, 389) has claimed that "defeating incumbents is not easy" in Brazil, implying that incumbents have advantages that derive from possession of a seat (see also Geddes and Ribeiro Neto 1992; Avelino Filho 1994; Ames 1995b).

It is true that deputies spend a good deal of their time pork-barreling and seeking jobs for their associates. However, we have good reasons to wonder whether they do so as part of a reelection strategy. As I have shown in this chapter, even given institutions that promote incumbency, a substantial portion of deputies choose not to run for reelection, electoral insecurity appears high even for those who do choose to run, and no advantage in terms of probability of reelection accrues to deputies who stay long in the Chamber. Moreover, deputies have not developed institutions that reflect a desire for repeated reelection. In short, on a variety of measures, Brazilian

---

[57] This was Michel Temer (PMDB-SP), who was by no means a political novice: he had served as Attorney General of the state of São Paulo and state secretary twice. He had served as a *suplente* for most of the 1987–90 legislature and again in the 1991–4 legislature, but he only won election outright for the 1995–8 legislature.

deputies do not exhibit behavior consistent with an assumption that they primarily desire a long-term career in the Chamber.

If a seat in the Chamber has low office benefits, why run for reelection at all? Moreover, why do deputies spend so much money to win (re)election, if the position comes with an apparently uncertain political payoff? (Samuels 2001a, 2001b, 2001c). The answer is that although deputies may spend a lot to reach the Chamber, this does not mean that they desire to *stay* there over the long term. A politician on the way up in Brazil sees the Chamber as a springboard to even higher office (Fleischer 1981). By investing huge sums of money under conditions of high uncertainty, ambitious Brazilian politicians signal a willingness to move to an even higher level later on. To bolster this claim about the nature of political ambition in Brazil, I elaborate on the structure of deputies' careers in the next two chapters.

The absence of careerism in the Chamber of Deputies should change how we think about deputies' goals and what they do to achieve those goals while serving in the Chamber. Instead of assuming a desire for reelection and deriving behavioral expectations from that assumption, we might instead assume that Brazilian deputies see their long-term career as mostly linked to state and/or municipal government. This approach would force us to reexamine many questions about legislative behavior in Brazil, most prominently as to why deputies spend so much energy seeking pork. Instead of using pork for reelection, deputies might be laying the groundwork for advancing to a state or municipal position. I investigate this possibility in chapters 6 and 7.

Chapter 3

Progressive Ambition and Congressional "Hot Seats" in Brazil, 1945–1998

INTRODUCTION

I have argued that Brazilian deputies do not aim to build a political career within the Chamber of Deputies. Instead, they are "progressively" ambitious and focus their energies while *in* the Chamber on ways to continue their careers *outside* of the Chamber. In this chapter I provide evidence of another manifestation of deputies' progressive ambition, what I call "Congressional Hot Seats." I explore how deputies rotate out of the Chamber to take national-, state-, or municipal-level political positions *immediately following their election as Deputy, during their terms*. In recent legislatures, over one-third of all sitting deputies have either rotated out or have manifested a desire to find a position outside of the Chamber during the term, and we might suppose that the percentage of deputies who would like to rotate out is actually much higher – a notion that politicians support when interviewed. If deputies were generally interested in developing a career within the Chamber, this "Hot Seat" behavior would be extremely puzzling. However, given progressive ambition, it is perfectly understandable.

In the first two chapters I argued that when careers are short, few deputies have incentives to institutionalize a hierarchy of positions within the legislature and a system of norms that regulates access to those positions. In this situation, the relative value of a seat in the Chamber does not increase with time served. Consequently, few incentives exist for deputies to develop a career in the Chamber. However, this internal dynamic tells only half of the story. Deputies not only have weak incentives to develop a career *within* the Chamber, they also have strong incentives to develop a career *outside* the Chamber. In particular, deputies seek municipal- and/or state-level positions, because the probability of attaining and maintaining political power at the national level is relatively slim while the opportunities are much greater – and the positions also quite attractive – at the municipal or state level. In this chapter I show that if the opportunity arises, a deputy will abandon the legislature – even after expending significant energy and money getting there – to take another political job. The empirical findings in this chapter thus strengthen my claim that extra-Chamber and primarily subnational incentives drive Brazilian deputies' career goals, even when they are serving in the Chamber.

The "Hot Seat" phenomenon of rotation from Congress to other offices is not unique to Brazil, and its presence elsewhere illustrates the importance of carefully depicting the structure of political careers when exploring legislative politics. For example, Kernell (n.d.[b]) and Young (1966) have described a similar dynamic in the nineteenth-century U.S. House of Representatives, and Payne (1968) has described how Colombian legislators in the 1960s also often abandoned the national legislature for other positions directly after election.

The parallels between the nature of political careers in the nineteenth-century United States and contemporary Brazil are quite clear. In the nineteenth-century United States, the budgets of the larger states even exceeded that of the federal government, and state- and local-level clientelistic networks were relatively more important then than they are today. The political career ladder reflected this context: politicians valued state-level offices much more highly than congressional office. Consequently, long-term congressional careers were uncommon, and the House remained relatively poorly institutionalized. Kernell concludes that office holding in the nineteenth-century United States resembled a "fast game of musical chairs" (ibid., 11). In fact, many early nineteenth-century U.S. House members failed to complete their terms, and "over half of those who resigned went directly to state government, with most of the rest accepting a federal appointment in the states" (ibid., 6). Until exogenous forces acted on this equilibrium and pushed the transition to the modern House, politicians in the United States sought to leave Congress after a short stint in office, rather than build a long-term congressional career. A similar dynamic characterizes contemporary Brazil, for similar reasons. In the next section I describe this dynamic.

"CONGRESSIONAL HOT SEATS" IN BRAZIL

Since 1945, Brazilian federal deputies have had the right to take a leave of absence from their seat in the Chamber to take nonelective positions in municipal, state, or national government. Deputies can also resign their seat if they run and win election to another office, such as municipal mayor or state governor.[58] When a *titular* (an incumbent deputy) takes a leave,

---

[58] This occurs due to nonconcurrent election calendars for mayors and for governor in some states in the 1945–64 period.

a *suplente* (substitute) takes the seat and gains all rights bestowed on the
titulares.[59] Examples of the "Hot Seat" phenomenon include:

- Deputy Adroaldo Mesquita da Costa (PSD-Rio Grande do Sul) takes a
  leave of absence during the 1945–50 term to become Minister of Justice
  (national level).
- Deputy Jutahy Junior (PFL-Bahia) takes a leave of absence during the
  1987–90 term to become Secretary of Justice (state level).
- Deputy César Maia (PMDB-Rio de Janeiro) resigns his seat from the
  1991–4 term to become mayor of the city of Rio de Janeiro (municipal
  level).

Given my argument from Chapter 1, when positions such as these are
available, progressively ambitious Brazilian deputies ought seek them. To
assess the extent of the "Hot Seat" phenomenon, I gathered data on every
resignation and leave of absence deputies took from 1945 to 1998, and calculated the percentage of deputies who took leaves as a portion of all deputies
in the legislature. Table 3.1 details the percentages of deputies who actually left the Chamber for either a national, state, or municipal-level position
since 1945.

Table 3.1 reveals three things. First, during democratic periods a sizeable
portion of deputies have resigned their seats to take extralegislative positions. Currently, about 20 percent of deputies leave the Chamber during
each term, even after a long and expensive campaign. Unfortunately, I could
not find complete information from 1945 to the present on deputies who put
themselves up as candidates for other positions during a term, but who do
not actually leave. If we knew this number, the figures in Table 3.1 would
be substantially higher. This information becomes more precise after 1986.
Since that time, the proportion of deputies who leave or who attempt to leave
(by running for an office such as municipal mayor) approaches 40 percent
of the total in each legislature, a significant number by any measure.[60]

Second, Table 3.1 permits comparisons of the relative percentage of deputies who go to each level of government. The number of deputies who
have left for state-level positions has historically been largest, and since the
1970s, the number of deputies who have left for municipal-level positions
has approached the number leaving for state-level positions, and is now

[59] However, if the *titular* desires to return to the Chamber, the *suplente* must leave. On the other
hand, if a deputy is *elected* to another position during the legislature, he must resign, and a
suplente is sworn in as *titular* for the remainder of the term. *Suplentes* take office in order of
their finishing on the district list. For example, if a list in district X has ten candidates and
wins five seats, it has five suplentes. The first suplente is the candidate who came closest to
winning a seat outright, and so on.
[60] The phenomenon has continued into the 1999–2002 legislature. In 2000, 106 deputies
(20.7 percent) ran for mayor and through July of 2001, a total of 86 deputies (16.8 percent)
had resigned or taken a leave of absence to take an extralegislative position.

TABLE 3.1 *Incumbents Taking Leaves for Municipal, State, or National Positions*

Legislature	% Municipal	% State	% National	% Total
1945–50	0.0	11.2	4.3	15.5
1951–54	0.3	5.3	3.0	8.6
1955–58	0.9	7.1	2.8	10.7
1959–62	0.0	7.7	7.1	14.7
1963–66	0.2	5.4	3.9	9.5
1967–70	0.5	5.4	2.2	8.1
1971–74	1.3	1.6	0.0	2.9
1975–78	3.0	5.2	0.6	8.8
1979–82	0.7	8.8	0.7	10.2
1983–86	3.6	9.0	1.9	14.4
1987–90	4.7	8.8	2.5	16.0
1991–94	6.8	11.1	3.0	20.9
1995–98	7.8	8.0	1.4	17.2

Source: Author's compilation.

significantly higher than the number of deputies who have left for national-level positions.

Third, we can observe and attribute a trend to the influence of the 1964–85 military regime. While deputies have rotated out of the Chamber since 1945, the military regime limited deputies' range of action. The military virtually eliminated deputies' ability to land national-level positions for about fifteen years, handing out only four ministerial positions to deputies in the 1967–70 term, zero positions from 1971 to 1978, and two for the 1979–82 term. After the military relinquished control, deputies regained access to national-level positions.

Military rule also limited deputies' access to state-level positions, but for a shorter period. Following its allies' disastrous performance in the 1974 elections, the military recognized the need to reincorporate its civilian allies into state politics, to bolster its own support. So, the military began to allow deputies to regain access to the halls of power at state level: by the 1975–8 term, deputies were choosing to leave the Chamber for state-level politics, and did so at the same rate as in the 1967–70 legislature. The percentage of deputies taking state-level positions has continued to increase since then, averaging about 10 percent in each legislature.

In the next three sections I explore the pattern for each level of office, in order to tie the "Hot Seats" dynamic to my argument about political careerism in Brazil. Although Brazil has experienced dramatic social, economic, and political transformations over the last half-century, the incentives to seek a state- or municipal-level position have remained high or even increased (as in the case of municipal-level positions). On the other hand, while the incentives to obtain a national-level position remain undoubtedly very high, a deputy's chances of reaching (and remaining at) a national-level position have undergone a relative decline, indicating that national-level positions are actually less important now than they were during the 1945–64 period.

National-Level Positions

In terms of the calculus of careerism for each individual deputy, the crucial variable regarding national-level positions is the probability of access. As in other countries, a Brazilian deputy's probability of landing a national-level position is relatively low because these positions are in short supply relative to state and municipal positions, and because no norm regulates access to them. Consequently, national-level positions remain attractive as *part* of a career, but deputies do not consider a national-level position their primary career aspiration.

Short Supply of National Positions. The first reason that the probability of landing a national position is low is because supply remains short. There are simply very few ministries relative to the number of deputies who might aspire to be minister. There were eleven ministries on average from 1946–64 and seventeen from 1987–present (FGV n.d.). Compared to the possibility of landing a position in the state-level secretariat, the probability of landing a ministerial position is much lower. Deputies weigh both the probabilities of obtaining the position and the benefits (or costs) of achieving the position when considering whether to expend effort to seek a political position. Consequently, even though a ministerial position is more prestigious, deputies discount their chances of obtaining a ministry relative to their chances of obtaining a state-level position.

Deputies have obtained relatively fewer national-level positions during the current democratic period relative to 1946–64. What accounts for this trend? While the Chamber of Deputies was smaller from 1946–64 than it is today, the number of ministries from 1946–64 was also smaller; this comparison is inconclusive. On the other hand, the supply of positions has declined because contemporary presidents nominate more "technical" professionals (those without party affiliation) on average (31.3 percent) than they did during the 1946–64 period (24.0 percent) (Amorim Neto 1995). Moreover, tenure in ministerial office, while short to begin with, has gone up slightly during the contemporary period. Ministers stayed an average of 10.2 months in office from 1946–64, but from 1987–94 they remained in office on average for 12.1 months (calculated from FGV n.d.). These factors result in fewer national positions being available for deputies.

Relatively few deputies obtain national-level positions. In some countries supply could be greater if high-level permanent bureaucratic sinecures at the national level comprised a rung on a substantial proportion of deputies' career ladders, but this is only rarely the case in Brazil. National-level positions are undoubtedly politically plum prizes, and many deputies will take one if it were offered, but deputies weigh the relatively low probability of attaining such a position when assessing how to expend their scarce resources on advancing their careers. Consequently, they tend to discount national-level positions.

Absence of Norms Regulating Access to National Positions. A second factor that encourages deputies to discount the utility of seeking a national-level position is the absence of norms that regulates access. Countries with legislative-based career structures or hierarchically organized national parties ought to develop a norm whereby only more senior members have access to high-level positions (Epstein et al. 1997). Thus, politicians in many countries typically spend considerable time "paying their dues" before they reach cabinet or ministerial status. For example, in Japan, a Diet member cannot hope to obtain a cabinet position until his fifth or sixth term (Ramseyer and Rosenbluth 1993, 86). Moreover, access to ministerial positions is predicated on a long-term link to a *national* party organization. Similarly, in Mexico, national-level factions (called *camarillas*) are well established within the PRI. The relationship between the individual and a *camarilla* is long term, and serves as the basis for a political career from beginning to end (Smith 1979; Langston 1995).

In contrast, in systems that lack institutionalized legislative career structures or hierarchically organized national parties, the converse holds: no norm such as seniority should determine who gains access to prominent national positions. This is true in Brazil. Although deputies appointed as minister do tend to have longer-than-average congressional careers, no norm regulates access to top-level national positions. In fact, it is not uncommon for "freshmen" legislators to become ministers of state. A good example of this is President Cardoso's Minister of Planning from 1996–98, Antonio Kandir, who won election as deputy in 1994. Kandir had a "technical" career prior to his first election victory: he had earned an economics Ph.D. and had previously been appointed to several government posts. He gained popularity as a radio, television, and newspaper commentator on the national economy, and won ministerial appointment through his association with President Cardoso and his São Paulo associates, not through diligently and patiently climbing a party or legislative career ladder. In Brazil, long-term membership in and leadership of a national party organization are not prerequisites for reaching high national office. In short, deputies discount the probability of attaining a national-level position because few exist and because no clear norm regulates access.

State-Level Positions

As I explained in Chapter 2, appointed positions in the state-level executive branch are particularly attractive to career-minded deputies. In relative terms, deputies perceive state-level positions as more attractive than national-level positions because of greater probability of access and because the benefits are also quite high. As Table 3.1 indicated, a larger percentage of deputies each legislature take state-level positions than national or municipal positions. Eighty-three percent (288/345) of the state-level positions that deputies took were in state-level secretariats modeled after the national ministry. Deputies who seek a state-level portfolio typically have close ties to the elected governor, or are leaders of state-based factions in alliance with the governor.

Relative to national-level positions, deputies have a higher probability of obtaining a state-level position. While there is only one national ministry, each state has a secretariat. Thus, while an individual deputy has about a 3 percent chance (about 15 of 513 deputies) of gaining access to a ministerial post in any given legislature, he or she has a much higher probability of gaining a state-level position because there are only between eight and seventy deputies from each state.

Additionally, as has the federal government over the last 50 years, state governments have also expanded their ranks. L. Graham (1990, 79) notes that growth of the public sector at both the federal and state levels in the 1970s was "unrestrained" and resulted in the creation of "literally hundreds of new public enterprises." This implies that state governments expanded their role as suppliers of political patronage jobs during this period (Medeiros 1986, 182). Unfortunately, research on the growth of state-level administration in Brazil is virtually nonexistent.[61] I gathered data on the growth of the state government in the state of São Paulo, which may not be a representative example, but the findings are nonetheless suggestive: São Paulo had eleven secretariats in 1947, seventeen in 1976, and twenty-one in 1994 (Sonnewend 1975, 49; São Paulo n.d., ii). Splitting secretariats provides the governor with a larger "pie" to divide among his cronies.[62]

Calculations of utility involve costs, benefits, as well as probability of achieving the desired goal(s). Deputies ought to regard the utility of seeking a state-level position more highly relative to the utility of seeking a national-level position because of a higher probability of access and because state-level positions also provide significant political benefits.

Municipal-Level Positions

As Table 3.1 indicates, although almost no deputies resigned their seats during the 1945–64 legislatures to take municipal-level positions, the number of deputies leaving the Chamber for municipal-level positions started to

---

[61] I know of no comprehensive research on the structure and evolution of Brazilian state governments.

[62] Privatization has probably had a similar effect on patronage at the state and national levels.

increase in the 1959–62 legislature. By the 1995–8 legislature nearly 8 percent of deputies abandoned their seat to take a municipal-level position (nearly all as mayor). While a deputy's probability of winning a mayoralty race is necessarily low, the benefits to winning are quite high. In the following text, I discuss why we have seen an increase in number of deputies leaving for municipal-level positions.

Why the Over-Time Increase in the "Municipal" Trend? The percentage of deputies taking municipal-level positions moves upward independently of regime type: the increase begins before the 1964 coup, and proceeds apparently unimpeded up to the present. Deputies' increasing desire over time to take municipal-level positions becomes more evident when we include data on those deputies who not only *win* but those who *seek* election as mayor during the off-year municipal elections. Accurate data exist beginning with the 1987–90 legislature that detail the percentage of deputies who run for mayor or vice-mayor during each term.[63] These percentages were 22 percent in 1988 (DIAP 1988),[64] 16.3 percent in 1992 (DIAP 1992), 23 percent in 1996 (OESP 1996), and 20.7 percent in 2000 (DIAP 2000).[65]

While most municipalities in Brazil are dirt poor and continue to hold few political attractions for career-minded deputies, the political importance of medium and large municipalities has increased dramatically since 1945. As a reflection of this transformation, municipalities were given status as federal entities for the first time in the 1988 constitution. Three factors explain the "political rise of the municipalities" in Brazil: structural demographic changes, and two policies that the military regime introduced (Samuels 2000a).

First, urbanization and industrialization spread beginning particularly in the 1950s. These changes concentrated voters in cities, whereas the countryside had dominated politics previously. In 1950, 36.2 percent of Brazil's population of 52 million lived in urban areas, whereas by 1991, 77.1 percent of its population of 150 million lived in urban areas (M. Santos 1994, 29). In particular, urban population growth increased most rapidly in the 1970s, growing faster than overall population growth (ibid., 30). Unlike other Latin American countries, which have few large urban centers, Brazil in 1992 had twelve cities with a population of over 1 million, and 183 cities with a population over 100,000. Most importantly, although the Southeast region is the most urbanized (82 percent), the growth of mid-sized cities has begun to spread throughout the country. Mid-sized cities (population between

---

[63] See Chapter 4 for information on deputies who run for mayor *after* their term is finished.

[64] I should note that the source counts deputies and senators together when calculating the percentage. Typically fewer than a half-dozen senators run for mayor, so the number of deputies would not be lower than 20 percent.

[65] Of these, 20/120 (16.7 percent), 27/82 (32.9 percent), 32/116 (27.6 percent) and 22/106 (20.8 percent) won.

100,000 and 500,000) currently are growing faster than the largest cities (ibid., 81).

Urbanization and industrialization increased the supply of politically attractive municipal-level positions. Together, the mid-sized cities and the state capitals comprise the political prizes that federal deputies seek: the larger the city, the more likely its mayor has a large bureaucracy and a large budget to control. While 87.4 percent of all Brazilian municipalities depend on state and federal government transfers for more than half of their revenue (Bremaeker 1995, 21), even when dependent, the mayor makes the final call on hiring and firing, and gains political credit for implementing public-works projects within the municipality. Thus, mayors have far more political weight within their municipalities' borders than deputies do; deputies only act as intermediaries *on behalf of* mayors, attempting to pry resources from federal and state governments. The growth of mid-size and large cities means more plum political prizes for ambitious politicians.

Second, in combination with the socioeconomic changes, two policies the 1964–85 military government adopted ironically increased the attractiveness of a municipal-level position. First, the military continued to hold elections in nearly all municipalities throughout its rule. Although the military-nominated state governors nominated the mayors of state capitals, all other mayors were directly elected.[66] As a result, while the military emasculated Congress' powers and reduced municipalities' fiscal resources, mayors continued to depend on popular approval and retained substantial executive power. Particularly relative to the power of a federal deputy, the power of a municipal mayor increased during the military period. Especially after the 1974 election, which proved disastrous for the military regime, the government increased the distribution of patronage to its allies at the local level (Medeiros 1986; Ames 1987). In contrast, deputies were cut off from budgetary pork-barrel goods throughout the military period. Thus, winning election at the municipal level became more politically profitable during the military regime relative to winning election as a federal deputy.

Third, the military increased the political attractiveness of municipalities by deliberately sidestepping state governments' traditional role as the intermediary between federal and municipal governments. This had historically lead to state governments "diverting" resources and low rates of program success (Schmitter 1973, 220; Cammack 1982, 67; Medeiros 1986). In attempting this end-around of state elites, the military began to deal directly with municipal governments, contributing to mayoral political autonomy from state-government tutelage during the dictatorship. As a result of all these changes, the political attractiveness of municipal-level political office has increased relative to the 1945–64 period.

---

[66] Except in several municipalities designated as "vital to national security."

In sum, because of demographic changes in population and industrialization, urban centers have become more attractive politically over time. In addition, policies that the military regime implemented made municipalities even more politically valuable to ambitious politicians. These factors increased the political autonomy and political attractiveness of municipalities, both in the aggregate and relative to other high-level political positions, and explain why currently about 20 percent of sitting federal deputies attempt to win election at the municipal level during each legislature, as well as why many deputies see municipal positions as part of their long-term career goals (see Chapter 4). Differently from the 1945–64 period, federal deputies increasingly see the benefits of holding municipal-level office as part of their political career not only before, but also during and after their terms in the national congress.

CONCLUSION

In this chapter I explored the phenomenon of "Congressional Hot Seats." I demonstrated that during democratic periods, a substantial portion of sitting Brazilian federal deputies choose to abandon their recently won seats to take political positions outside the Chamber, principally at the state and municipal levels. Currently, between 15 to 20 percent of all deputies do so during each term, and about the same number run for municipal office, but do not succeed. Thus, between 35 to 40 percent of sitting deputies have either exhibited a preference to leave the Chamber or have actually done so. The real number who desire to leave the Chamber is probably even higher, as the number of deputies who seek a state- or national-level position but who do not obtain one remains unknown, and some deputies who desire a municipal-level position desist from their candidacy after examining the political situation. In any case, 35 to 40 percent is a substantial proportion of all deputies. If the position of deputy were higher on the career ladder in Brazil, we would not expect such a large portion of incumbents to seek to leave the Chamber after expending substantial resources to get there. This finding thus bolsters the argument that deputies desire extralegislative positions, principally in the executive branches of state and local government, more intensely than they desire to develop a career in the Chamber.

Chapter 4

Labyrinths of Power, Brazilian Style: Post-Chamber Political Careers

INTRODUCTION

I argue that one cannot assume that Brazilian politicians desire a career within the Chamber of Deputies. Instead, political careerism among Brazilian legislators is largely focused on positions outside the Chamber, and mainly at the subnational level. I have already demonstrated that Brazilian deputies do not develop long careers in the Chamber, that they have not created institutions that would enhance the status of a seat in the Chamber, and that they often rotate out of their legislative seats to take a position in state or municipal government, even during their term. Taken together, this evidence strongly supports the notion that political careers in Brazil are not primarily built within the Chamber of Deputies. In this chapter, I complete the picture by providing evidence that Brazilian politicians exhibit largely state- and municipal-directed "progressive ambition" *following* their stints in the Chamber.

In the United States, scholars have argued that the House of Representatives is perfectly designed to suit members' reelection goal (Mayhew 1974, 82). The U.S. literature takes this as given, and thus explores the institutions and rules that House members have created in their attempt to assure repeated reelection. The literature's focus leaves us with very little knowledge of what Representatives do after leaving the House. The Mayhewian dictum that House members care utmost about reelection has apparently forestalled research on this topic. To my knowledge, only one scholarly article explores post-House careers. This research found that more than half of retiring or defeated House members left politics entirely, and of the remaining group most remained politically linked to *national*-government politics. Herrick and Nixon (1996) found that 9 percent of ex-House members retired from the workforce completely, 24 percent went into private legal practice, 20 percent went into business, 13 percent lobbied the federal government, 14 percent worked in the federal bureaucracy, 6 percent were educators,

2 percent became political consultants, 2 percent worked for an interest group, and 2 percent took a position in a state-government bureaucracy.[67]

Despite suggestions that a seat in the Brazilian Chamber of Deputies serves as a "political trampoline" and that careers in Brazil embody some kind of "zig-zag" pattern (e.g., Fleischer 1981), no research on Brazil has ever tracked post-Chamber careers, possibly because the U.S. model of the "ideal" legislature as one populated by long-term residents has driven the questions researchers have asked.[68] This lacuna has shaped how scholars perceive Brazilian legislators' goals. In order to properly understand the decisions that Brazilian legislators make regarding both legislative organization and policy choices, we must understand their career motivations. Studies that explore deputies' background provide little help here. Instead, we need to explore what deputies do – and what they desire to do – *after* they serve in the Chamber.

My findings reveal that most Brazilian deputies do continue their political careers, or at least attempt to do so, after serving in the Chamber, and that most of them do so at the subnational level. In addition to the evidence already presented, these findings highlight the inapplicability of the reelection assumption for analyses of Brazil, confirm the validity of an approach that focuses on the importance of subnational politics, and should encourage research on political careerism in other systems.

RESEARCH DESIGN

Hypothesis and Operationalization of Progressive Ambition

I define progressive ambition as a politician's desire to build a political career outside of the Chamber of Deputies following election as deputy. In this chapter, a deputy who demonstrates progressive ambition is one who is observed seeking or winning an appointed or elected position in municipal, state, or federal government, or serving in a state or national party executive organ after his or her first election to the Chamber of Deputies.[69]

Case Selection

I am exploring a population of the total of 2,837 people who won election outright as federal deputy in Brazil from 1945 to 1994 (and who

---

[67] Nine percent listed "other" occupations. Herrick and Nixon relied on a survey of ex-members for their information, and only reported what ex-members said was their first post-House job.

[68] Research on congressional careers has focused on what deputies did *before* entering the Chamber. See F. Santos (1999) for a review of the literature on Brazilian political careers.

[69] See Appendix 1 for a coding of positions.

thus served through 1998). This excludes *suplentes*. I selected a sample of 1,057 deputies (37.3 percent) from this population, and tracked these deputies' post-Chamber political careers. This sample is not random; I selected on a geographic basis. Social scientists divide Brazil into five regions that differ on socioeconomic, political, and cultural lines: North, Northeast, South, Southeast, and Center-West. To get a good cross section, I tracked the careers of all deputies who served from seven of Brazil's twenty-seven states, choosing at least one state from each region: Santa Catarina from the South; São Paulo and Minas Gerais from the Southeast; Goiás from the Center-West; Tocantins from the North; and Ceará and Piauí from the Northeast.

The inevitable difficulties of field research in a country as massive as Brazil imposed these constraints. I could not have taken a random sample of all deputies from all states, or gathered data on the entire population of deputies, because I lacked resources and time to travel to and conduct research in all states. These states vary from large to small, from economically and politically powerful to much less powerful. Table 4.1 provides some basic statistics on each state, and subsequently I provide a brief description of each state.

São Paulo is Brazil's richest and most-populous state, and has historically played a crucial role in Brazilian national politics (Schwartzman 1975; Love 1980). São Paulo is the financial "Wall Street" of Brazil as well as its industrial powerhouse. As one can see from Table 4.1, although São Paulo accounts for 20 percent of the national population, it generates almost 40 percent of Brazil's Gross Domestic Product (GDP). Historically, the state has been the "engine" dragging the other (empty, it is said) "boxcars" of the Brazilian federation along, and indeed to this day a good portion of São Paulo's wealth gets redistributed to poorer states. São Paulo is highly urbanized, and contains Brazil's largest city and metropolitan area (greater São Paulo City, population approximately 18 million). The state has forty-seven other cities with a population over 100,000, and 68 percent of the

TABLE 4.1 *State Statistics*

State	# Deputies in Sample	Seats in 1995–99 Congress (%)	% of Brazil's Population	% of Brazil's GDP
São Paulo	378	70 (13.6)	21.6	37.5
Minas Gerais	279	53 (10.3)	10.6	13.1
Ceará	128	22 (4.3)	4.3	1.6
Santa Catarina	106	16 (3.1)	3.1	3.4
Goiás	95	17 (3.3)	2.8	2.2
Piauí	58	10 (1.9)	1.7	0.4
Tocantins	13	8 (1.6)	0.6	0.2

Source: Author's compilation from TSE (1999) and IBGE (1998).

state's population resides in these cities. Only the state of Rio de Janeiro has a greater urbanization rate (M. Santos 1994, 145).

After São Paulo, historically, Minas Gerais has arguably been Brazil's second-most important state both politically and economically (Wirth 1977; Hagopian 1996). *Mineiro* politicians pride themselves on their state's indigenous political style that combines reticence and cunning, and they seek to maintain their state's role as the historical keystone of the Brazilian federation. Economically, Minas combines industrial production (metallurgical industries, textiles, and automobile manufacturing are prominent) and a booming agro-industrial complex. Moreover, as belies its name ("General Mines" in English) the state still produces a great deal of precious and semiprecious stones and other minerals. Analysts also believe that, given recent infrastructural improvements (e.g., highway and railroad extensions) Minas has gained from the expansion of industry out of São Paulo (Sá 1993). Minas Gerais is moderately urbanized, with eighteen cities with a population greater than 100,000, but residents of these cities comprise only 35 percent of the state's total population (M. Santos 1994, 141).

Santa Catarina is a relatively wealthy but small state in Brazil's Southern region. Historically a small number of political families have dominated the state. Along with São Paulo and Minas Gerais in the sample, it has a greater portion of Brazil's GDP than corresponds to its population. Like the other two states in the Southern region (Rio Grande do Sul and Paraná), family farms rather than plantation agriculture characterized the state's economy during Brazil's early development. Consequently, the state and region attracted a good number of European immigrants, and to this day Santa Catarina and its neighbors have relatively fewer people of African descent than other states in Brazil. Santa Catarina has eight cities with a population of greater than 100,000 and these cities contain 33 percent of the state's population.

The two states in the Northeast present a good deal of contrast. On the one hand, Piauí is Brazil's poorest state, and it reflects the worst of the Northeast region's problems of underdevelopment. The state has little industry, and its agricultural sector has been slow to modernize. Of the sample of seven states, Piauí has the lowest urbanization rate, with only two cities that have more than 100,000 people (M. Santos 1994, 139). Piauí's stagnant economy is also reflected in the lack of turnover among the state's political elite: Gonçalves (1995) argues that continuity and homogeneity characterize the Piauense political elite during the twentieth century.

On the other hand, while Piauí's neighbor Ceará is still quite poor relative to São Paulo or some of the southern states, Ceará's state governments since 1986 have won international praise for effective and progressive policy making (Tendler 1996). Since that year, Ceará's governors have emerged from a group of businessmen who style themselves as different from the state's "traditional" political elite, and Ceará does differ from Piauí in that its political elite are more factionalized (Lemenhe 1995; Gonçalves 1995). Despite this intraelite squabbling (or perhaps because of it), in the last fifteen years, Ceará has had relatively good success in attracting investment, particularly in tourism services. Ceará has five cities with more than 100,000 people, and these cities contain 37 percent of the state's population (M. Santos 1994, 139).

Goiás is a rapidly developing frontier state in Brazil's Center-West region, but still has a lower share of Brazil's GDP than average. The state is best known for agricultural production, particularly cattle raising. Goiás has four cities with a population of more than 100,000, and these cities contain 38 percent of the state's population (M. Santos 1994, 147). Tocantins was carved out of the northern half of Goiás in 1988, and many of Tocantins' prominent politicians were active in Goiás politics prior to their state's creation. The state is very poor, has very little agricultural or industrial development, and has little infrastructure (more rivers than roads crisscross the state). Nevertheless, Tocantins' planned capital, Palmas, is one of Brazil's fastest-growing cities.

Overall, these seven states present a great deal of contrast, from backward frontier regions to densely populated, highly industrialized areas. While I have not captured the totality of variation across Brazil's states, I believe that given this sample, my findings about political careers ought to generalize across Brazil.

POST-CHAMBER POLITICAL CAREERS: THE DATA

To discover whether incumbent deputies ran and won elective office other than federal deputy, I first employed data published by Brazil's national electoral court, the *Tribunal Superior Eleitoral*. From these sources I created a database of the names of all candidates (both winners and losers) since 1945 for all elective offices: state deputy, federal deputy, president, vice-president, governor, vice-governor, senator, *suplente* senator, mayor, and vice-mayor. This excludes only one elected office in Brazil, that of city council-member.

For all states (not just the seven I chose), these data are complete, and I have no reason to suppose that these data are biased or unreliable, with the exception of municipal election data. For mayoral and vice-mayoral positions, the TSE data proved inadequate, so I relied on archival research at the electoral courts in each state. I gathered data only for municipalities that had over 30,000 voters, reasoning that deputies would not seek to become mayor of very small cities, but would instead focus on larger cities that had larger budgets and more power to hire and fire.

I also searched for the names of incumbent deputies as appointed members of the federal- or state-government administration or the administration of their state's capital city. This involved additional archival research, consultation of secondary sources on the history and politics in each state, and interviews with active and ex-politicians.[70] Finally, I gathered data on whether deputies also held positions in the "executive organ" of the national party or a state-level political party branch, at the TSE and the state TREs. State-party leaders wield tremendous power to choose candidates for executive and legislative offices. Typically, the president of a state-party branch is considered a precandidate for governor or senator. National party executives choose only the party's candidate for president.

After compiling this information, I matched names to dates and offices. I gathered at least some information on every deputy in the sample. Nevertheless, and this is important to note, the results probably *underestimate* the percentage of deputies who held positions outside the Chamber following their terms. Despite my best efforts, I undoubtedly came up short in gathering complete information on the career of every single deputy who had served in the Chamber from these seven states from 1945–98. As noted for example, the mayoral candidate records contain some gaps.[71]

Nevertheless, I do not believe that any gaps in the data damage my argument. On the contrary, my success despite the sometimes frustrating research conditions demonstrate the strength of my argument about progressive ambition in Brazil. Assuming that I missed some information only implies that the data underestimate the percentage of deputies who exhibit progressive ambition, especially relative to the number of deputies who attempt a career in the Chamber, for which I have complete data. In short, none of the methodological problems I confronted ought to seriously affect the validity or reliability of my claim about political careerism in Brazil.

POST-CHAMBER CAREERS: IDEAL TYPES

Before presenting the aggregate results, I provide several examples of deputies' careers, in order to characterize several ideal-typical career paths and to put some meat on the dry bones of the aggregate data. Deputies' careers exhibit a great deal of variation, and the distinction between a "state-based" career and a career in the Chamber is not necessarily cut and dry. Nevertheless, we can posit several ideal types, provide plausible examples, and then move to the aggregate data to see how the broad trends confirm my hypothesis. Let me suggest four ideal-type Brazilian political career paths.

* *Congressional-Local*: this deputy would resemble in some ways the U.S. "model" legislator: a deputy who spends most of his or her political career

[70] Secondary sources included Araújo (1984); Bastos (1994); Beloch and Abreu (1983); Coutinho (1982); Diógenes (1989); Freire (n.d.); FGV (n.d.); W. Gonçalves (1992); R. Gonçalves (1995); Kugelmas (1985); Lemenhe (1996); Lenzi (1983); Loyola (1980); Piazza (1994); Sallum Jr. (1996); Sampaio (1982); Sautheir (1993); Teixeira (1983); as well as various government publications.
[71] See Samuels (1998), Chapter 4, for additional information.

in the Chamber, and who attempts to bring particularistic goods to his or her vote base in order to insure continued reelection.

* *Congressional-National*: deputies of this type would also have long congressional careers, but would instead focus their energies on partisan politics or national political issues.
* *State-Directed*: these deputies would use their time in Congress as a stepping-stone to advance their state-level career ambitions.
* *Municipal-Directed*: these deputies would use congress as a political trampoline to seek municipal-level office.

Very few deputies fit one type perfectly. However, trends do emerge from the data. Most importantly, my findings indicate that very few deputies fit the first two ideal-types, while a substantial portion correspond to the latter two types.

Congressional-Local

Most Brazilian deputies do attempt to service their local constituent bases, even though very few make a long-term career in the Chamber out of local constituency service (see Chapter 2). Here I provide an example of a long-serving deputy who appears to fit this type very well, but when we examine his career more carefully we see that he has harbored extra-Chamber ambition all the while, becoming especially involved in state politics.

Our example comes from the state of Ceará: Antônio Paes de Andrade. Andrade was born in 1927, and first attempted to enter politics in 1950 by running for state deputy. He lost, but won election as state deputy in 1954, and again in 1958. During his second term he solidified links with the state government by serving as State Secretary of Interior and Justice. In 1963 he began a long career in the Chamber of Deputies, where he served consecutively until 1990, and won election again in 1994. Andrade is an almost stereotypically "pork-oriented" deputy who desires most to serve his hometown of Mombaça, in the interior of his state.

Despite Andrade's "localistic" reputation and the length of his service in the Chamber, his career path is not so clear. During his time in Congress he has taken four different leaves of absence to serve in state government. In addition, in 1985 he ran and lost for mayor of Fortaleza, Ceará's capital; and in 1990 he ran for senate and lost. In 1994 he returned to the Chamber of Deputies, and in 1995 he even gained some national prominence by winning election as president of the national executive of the PMDB, one of Brazil's largest political parties. In 1998 Andrade once again considered running for governor of Ceará (*OESP* 4/24/98, p. A-6), but ended up running (and losing badly) for senate. Andrade has served far longer than average in the Chamber, and this makes him quite exceptional in that regard, but despite this long congressional career he has cultivated links with state government all along, and for over a decade he has been (unsuccessfully so far) attempting to move beyond the Chamber, to either municipal- or state-government office. I use this example for two purposes: to provide an example of a long-serving deputy (a rarity to begin with), but also to illustrate that even those deputies who do serve long periods in the Chamber are often both intimately linked with state and municipal governments and seek political offices at those levels of government, often even as they are serving long periods in the Chamber.

Congressional-National

As in most countries, even though they often figure prominently in the media, very few Brazilian deputies conform to this ideal type, the famous "citizen legislators" who appear to have nothing but the general public's interests at heart. Nevertheless, it is useful to provide examples, no matter how rare these characters are in real life (readers familiar with Brazilian politics will recognize my examples, and appreciate how truly rare this type is).

Without a shadow of a doubt, the archetypical Congressional-National deputy in Brazilian history was Ulysses da Silveira Guimarães. Guimarães was born in 1916, and began his career in 1940 as the 1st Vice-President of the National Student Union. In 1947, he won election to the São Paulo state legislative assembly, where he served one term. In 1950, he began his career in the Chamber of Deputies, and would win ten consecutive terms, serving for forty-two years until his death in a helicopter accident in 1992. Guimarães holds the record for most consecutive wins to the Chamber of Deputies and most years served since 1945.

Guimarães served as Minister of Industry and Commerce in 1961-2, and following the 1964 military coup he quickly rose through the ranks as moderate leader of the opposition MDB party. He was elected national president of the (P)MDB in 1971 and served for twenty years in that capacity. In 1973 he ran as the Quixotic "anticandidate" for president of Brazil against the military's candidate. Guimarães served also as president of the Chamber of Deputies from 1987 until his death. He presided over the 1987-8 constitutional convention, and following that success, ran for president of Brazil in 1989 on the PMDB ticket. However, he finished embarrassingly poorly despite his national prominence, and in 1990 barely won reelection to the Chamber of Deputies. Guimarães vote base consisted of a segment of the city of São Paulo's business and liberal elite.

A second example, more to the left of the political spectrum, is José Genoíno, from the Workers' Party (PT). Genoíno was imprisoned during the military regime, and then amnestied in the late 1970s. He won election to the Chamber in 1982 and has served ever since. Genoíno is one of the very few deputies elected solely on the basis of "votes of opinion." He has no personal links to either municipal or state government due to his career trajectory, and does not attempt to bring "pork" to his hometown of São Paulo. However, newsmagazines and think tanks consistently rate him as one of Brazil's best parliamentarians, and even his conservative antagonists respect his political acumen. Because Genoíno is so clearly intelligent and articulate, the media often consult him when they want the "opposition's" opinion, and as a result he often appears on television, or in the newspapers or newsmagazines. In addition, unlike many of his PT colleagues, Genoíno has never exhibited any desire to leave the Chamber. In an interview, Genoíno confirmed this vision of his career, stating "I *live* to be here in Congress, even though my side never wins. I don't know if I would like the executive branch, really." Genoíno was the only politician among forty interviewed who stated such a preference.[72]

Genoíno and Guimarães are examples of extremely prominent politicians. However, their very prominence highlights their rarity: as in any country, politicians who truly "think globally" are few and far between.

State-Directed

An example of a state-directed deputy comes from Santa Catarina. Antônio Carlos Konder Reis, born in 1922, is the proverbial scion of a politically powerful family, and became one of the state's most historically prominent politicians. He began his career at the age of twenty-three, when he was elected state deputy. He was reelected to the state legislature in 1950, but in 1951 he took a position as Head of the Economic Forestry Division in the National Pine-Nut Institute in Rio. Pine-nuts are an important agricultural product for Santa Catarina, and a *Catarinense* politician often directed the institute, which helped organize production and marketing.

From 1952 to 1954 Konder Reis served as the *chef-de-cabinet* of the Minister of Agriculture, a national position. He appeared to be on a "national" career track when he won election to the Chamber of Deputies in 1954, but he quickly took a leave of absence from the Chamber to become his state's Secretary of Finance. In 1958 and 1962 he was reelected as federal deputy. From 1961 through the extinction of existing political parties in 1966 by military decree, Konder Reis served as a member of the state executive committee of the UDN, a party formed to oppose the political machinations of ex-dictator Getúlio Vargas. In 1962, he was elected senator from Santa Catarina by the UDN, but in 1965 he campaigned and lost election as governor, also on the UDN ticket. When the military created the

---

[72] Interview with José Genoíno. However, even at this early date (the interview was conducted in July 1999), rumors abounded about Genoíno's behind-the-scenes articulation to win the PT's nomination for the 2002 race for São Paulo governor. If Genoíno does come to seek this position, it would simply provide additional confirmation of my main point: even those deputies who *appear* to have "national-legislative" trajectories may actually aspire to *sub*national executive office.

progovernment ARENA and the opposition MDB parties in 1966, Konder Reis joined ARENA. He was reelected senator in 1970. He cut his senatorial term short, however, when he was nominated state governor in 1974. He served until 1978, and then got his nephew Jorge Konder Bornhausen nominated as his successor in the statehouse.

In 1982 Konder Reis considered a run in the first direct elections for governor following redemocratization, but decided that his chances were not good and desisted. In 1983 he became a member of the state executive committee of the newly created conservative PDS party, and that year the governor appointed him Extraordinary Secretary of Reconstruction, a state-level cabinet position, and he served in that capacity until 1985. In 1986 he returned to the Chamber of Deputies, serving in the constitutional congress, but in 1990 he ran and won election as vice-governor, serving until 1994. In 1998, Konder Reis once again returned to the Chamber of Deputies. Thus, Konder Reis served three consecutive terms in the Chamber in the 1950s and 1960s, another term in the 1980s, and another in the 1990s, but he has spent the majority of his political career intimately tied with Santa Catarina state politics as representative of the state's agricultural interests in the national government, state secretary, state party executive member, governor, vice-governor, and senator (Beloch and Abreu 1983, 2912).

Municipal-Directed

A number of deputies run and often win election to the Chamber in an attempt to "stay alive" in politics simply so that they can pursue their higher career goal, election as mayor. The state of São Paulo provides the greatest number of this type of deputy, so my example comes from that state: Francisco Chico Amaral. Without knowing the details, Amaral might appear to fit in one of the two congressional ideal-types, because he has won election to the Chamber of Deputies five times: in 1966, 1970, 1974, 1982, and 1986 (and ran and lost twice more). However, the quest to be mayor of the city of Campinas, São Paulo state's "second city," has dominated his political career. Moreover, he has also played a role in state politics. Amaral ran for mayor of Campinas during each of his first two terms in Congress, on the opposition MDB ticket, and lost both times. From 1969 to 1972, he served as vice-president of the São Paulo state PMDB, and during this third term in congress, he was elected as "chair" of the São Paulo state delegation of deputies, a position of prominence as the state delegation's representative and spokesman in the Chamber. In the late 1970s he became particularly close to senator, vice-governor, and, subsequently, governor Orestes Quércia, who constructed a relatively successful statewide political machine (Beloch and Abreu 1983, 113; Melhém 1998, 140).

However, in 1976, Amaral abandoned his seat in the Chamber and position as state delegation chair because he won election as Campinas' mayor, where he served until 1982, when he returned to the Chamber of Deputies. He won election as deputy again in 1986, but lost reelection in 1990. In 1991, he found a position in state government as Administrative Director of the São Paulo State Assurance Company (*Compania de Seguros do Estado de São Paulo*). He ran and lost for federal deputy in 1994, but in 1996 he again was elected mayor of Campinas. Amaral has survived his mentor's political decline and remains successful at the municipal level.

These examples provide an image of four types of Brazilian political careers. They are not exhaustive, and as ideal types they are not always perfect fits, but as I will demonstrate in the next section the aggregate data tend to confirm my hypothesis that deputies do continue their careers after serving in the Chamber, and that they most often attempt to do so at the state and/or municipal levels of government.

POST-CHAMBER CAREERS: OVERALL FINDINGS

Table 4.2 provides the percentage of all deputies in the sample who sought or obtained different political positions. This evidences demonstrates that a significant percentage of deputies sought to continue their political careers at the state and/or municipal levels of government, and that a much smaller percentage sought careers at the national level.

Percentages in Table 4.2 do not add up to 100 because deputies often held more than one position. Controlling for this, overall, 52.7 percent of all

TABLE 4.2 *Post-Chamber Positions Sought or Held – Full Sample*

Position Sought/Held	% Deputies
State	
Governor or Vice-Governor Candidate	9.6
Senator or *Suplente* Senator Candidate	9.7
State Deputy Candidate	6.3
State Secretary or other State-Level Position	21.0
State Party Executive Member	27.7
Municipal	
Mayor/Vice-Mayor Candidate	16.3
Municipal Position or City Council	2.6
National	
Minister of State	4.1
Other Federal-Government Position	8.5
President/Vice-President Candidate	1.2
National Party Executive Member	2.9

Source: Author's compilation.

deputies sought or held at least one state-level position,[73] 18.4 percent sought or held at least one municipal-level position, and 13.7 percent sought or held at least one national-level position.[74] Overall, 64.7 percent of deputies in the sample pursued some kind of position after serving in the Chamber.[75] I do not count "leaves of absences" as per Chapter 3 in this calculation. The numbers here are *in addition to* any national-, state-, or municipal-level position deputies may have held during a term. This finding contrasts quite starkly with the figures presented for post-House careers in the United States, and confirms that we ought not assume that deputies are primarily driven by a desire for reelection. Instead, after spending a short portion of their political career in the Chamber, most ex-deputies continue their careers at the subnational level.

POST-CHAMBER CAREERS BY STATE

The overall findings may obscure important state-by-state variation in post-Chamber career patterns. For example, the deputies from one or two of the larger states may be swamping the overall results. Consequently, here I break the aggregate data down by state. Table 4.3 presents the percentages of deputies from each state who sought or held positions at each level.

Significant state-by-state variation does exist in post-Chamber careers. For example, the fewest deputies who seek a statewide elective office come from São Paulo. We can attribute this finding to two factors. First, São Paulo elects the most deputies of all states in Brazil. Given that deputies compete in at-large, statewide districts, a *Paulista* who seeks election as deputy needs the fewest votes as a portion of all votes in his or her state to win relative to what candidates in other states need to obtain. We can reasonably suppose that for an individual deputy, the leap to statewide elective office in São Paulo would therefore be the most difficult. On the other hand, several ex-deputies from São Paulo appear to consider taking a step "down" the career

---

[73] If we remove membership in a state party from this calculation, 37 percent of all deputies in the sample sought or held a state-level position.

[74] Senator is counted as state-level for three reasons: one must win a statewide election to become senator, senators represent state interests in the national government, and because senators are often regarded as leaders of statewide political cliques.

[75] If we explore the careers of deputies who held positions at more than one level, we see that 112 deputies (10.6 percent of the sample) sought or held both state and municipal positions, 95 (8.9 percent) sought or held both state and federal positions, 20 (1.9 percent) sought or held both federal and municipal positions, and 16 deputies (1.5 percent) sought or held positions at all three levels. Thus, although many deputies appear to have progressive ambition that heads in multiple directions, most often state-level ambition dominated: of the 145 deputies who sought or held a national-level position, almost two-thirds of them (95) also held a state-level position, while of the 558 deputies who sought or held a state-level position, only 20 percent also held a national-level position.

TABLE 4.3 *Percentages of Ex-Deputies in Each State Seeking or Holding Extra-Chamber Positions*

Position	% of Deputies Holding Position						
	São Paulo	Minas Gerais	Santa Catarina	Goiás	Ceará	Piauí	Tocantins
State Level							
Candidate/Governor or VG	5.3	10.1	14.1	20.0	9.4	12.1	7.7
Candidate/Senator	6.1	7.6	17.0	13.7	10.9	22.4	7.7
Candidate/State Deputy	8.7	5.4	6.6	6.3	3.1	3.4	0.0
State Secretary/other	13.2	32.5	22.6	15.8	17.2	31.0	23.1
State Party member	24.6	26.0	38.7	27.4	29.7	31.0	38.5
Municipal Level							
Candidate/Mayor or VM	20.6	10.4	19.8	13.7	13.3	17.2	30.8
Other Municipal	4.5	2.2	0.9	1.1	2.3	0.0	0.0
National Level							
Minister	3.7	6.5	2.8	1.1	4.7	1.7	0.0
Other Federal Job	4.8	14.4	3.8	13.7	7.8	8.6	0.0
Candidate/President or VP	1.9	1.8	0.9	0.0	0.0	0.0	0.0
National Party member	3.2	1.8	0.9	3.2	5.5	1.7	15.4

Source: Author's compilation.

ladder a safe bet and a good career move. Nearly one in ten ex-deputies from São Paulo attempt to stay in state politics by running for a seat in the state legislature. Table 4.3 also shows that São Paulo's ex-deputies direct their progressive ambition relatively more toward the municipal level than any other state's deputies. Almost 25 percent of ex-deputies have sought or held a municipal-level position following service in the Chamber.

In contrast to the relatively more municipal-directed São Paulo deputies, deputies from Minas Gerais confirm their historical reputation as highly state-oriented (see e.g., Hagopian 1996). While relatively few *Mineiros* run for statewide *elective* office (compared to other states), almost one-third of ex-deputies subsequently held an *appointed* position in state government. On the other hand, despite the relatively high number of large cities in Minas, *Mineiro* ex-deputies sought municipal-level positions least often among the seven-state sample. Santa Catarina contrasts with both Minas Gerais and São Paulo in that its deputies seek out both state- and municipal-level positions relatively often. In the Northeast, deputies from Piauí appear to generally have a greater propensity to seek positions both at the state and municipal level than do deputies from Ceará, while deputies from Ceará manage to insert themselves at the national level with greater frequency than Piauense deputies.

In sum, some cross-state variation in post-Chamber careers exists. This is to be expected, given the size of the state, its level of urbanization, its political prominence within the Brazilian federation, and its particular history. In any case, both the aggregate data and the state-specific data tend to confirm my hypothesis that Brazilian deputies exhibit progressive ambition.

POST-CHAMBER CAREERS: RETURN TO THE CHAMBER?

Table 4.2 revealed that about two-thirds of all deputies in the sample exhibited some form of "progressive ambition" after their stint in the Chamber of Deputies ended. However, one might wonder whether this same number of deputies also ran for federal deputy *again*, after one or two terms had elapsed, and after they had served in some position outside the Chamber. If this were true, I might have to qualify my claim about the nature of political ambition in Brazil. However, even if this were true, it would still not indicate a desire to develop a long-term political career *within* the Chamber – and of course the very fact that time had elapsed between one Chamber term and the next would make such a feat impossible.

In fact, 245 (23.2 percent) of all ex-deputies in my sample attempted to return to the Chamber after their initial departure. However, only 45.7 percent of this group managed to win a return trip, a lower percentage than those who run for immediate reelection. This means that 12.5 percent of all deputies in the sample returned to the Chamber after an absence of at least one term. An exploration of what these deputies did in the interim period bolsters my argument about the importance of holding positions in the executive branch, especially at the subnational level.

Of the 245 deputies in the sample who ran for deputy again after missing at least one full legislature, 20 had been forced out of office for political reasons during the military regime. When they regained their political rights and ran for deputy again (often fifteen or more years later), ten managed to win reelection (50 percent).

Of the remaining 225 ex-deputies, 113 held no position at all or ran for no other office after either losing a reelection attempt or deciding to step down from the Chamber. Of this group, only 27.5 percent managed to win a return to the Chamber and continue their political career. In contrast, 112 deputies held a position in national, state, or local government, or were a candidate for a position at one of those levels, following their stint in the Chamber. Of this group, 66.1 percent managed to return to the Chamber. This suggests that holding or even running for executive-level office perpetuates one's political career in Brazil (of course, many who return to the Chamber turn around and take a leave of absence again just as quickly!).

Breaking down the information about the sources of a successful "return to the Chamber" supports my contention about the importance of holding *subnational* executive office as part of a successful long-term political career in Brazil. One can classify the ex-deputies by the kinds of jobs that they held after serving in the Chamber. Fifteen of the 112 ex-deputies held or ran for positions at multiple levels before attempting to return to the Chamber, making identification of the sources of their success difficult. Let us explore the comparative ability of the remaining 97 ex-deputies to return to the Chamber, given the positions they held or ran for following their terms.

Of the ten ex-deputies who held or ran for national positions of some kind, four managed to win a return trip to the Chamber (40 percent). Of the sixty-three deputies who held or ran for a state-level position before running for deputy again, forty-four managed to win reelection (69.8 percent). Of these, eighteen of nineteen who served as governor, vice-governor, senator, or even *suplente* senator won a return to the Chamber. Even eleven of eighteen who were *candidates* for any of those positions but who lost eventually won reelection to the Chamber (61.1 percent). Finally, of the twenty-four deputies who continued or attempted to continue their career at the municipal level, fifteen eventually managed to win reelection to the Chamber (62.5 percent).

Although the law of small numbers makes any definitive conclusion impossible, these numbers imply that if a Brazilian deputy leaves the Chamber and then wants to return, then activity at the state or municipal levels of government is more likely to provide the necessary political sustenance compared to holding a national-level office. This is because a subnational executive office provides a higher payoff in terms of keeping politicians closer to

TABLE 4.4 *Post-Chamber Careers: Changes over Time*

Position	Time Entered Congress		
	1945–63	1964–81	1982–94
State Level			
Candidate Governor/VG	13.8	9.6	5.7
Candidate Senator	15.3	10.4	4.0
Candidate State Deputy	5.8	10.0	4.7
State Secretary/other	27.0	29.5	10.0
State Party executive	17.3	31.0	36.4
Municipal Level			
Candidate Mayor/VM	5.0	21.1	24.4
Other Municipal	2.5	2.8	2.8
National Level			
Minister	7.3	3.2	1.5
Other Federal Job	18.7	3.2	1.7
Candidate President/VP	1.8	0.8	1.7
National Party executive	4.5	0.7	2.5

Source: Author's compilation.

their vote bases and political networks. In short, as deputies often indicated in interviews, serving in the Chamber or in an other national office takes one "away from one's political base" and may even *endanger* one's political career, whereas serving in state or local government provides a much better political return.

POST-CHAMBER CAREERS: CHANGES IN THE CAREER LADDER SINCE 1945

I suggested previously that although deputies tend to rotate out to state-level positions at the same pace in the current democratic period as they did during the 1945–64 period, the number of deputies who now seek a municipal-level position has increased. Data from my sample of post-Chamber careers provides additional confirmation of this claim. Table 4.4 relates the percentages of deputies from each state who sought post-Chamber positions during the three political regimes since 1945: democratic from 1945–63, authoritarian from 1964–81, and democratic again from 1982–present.[76] For this table, a deputy elected in 1958 but who ran for governor in 1970 would fall in the 1945–63 column. That is, I count the deputy from his or her first election to the Chamber. These figures should be taken with a large grain of salt. Because I include deputies elected in 1994, many deputies in the contemporary

[76] For this table, I considered every politician elected to a position as having been a candidate for that position (to account for deputies the military appointed governor or vice-governor).

period may not have moved on from or attempted to win a position outside of the Chamber yet.

The evidence shows a decline in the number of deputies seeking or holding state-level positions, but this could be artificial because some deputies in the current period haven't manifested progressive ambition yet. The same could hold true for national-level positions, although the starker relative drop may indicate that national-level positions have truly lost their luster for deputies. On the other hand, even given that some contemporary deputies may not have exhibited progressive ambition yet, the dramatic increase in municipal-directed ambition beginning with the cohorts of deputies elected during the military period provides additional confirmation of my claim that an increase in progressive ambition directed at the municipal level is a major new development in the "direction" of Brazilian political careers.

CONCLUSION

Along with the evidence I presented in chapters 2 and 3, the career-path data presented here bolster my claim about the direction of political ambition in Brazil. Of my sample of over one thousand Brazilian federal deputies, over half returned to state politics – in an elected office, a partisan office, or an appointed position – and almost 20 percent returned to municipal politics. In contrast, fewer than 15 percent continued on at the national level – and of this group nearly two-thirds also held state-level positions. Thus, despite sometimes serious limitations in the data that probably underestimate the extent of progressive ambition in Brazil, I can confidently confirm that while Brazilian politicians do not develop long-term careers in the Chamber of Deputies, the Chamber serves as a middle-level rung on a career ladder that for most politicians has both its bottom and top rungs at the subnational levels of government.

I therefore also conclude that not only do the *congressional* careers of Brazilian deputies' differ from those of members of the U.S. House in their length, but also that postcongressional careers in Brazil contrast starkly with those of members of the House. In the United States, over half of those who retire from the House leave politics completely, and most of those who remain active in politics stay involved in national-level affairs.

If a politician's behavior is a response to his office goals, as Schlesinger (1966, 9–10) argued, then my findings about Brazilian postcongressional careers confirm the descriptive accuracy of my hypothesis that Brazilian deputies do not behave like the stylized members of the U.S. House, who act as "single-minded seekers of reelection." Instead, political ambition in Brazil takes on a different form. Brazilian deputies do not attempt to develop a long-term career in the Chamber, but rather strive to move *up* the career ladder by moving *down* to subnational politics after a relatively brief stint in the Chamber of Deputies. Given this shape of political careers, the assumptions we make about the behavioral incentives of Brazilian deputies must also differ. If Brazilian deputies have extra-Chamber office goals, then we must assume that these career goals shape their behavior while they are serving as deputies. In the next section, I demonstrate the tremendous influence that federalism has in Brazilian electoral politics. Subsequently, I link this finding with the results of chapters 1 through 4, in an effort to explore the implications of careerism and federalism in Brazil.

INTRODUCTION

I n Section 1 I demonstrated that Brazilian federal deputies do not seek
long-term careers in the Chamber. Instead, many are willing to abandon
their seats after winning the election in order to take a position in state or
local government, and the majority also continue their political careers at
the state and/or municipal level after finishing their time in the Chamber. Because politicians' future career goals shape their present behavior, the career
structure in Brazil thus tends to generate behavioral incentives for incumbent
legislators to "represent" municipal and state governments' interests in the
national legislature. By acting as advocates for their state and/or local governments, deputies also are strategically seeking ways to potentially advance
their own careers at those levels. A few deputies may seek national positions,
but most of those who do land a national position also end up returning to
state or local politics, meaning that even the deputies who seek to reach a national position also have incentives to represent state and municipal interests
in the legislature.

In this section I begin to connect these individual-level incentives to
broader phenomena. Although the study of elections has gained prominence
in the (re)emerging Latin American democracies and across the globe, we
still know relatively little about some of the primary factors driving these
elections. In this section, I explore how federalism in Brazil produces a particularly state-level dynamic in legislative elections. Combining the impact
of politicians' ambitions with the "federalizing" incentives of electoral competition in Brazil helps explain the policy processes to which I turn in the
final section of the book.

Chapter 5

The "Gubernatorial Coattails Effect": Federalism and Congressional Elections in Brazil

"Stumping for candidates is a thing of the past, it's a figure of speech. These days, if you advertise that you're going to vote for this guy or that guy, it doesn't change anything."
> —Brazilian President Fernando Henrique Cardoso, expressing his belief that presidential coattail effects do not exist in Brazil

"If every politician's first rule is to survive, then we reach the following conclusion: it is useless to discuss national issues in the electoral process."
> —Nelson Jobim, two-term federal deputy, former Minister of Justice, and current Supreme Court Justice

INTRODUCTION

In January 1999, Fernando Henrique Cardoso became the first Brazilian president in history to pass the presidential sash to himself. He won a smashing first-round reelection victory in October 1998, defeating his nearest rival by over 20 percent, and the parties in his alliance also won sizeable majorities in both houses of Congress. By all rights, Cardoso's reelection ought to have rejuvenated his efforts to maintain Brazil's economic stabilization program (the *Plano Real*) and to pass extensive political reforms. On top of the prestige due from his relatively easy victory, soon after the election the IMF agreed to provide Brazil with U.S.$42 billion to give Cardoso extra political and economic breathing room to maneuver for reform. Superficially, President Cardoso appeared to possess significant political capital upon the start of his second term.

However, Cardoso experienced no "second honeymoon." Quite the contrary; his second term began as a nightmare. Within weeks of his inauguration, the *Real* collapsed, losing half its value and raising fears of a return to Brazil's infamous days of hyperinflation; the country's foreign currency reserves were drained; two Central Bank presidents resigned in succession; the Brazilian stock markets went into a free fall; and former President

Itamar Franco, elected governor of the important state of Minas Gerais, effectively defaulted on his state's debts owed to domestic and international creditors. This "last straw" forced the central government to cover Minas' debts in order to stave off the perception of a generalized government default. The *New York Times* soon concluded that despite Cardoso's victory, "Brazil is struggling against its worst financial crisis in years" (NYT 1/25/99, p. A-8). Moreover, as the largest economy in Latin America and the eighth largest in the world, Brazil's troubles reverberated throughout the region: leery investors feared that Brazil's problems could unleash "new global turmoil" (*NYT* 2/11/99, p. A-9) or even precipitate a "global financial meltdown" (*The Economist* 1/16/99, p. 17). Brazil's economic crisis generated a political crisis, and after his inauguration Cardoso's postelection political halo quickly vanished as the president's prestige slipped both with voters and within the halls of Congress.[77]

Why was Cardoso's second honeymoon cut short so abruptly? While many factors were at play, one clearly stands out: the way in which Brazil's federal institutions constrain presidential leadership and impede smooth executive-legislative relations. The *Plano Real* entailed serious consequences for intergovernmental relations in Brazil: to keep inflation in check, the plan kept domestic interest rates at extremely high levels, which since 1994 dramatically increased the debt burden on Brazil's states (Abrucio and Costa 1998). That is, the *Real* fixed one problem and exacerbated another. The bubble burst when Franco and several other governors demanded debt relief in January 1999. Creditors suspected the central government's fiscal credibility and doubted whether Cardoso had the congressional support to pass needed reforms, especially in terms of fiscal policy. Consequently, economic and political crises erupted. This view was widespread: recognizing the federal root of the problem, one *New York Times* headline even reported that "Brazil's Economic Crisis Pits President Against Governors" (1/25/99, p. A-8).

This interpretation jibes fairly well with scholarly opinion about Brazil's comparative inability to institutionalize political and economic reforms. While Brazil's presidency ranks among the world's most institutionally powerful (Shugart and Carey 1992) and this concentration of power might lead one to suppose that governing ought to be relatively easy; multipartism, fragmented parties, and strong federalism impede smooth executive-legislative relations (Abranches 1988; Mainwaring 1999; Power 2000; Ames 2001). The fragmentation of Brazil's party system and Brazilian parties' lack of cohesion force the president to struggle to construct very broad legislative coalitions with each new policy proposal (cf. Figueiredo and Limongi 2000a). Scholars typically point to Brazil's electoral system – its use of open-list proportional representation with a low threshold for achieving

---

[77] See for example *The Economist* 2/6/99, p. 34; *The Economist* 3/27/99, NYT 1/8/99, p. C4; NYT 1/17/99, p. WK4; NYT 2/11/99, p. A9; NYT 1/25/99, p. A8; *The Economist* 1/16/99, pp. 17, 33; *The Economist* 2/27/99, pp. 33–77.

representation and high district magnitudes – as the source of party-system fragmentation and party weakness, and of the president's consequently reduced capacity to get what he wants from the legislature.

Brazilian federalism, by generating incentives for legislators to pay close attention to state-based issues and scant attention to national partisan issues, also contributes to partisan fragmentation and uncohesiveness, making legislative coalition building even more difficult. State governors also possess resources, such as pork-barrel funds and the power to hire and fire, to influence legislators from their state. Given these state-based political loyalties and gubernatorial influence over congressional deputies, presidents must negotiate with state governors to build legislative support. This gives governors influence in national politics and restricts the president's range of action (Abrucio 1998).

Even given these institutional constraints, the rapid collapse of the *Real* and the abrupt return of a feeling of generalized crisis in Brazil conflict with the optimistic expectations that Cardoso's victories generated. For example, Linz and Stepan (1996, 188) argued that Cardoso would enjoy smoother executive-legislative relations than former president Fernando Collor (1989–92) because he brought "great legislative prestige and experience" to the presidency and because he enjoyed wide popular support. Likewise, Abrucio (1998, 227) claimed that the concurrence of presidential and legislative elections in 1994 and 1998 would strengthen Cardoso's hand vis-à-vis Congress and facilitate passage of his agenda. Finally, Mainwaring (1997, 106) deliberately distinguished the chaotic 1985–94 period from Cardoso's presidency and argued that because of Cardoso's first-term success passing some reforms, "it seems likely that institutional constraints will loom as less deleterious" in the future.

Given these expectations, the question I ask in this chapter is whether federalism helps explain the rapid end to Cardoso's second honeymoon. By extension, the argument also offers insight into why Cardoso's reform efforts succeeded in some areas but failed to advance in others, as well as offer predictions about the potential for governability in future administrations.

This chapter offers a different interpretation of how federalism and weak partisan powers constrain presidential leadership in Brazil and make construction of stable legislative coalitions difficult. I address a previously neglected aspect of Brazilian electoral politics: the absence of presidential "coattail effects," and the presence of what I call "gubernatorial coattail effects." Because presidential coattails are so short in Brazil, the president cannot use his personal electoral popularity as a tool to influence Congress. In contrast, governors have long electoral coattails in their state's *national* congressional race. Gubernatorial coattail effects therefore explain how federalism directly impacts national executive-legislative relations in Brazil.

This attempt to understand the electoral roots of governability in Brazil is new, but fits well with our understanding of federalism's political importance in Brazil. While several scholars have recently explored Brazilian federalism, and some have intimated the importance of the electoral link between the governor's race and national legislative elections,[78] none have looked for presidential coattails, and none have empirically explored how gubernatorial coattails drive national legislative elections and consequently affect both the contours of the national party system as well as national-level executive-legislative relations.[79]

This chapter is organized as follows. In the next section I explain why coattail effects are important for understanding executive-legislative relations. Subsequently I explain why we have good reason to believe that coattail effects in Brazil are gubernatorial and not presidential. I then provide evidence that a state-based dynamic does drive national legislative elections, and I conclude offering insights as to how gubernatorial coattails affect governance in Brazil.

PRESIDENTIAL COATTAILS AND PRESIDENTIAL GOVERNANCE

Presidential leadership in both the electoral and legislative arenas provides the key to understanding executive-legislative relations in separation-of-powers systems. In the United States, both politicians and scholars have

---

[78] For example, compare the analysis here and its implications for the party system with Lima Jr. (1983), Lima Jr., ed. (1997), or Lavareda (1991).

[79] No literature on "coattails effects" exists for any Latin American country except for Ames (1994), who argued that in Brazil we see a "reverse" coattails effect, where *municipal*-level elections drive the presidential election. This argument is problematic, both theoretically and empirically. Theoretically, coattail effects are more likely to be top-down than bottom-up (see text). Empirically, Ames' hypothesis implies that in Brazil we expect candidates whose parties have a solid base of support at the municipal level to do relatively well, *ceteris paribus*, in the subsequent presidential election. Yet in 1989, Lula's PT controlled only 38 municipalities and Collor's PRN only 3, of more than 4,000 total municipalities. The parties of the three candidates who together obtained 60.2 percent of the popular vote in the first round of the presidential election (PRN, PT, PDT) controlled only 5.5 percent of all of Brazil's municipalities, which contained only 25.5 percent of the country's population (and much of that was in just two cities, São Paulo and Rio de Janeiro, controlled by the PT and PDT at the time). In contrast, the presidential candidates of the country's four largest parties (PSDB, PFL, PMDB, and PDS) obtained only 24.3 percent of the vote in the first round, while they held 73 percent of all of Brazil's municipalities, which contained 54.6 percent of Brazil's population. Thus, in contrast to Ames' hypothesis, in 1989 we see a negative correlation (−.15) between a presidential candidate's national vote total and the percentage of the electorate that that candidate's party controlled, as well as a negative correlation (−.34) between a presidential candidate's vote total and the number of municipalities that his party controlled. This generates a puzzle: why did some candidates (e.g., Lula, Brizola, Collor) do relatively well *despite* having relatively little municipal-level support, while other candidates (e.g., Ulysses, Chaves, Maluf, Camargo) did very poorly despite the fact that their parties possessed widespread support at the municipal level? These observations might lead one to believe that local party organization matters in quite the opposite way that Ames suggests, that is, that local party organization and national elections are *not* well-linked in Brazil. In the end, both Collor's and Lula's success in 1989 rested on something besides the extent of their parties' (or even allied parties') ostensible level of municipal-level strength.

long known about the potential importance of presidential coattail effects.[80] Coattail effects in American politics are defined as "the ability of a candidate at the top of the ticket to carry into office ... his party's candidates on the same ticket" (Beck 1996, 251), and the concept typically is operationalized as a correlation between the presidential and legislative vote in a given constituency. In comparative politics, research on executive-legislative relations has focused on *post-election* institutional arrangements (e.g., Shugart and Carey 1992), while comparatively little research has explored how the relationship between executive and legislative elections subsequently affects postelection relations between branches (Shugart 1995; Jones 1997). Moreover, this existing research has explored the relationship between the "effective number of candidates" (or party lists) in executive and legislative elections, as opposed to looking for actual vote correlations between levels of elections.[81] In this chapter, I test for correlations between both votes as well as effective number of candidates.

Coattail effects in the United States are assumed emanate from the more important to the less important offices, linking the fates of congressional candidates to the fate of their party's presidential candidate. The theoretical rationale behind this assumption is as follows: because presidential candidates typically obtain the lion's share of campaign finance and of national media attention, and because the national party organizes presidential nominations, candidates for legislative office seek organizational and financial support from the national party and/or its candidate. Moreover, voters seek "information shortcuts" and tend to pay greater attention to executive-office campaigns, which have a national focus and which embody broader national issues. This creates a focal point around which legislative candidates can coordinate their own campaigns.

In this way, the relative importance of the presidential campaign creates strong incentives for congressional candidates to line up behind the presidential candidate of their party. When executive and legislative elections are thus linked, executive candidates will sweep legislative candidates into office on their "coattails" (or not, depending on the performance of the executive-office candidate). On the other hand, if congressional candidates made no such effort to coordinate with an executive-office candidate (or if they actively distance themselves from their own executive-office candidate) we expect the results for the two elections to be independent of each other.

---

[80] Debate continues about whether coattails in the United States have declined in importance in recent decades. See for example Born 1984; Campbell 1986a, 1986b; Campbell and Summers 1990; Ferejohn and Calvert 1984).

[81] In general, the electoral studies literature tends to ignore the potential impact of subnational variables on the overall degree of fragmentation in the party system. See for example Rae (1971), Lijphart (1990, 1994).

When the presidential and legislative elections are linked, coattails can provide the margin of victory for individual congressional candidates. Coattail effects can thus affect the distribution of seats in the legislature. Consequently, when a presidential candidate helps elect members of his party, his subsequent task of constructing a stable legislative coalition is made easier. Once in office, legislators who believe the president helped elect them are more likely to cooperate with him, if not out of gratitude then out of a shared sense of fate. On the other hand, those who believe they were elected on their own merits have less reason to go along with presidential proposals (Jacobson 1992, 156). Furthermore, a partisan tide flowing from the presidential election sends a symbolic message that the electorate has spoken clearly, and might cow legislative opposition to the new president out of fear of future electoral punishment.

The degree of linkage between executive and legislative elections has potentially profound implications for national politics in separation-of-powers systems. Given the spread of presidential democracy, scholars ought to explore the extent to which coattails effects exist, and what factors drive them. For all of their historical importance in the United States, coattail effects – or their absence – might be even more important for the democratic process elsewhere.

PRESIDENTIAL VS. GUBERNATORIAL COATTAILS IN BRAZIL

How can we assess the linkage between executive – whether presidential or gubernatorial – and legislative elections in Brazil? To answer this we must specify more clearly what candidates for legislative office seek by associating with an executive-level candidate. First, they seek access to the ballot. Second, once on the ballot, they seek the resources that a larger campaign might be able to provide. I argue that a state-based dynamic drives both of these processes in Brazil, and that *gubernatorial* coattails explain the distance between presidential and legislative elections, the concomitant importance of the gubernatorial election to candidates for federal deputy, and therefore the importance of federalism in executive-legislative relations.

These factors focus renewed attention on the weakness of Brazil's national parties. Brazilian national party labels have historically been and continue to be weak, as are Brazilian national party organizations (Mainwaring 1999). Most voters and most politicians appear not to place much importance on long-term "affective" national partisan affiliations (Mainwaring and Scully 1995; Samuels 1999). Brazilian politicians change their partisan affiliation frequently (Nicolau 1996; Schmitt 1999), and create and extinguish parties frequently as well, making difficult any voter's desire to maintain a partisan attachment. Given these factors, as they would in any country, Brazilian candidates have few reasons to let national parties or partisan disputes determine their campaign strategies.

Ballot Access: a State-Level Game

In many countries, centralized party organizations choose both the presidential and congressional candidates. This would provide congressional candidates with a strong reason to line up behind their national leadership. In contrast, decentralized nomination control is among the most important factors that limit a national-level party's ability to espouse a consistent policy position across constituencies (Carey and Shugart 1995). In Brazil, the twenty-seven states of the federation serve as electoral constituencies for congressional elections. By law, nominations for all offices except president (and municipal-level positions) are decided at the state level. Typically, a small clique of state political bosses determines access to the ballot for federal deputy in each state; national party organs have no say. Consequently, candidates who seek access to the ballot must appease state-level political leaders. Interviewed politicians candidly detail stories of state political bosses attracting or impeding candidacies,[82] and newspapers often relate episodes of politicians barred from a party's nomination because their state-level rivals did not want the competition.[83] In short, at the very first stage of the electoral process – gaining a spot on the ballot – candidates have strong incentives to link their campaign to a state-based political machine, and few incentives to focus on the policy platform or personal electoral popularity of their party's presidential candidate.[84]

Campaign Resources and Gubernatorial Coattails

After gaining access to the ballot, candidates seek resources to boost their campaigns. Executive-office campaigns provide three kinds of benefits to office-seeking congressional candidates: information "shortcuts," organizational resources, and media exposure. Information "shortcuts" can include party labels or a popular candidate's name. Because voters have limited interest in acquiring extensive information about legislative candidates, these same candidates have tremendous incentives to provide information shortcuts to reduce voters' uncertainty (Popkin 1990). Association with a readily identifiable party label or with a well-known higher-office candidate is relatively cheap, and may provide a high return in terms of votes.

---

[82] Interviews with Ivo Wanderlinde, Marcelo Linhares, Carlos Estevam Martins, and Aldo Fagundes.

[83] See for example *FSP* 7/3/97, p. 4; *FSP* 1/8/97, p. 4; *OESP* 4/30/97, p. 6; *OESP* 4/21/97, p. 6; *FSP* 4/30/97, p. 4; *OESP* 5/14/97, p. 6, 8; *OESP* 3/22/97, p. 6; *FSP* 1/27/97, p. 5; *FSP* 9/18/96, p. 4; *FSP* 7/3/97, p. 4.

[84] Nomination control is not a necessary condition for presidential (or gubernatorial coattails): in the United States neither national parties nor presidential candidates influence the nomination process for House candidates, but we see presidential coattails. However, nomination control in Brazil is intimately linked to what may be a sufficient condition for coattail effects: the benefits of association with a broad-based campaign.

In Brazil, despite scholarly focus on the high degree of individualism and on the relative unimportance of party labels on the campaign trail (Ames 1995b; Samuels 1999), candidates do not simply desire to "go it alone." Instead, they seek to associate their own campaign with a broader campaign that might attract uncommitted and/or uninformed voters. Low party identification in Brazil means a relative absence of reliable national partisan "cues," forcing candidates seek other ways to provide voters with information shortcuts to increase their probability of success. While they may not seek to associate themselves with a party label, they do attempt to tie themselves to candidates for higher office.

Brazilian politicians recognize the incentive to provide voters with information shortcuts: "A deputy tends to want to insert himself in something larger, and thus tends to associate himself with a campaign for the executive," stated a deputy who had also served as governor and senator.[85] Given that congressional candidates do not rely on their national partisan affiliation to reap votes, the question is then which executive campaign – the presidential or the gubernatorial – provides relatively higher payoffs for an office-seeking candidate?

While presidential candidates may enjoy significant personal popularity, congressional candidates have few incentives to line up behind them. On the other hand, gubernatorial candidates possess the name recognition and organizational backing that congressional candidates seek. When asked, candidates for deputy affirm that because presidential candidates are political "outsiders" in every state but their own, association with a gubernatorial candidate – a trusted local – is a better political investment. For example, one candidate stated that

It's important to have a good candidate for the [state] executive. If he's good, then the association with his name can bring you votes. Everybody knows that there are voters out there who are indifferent to you. So, a candidate for deputy puts the candidate for governor's name on his campaign literature, because if the governor's name is on there, the voter might say "well, I don't really think too much of so-and-so, but he's with the guy I like for governor, so I'll vote for them both." The gubernatorial candidate's name brings in the votes.[86]

While presidential candidates are often seen as virtual "foreigners" who depend on state-based leaders to project their own campaigns – particularly given Brazil's dramatic regional disparities – gubernatorial candidates are typically better known "locals" who have developed a stronger and broader clientelistic network in their state. Even when gubernatorial and presidential elections occur simultaneously, this provides a strong reason for a candidate to strengthen his ties to a gubernatorial candidate. In short, in the absence of strong national party organizations and labels, candidates may seek

---

[85] Interview with André Franco Montoro.   [86] Interview with César Souza.

other ways to attract votes. In Brazil, candidates have incentives to associate their campaigns with the gubernatorial race, historically the "locomotives" pulling Brazilian congressional elections (Abrucio 1998).

The second and third kinds of benefits from "coattails" focus our attention on the importance of the state government for office-seeking politicians in Brazil. In general, higher-level campaigns can provide organizational support to relatively resource-poor congressional candidates. For example, executive-office elections typically reel in the lion's share of campaign finance, and their organizations can thus provide funds, personnel support to "get out the vote," or other organizational resources. Scholars agree that subnational actors in Brazil have historically held, and retain to this day, considerable political prerogatives (Abrucio and Samuels 1997; Abrucio 1998; Mainwaring and Samuels 1999). In particular, state governors control sizable budgets and retain extensive power to hire and fire. In countries with relatively autonomous subnational governments like Brazil, politicians may have incentives to respond to subnational rather than national political forces when campaigning, because gubernatorial candidates and/or incumbent state officials might be a better source of scarce electoral resources than presidential aspirants.

For example, in contrast to presidential candidates, gubernatorial candidates in Brazil typically control strong statewide clientelistic networks that can provide organizational support to vote-hungry deputy candidates. Interviews with politicians confirmed that deputies perceive that association with a national party's presidential candidate provides little electoral return, while association with a gubernatorial candidate provides a significant return.[87] One deputy confirmed that a popular presidential candidate can provide little organizational support, noting that "Our electoral base is in the state, it's not national. The presidential candidate can't pay attention to over 5,000 municipalities."[88] On the other hand, gubernatorial candidates do provide essential "get-out-the-vote" support. Another candidate stated that "It's important to have a tight relationship with someone strong at the state level in your campaign, because he can win over some municipal leaders, some bases of support for your own election."[89]

An additional incentive for congressional candidates to ally with a gubernatorial candidate is that if he allies with the winner, he can expect privileged access to pork-barrel funds and plum political jobs for his cronies later on. As Abrucio (1995, 141) argues, "political machines in Brazil tend to consolidate around their relationship with state executives, because the mayors and all the local leaders depend highly on the power of the governor. It is the state government, or the regional bosses, almost always linked to the state

[87] Interviews with César Souza, Ivo Wanderlinde, Waldeck Ornellas, Jarbas Passarinho, Alberto Goldman, Paulo Lustosa, Gonzaga Mota.
[88] Interview with Lidia Quinan.   [89] Interview with Sandro Scodro.

government machine, that organizes the local brokers and ward heelers." Thus, to assure his clients that he will be able to follow through on promised access, a candidate seeks out his own patron. If he picks a loser, he will have to initiate a rapprochement with the winning candidate, which is facilitated by Brazil's weak party legislation.

Finally, candidates for legislative office might benefit from publicity associated with the executive-office campaign. If the presidential or gubernatorial candidate visits his or her constituency, the legislative candidate may be able to free ride and gain significant exposure that would have otherwise been too costly to purchase. This free exposure associates the congressional candidate with the policies and personality of the executive-office candidate. In short, although Brazilian congressional candidates exhibit a good deal of electoral individualism, they have strong incentives to associate with a broader campaign in the hope of benefiting from coattail effects. Not only must Brazilian congressional candidates seek nomination in a state-level game, but they also obtain the resources necessary for their campaigns – information shortcuts, organizational support, and publicity – largely at the state level.

EVIDENCE OF GUBERNATORIAL COATTAILS

Alliance Patterns and Gubernatorial Coattails

When interviewed, Brazilian politicians highlight gubernatorial coattails, but candidates may say one thing while the election results reveal another. What other empirical evidence exists that congressional candidates act to coordinate their campaigns around a gubernatorial candidate and not a presidential candidate? State-based party branches control not only nomination but also have controlled the creation and composition of electoral alliances for all offices except president. Nearly all winning deputies win as members of a multiparty alliance – votes are pooled at the *alliance* level in each state, not the party level, for the allocation of seats. National parties have held negotiations about the presidential race separately from the state-level negotiations, which actually *precede* the nomination of candidates for federal deputy – once an alliance is formed, its members have to decide how to allocate the spaces on the list (this dynamic may change in the 2002 elections).

State-level alliance control has meant that a deputy alliance could parallel a gubernatorial alliance, a presidential alliance, both, or neither. State-level leaders have had the discretion to decide whether to follow national party dictates, or whether to organize races according to local conditions. This autonomy also has opened up the possibility that partisan alliances for the gubernatorial and deputy races could differ across states, severely limiting the ability of presidential candidates to conduct consistent national campaigns, because their national allies might be enemies at the state level. To further assess presidential versus gubernatorial coattails, we therefore need to discover the extent to which party alliances have been congruent across levels.

I define a congruent alliance as one in which all parties in the alliance support the same candidate for higher office, while an incongruent alliance is one in which the parties in the same alliance support different candidates for higher office.[90] For example, if parties AB and CD ally to run presidential candidates, congruent alliances would have AB and CD running gubernatorial and deputy candidates in a given state. In contrast, incongruent alliances might see AB and CD running presidential candidates while AC and BD ran gubernatorial and deputy candidates. AC and BD would be incongruent with the presidential race but congruent with each other because they support one gubernatorial candidate each but two presidential candidates each.

In states where deputy and gubernatorial alliances are congruent, we might expect gubernatorial coattails: the gubernatorial candidate would serve as a state-level rallying point who also possesses significant political connections and valuable electoral resources. On the other hand, where deputy and presidential alliances match, we might see presidential coattails, for the same reason. If the deputy alliances match both the gubernatorial and presidential alliances, we would have to statistically weigh the influence of each upon the deputy campaign. Finally, if we observe that a deputy race matches neither executive-office race, we might suspect that no coattail effects exist at all. Let us first examine the presidential elections. Table 5.1 lists the candidates, alliances, and national results for Brazil's presidential elections.[91]

In 1989, few parties allied. Winning candidate Fernando Collor's alliance (PRN/PST/PSL) consisted of three minuscule parties, while second-place finisher Lula's alliance consisted of the Workers' Party (PT) plus two tiny leftist parties. In 1994, more parties allied, but two of the four largest center-right parties fielded their own candidates – the conservative PPR (Paulo Maluf) and the centrist PMDB (Orestes Quércia) – while the centrist PSDB and conservative PFL allied with the PTB, a small center-right party. In 1998, the PMDB sat out the presidential race, while all the other major center-right

---

[90] Parties that run independently and do not support any candidate for executive office, or alliances of candidates that do not support any candidate for executive office, are not counted. On the other hand, two parties that support one candidate for governor could decide to create two separate lists for the deputy race, and both of these lists would be "congruent." There is a method to this madness: in some states, there are more willing candidates for deputy than there are slots on a single list (alliances can run one and a half candidates times the number of seats in the district). Thus, these candidates agree to form two lists instead of excluding some candidates from competition. Both lists then rally around the same gubernatorial candidate, even though the lists are competing against each other for deputy votes. I do not count single-party lists when calculating "congruence" because it is tautological.

[91] I include candidates who received more than 0.5 percent of the vote. See the front matter for full names of Brazil's parties, and Mainwaring (1997) for descriptions of Brazilian parties.

TABLE 5.1 *Presidential Election Results – Brazil 1989–1998*

Year	Candidates (Alliance Partners)	% of 1st-Round Vote
1989	Fernando Collor de Mello (PRN/PST/PSL)	30.5
	Luiz Inácio Lula da Silva (PT/PSB/PCdoB)	17.2
	Leonel Brizola (PDT)	16.5
	Mario Covas (PSDB)	11.5
	Paulo Maluf (PDS) (currently PPB)	8.9
	Guilherme Afif Domingos (PL/PDC)	4.8
	Ulysses Guimarães (PMDB)	4.7
	Roberto Freire (PCB) (currently PPS)	1.1
	Aureliano Chaves (PFL)	0.9
	Affonso Camargo (PTB)	0.6
1994	Fernando Henrique Cardoso (PSDB/PFL/PTB)	54.3
	Luiz Inácio Lula da Silva (PT/PSB/PCdoB/PPS/PV/PSTU)	27.0
	Enéas Carneiro (PRONA)	7.4
	Orestes Quércia (PMDB/PSD)	4.4
	Leonel Brizola (PDT)	3.2
	Espiridião Amin (PPR) (currently PPB)	2.7
1998	Fernando Henrique Cardoso (PSDB/PFL/PTB/PPB/PSD)	53.1
	Luis Inácio Lula da Silva (PT/PDT/PCdoB/PSB/PCB)	31.7
	Ciro Gomes (PPS/PL/PAN)	11.0
	Enéas Carneiro (PRONA)	2.1

Source: Nicolau (1998); Tribunal Superior Eleitoral (1999).

parties lined up behind Cardoso. On the left, in 1994 the PT (Lula) and PDT (Brizola) ran separate candidates, but in 1998 the PDT ran behind Lula and the PT, while the ex-communist PPS ran its own candidate (Ciro Gomes), whereas it had allied with Lula in 1994. To what extent were gubernatorial and congressional alliances congruent with the presidential alliances?

Despite his dramatic win in 1989, Collor failed to organize a national party behind him. What has remained less obvious is the degree to which a state-based partisan logic dominated the 1990 campaign for gubernatorial, senatorial, and congressional elections. The last column of Table 5.2 shows that in 1990, 95 percent of the gubernatorial alliances matched the alliances for federal deputy in each state (although these alliances varied significantly from state to state).

Given nonconcurrent presidential and legislative elections in 1990, we might have expected this state-driven result. Did this pattern change when elections became concurrent in 1994 and 1998? Stepan (1997) among others has specifically pointed to the lack of concurrent legislative and presidential

TABLE 5.2 *Congruence of Brazilian Elections – 1989–1998 (all states)*

Year	% Congruent Presidential/ Gubernatorial	% Congruent Presidential/ Deputy	% Congruent Gubernatorial/ Deputy	% Congruent for All 3 Levels
1989/90	N/A	N/A	95% (N = 82)	N/A
1994	28% (N = 86)	35% (N = 110)	97% (N = 93)	23% (N = 123)
1998	20% (N = 83)	29% (N = 92)	97% (N = 97)	25% (N = 99)

N/A = Not applicable.
Source: Calculated from Nicolau (1998); Goés (1999); TSE (1991, 1995, 1999).

elections as a source executive-legislative tension in Brazil, and Shugart and Carey (1992) have argued that nonconcurrence tends to increase executive-legislative tension generally. Yet despite concurrent presidential elections in 1994 and 1998 the gubernatorial races with the legislative races continued to overshadow any link between the presidential and legislative races. Table 5.2 provides strong evidence of the linkage between the deputy and gubernatorial races in both 1994 and 1998.

If presidents were able to rally their allies around their candidacies across the country, we would expect both the gubernatorial and deputy alliances to match the presidential alliances. However, columns two and three of Table 5.2 show that less than 30 percent of all gubernatorial and deputy alliances in 1994 and 1998 matched the presidential alliances.[92] Parties in the other alliances supported two or even three different presidential candidates, yet campaigned as a team for the gubernatorial and/or deputy race. Moreover, most of the congruent alliances were on the left of the political spectrum: 67 percent (28 total) supported PT candidate Lula, 12 percent (5 total) supported other leftists, and only 21 percent (9 total) supported center-right candidates (of these, seven supported Cardoso). The left holds only about 20 percent of the seats in Congress.

In contrast to the incongruence of gubernatorial and deputy alliances with presidential alliances, column five shows that the gubernatorial and deputy alliances matched each other in nearly every case in all three elections. In short, neither gubernatorial nor deputy alliances typically followed the presidential alliances. Instead, the deputy race tended to conform to the gubernatorial race.

[92] The level of congruence between president and deputy is a bit higher because in many states some insignificant alliances run candidates for deputy and support a presidential candidate, but do not join a gubernatorial coalition or launch their own gubernatorial candidate. The number of cases differs because in some states parties choose to run deputy candidates and a presidential candidate but not a gubernatorial candidate, or vice versa. For "all three levels" I counted all deputy list cases, including ones that had not run either a presidential or gubernatorial candidate.

Table 5.3 provides examples from three states of how congressional alliances tended to coordinate around the gubernatorial race in each state and
not the presidential race. The first column lists the state and the second
column the year of the election. The third column lists the gubernatorial alliances in the state at a given election, and the fourth column lists the alliances
for federal deputy. These can be compared to the alliances for president in
Table 5.1.

The examples I picked are typical across Brazil. In each state, there has
been a lack of relation between the presidential alliance and the gubernatorial and/or deputy alliance, but a strong connection between the latter two
alliances. For example, if the PRN ran candidates in 1990, it was usually as
a tertiary member of a coalition. Many other parties that had run opposed
in the 1989 presidential race allied in 1990, but in different combinations
across states.[93] Let us explore this dynamic in more detail across states,
within states, and for the 1998 election in particular.

Table 5.3 shows that alliance patterns vary considerably across states.
Take Cardoso's PSDB: in Piauí the PSDB ran no deputy candidates in 1990;
decided to ally with the PMDB, PDT, and PPS in 1994 (shaded to the left);
and then with the PT and PSB in 1998 (further to the left). In Goiás, the
PSDB allied with the PP and PTB in 1994 (shaded to the right), and then
with the PMDB, PPS, PSB and others in 1998 (a center-left coalition). These
examples are typical; the near-total absence of partisan congruence across
states demonstrates that national partisan issues did not define alliance patterns in Brazil. Rather, personalistic factions determined how parties lined
up at the state level. This limited the potential impact of a popular president
to sweep his copartisans into office on a national partisan tide that stems
from his popularity.

Because state-level political concerns tend to trump national issues, not
even the leftist parties were immune to this incongruence, and in 1998 several
national-level enemies allied at the state level. Most incongruously, the PT
and PSDB allied in two states, and the PDT and PSDB in six states, even
though the PT and PDT allied behind Lula in opposition to Cardoso and his
PSDB that year at the presidential level. The PT even allied with such right-
wing parties as the PPR and PTB in some states.[94] In short, alliance patterns
reveal a near-complete lack of national partisan direction across states. This
limited the ability of a presidential candidate to project a national image on
the campaign trail.

[93] There is an "extra" party in a few alliances, but this does not make the alliance incongruent.
[94] In 1998 Ciro Gomes could not even get his minuscule party to line up behind him: the PPS
supported the PSDB in eight states and the PT in six more. In one state (Bahia) it allied
with both the PDT *and* PSDB, and in another it allied with the PDT and PTB (which was
part of Cardoso's alliance). That is, several states saw one deputy or gubernatorial alliance
supporting *all three* major presidential candidates in 1998.

TABLE 5.3 *Alliance Patterns in Brazilian Elections (selected states)*

State	Year	Gubernatorial Alliances (candidate's party in bold)	Federal Deputy Alliances
Piauí	1990	1. **PPR**/PSC/PFL/PTB 2. **PMDB**/PDC/PL/PTR/ PRN/PSDB	1. PPR/PSC/PFL 2. PMDB/PDC/PL/PTR/ PRN/PSDB
	1994	1. **PFL**/PPR/PTB/PL/PP 2. **PMDB**/PDT/PPS/PMN/ PSDB/PCdoB 3. **PT**/PSB	1. PFL/PPR/PTB/PL/PP 2. PMDB/PDT/PPS/PMN/ PSDB/PCdoB 3. PT/PSB
	1998	1. **PT**/PSB/PSDB 2. **PDT**/PTB/PMDB/PPS/PSDC/ PRONA/PCdoB 3. **PPR**/PFL/PRP/PTdoB	1. PT/PSB/PSDB 2. PDT/PTB/PMDB/PPS/ PSDC/PRONA/PCdoB 3. PPR/PFL/PRP/PTdoB
Goiás	1990	1. **PPR**/PTB/PDC/PSC/PFL/ PRN/PSD/PRP/PST/PTdoB 2. **PMDB**/PPS/PTR/PL	1. PPR/PTB/PDC/PSC/PFL/ PRN/PSD/PRP/PST/PTdoB 2. PMDB/PPS/PTR
	1994	1. **PFL**/PPR 2. **PMDB**/PL/PRN/PRP 3. **PT**/PSTU/PPS/PMN/PV/ PCdoB 4. **PP**/PTB/PSDB	1. PFL/PPR 2. PMDB/PL/PRN/PRP 3. PT/PSTU/PPS/PMN/PV/ PCdoB 4. PP/PTB/PSDB
	1998	1. **PT**/PDT/PCdoB 2. **PPR**/PTB/PFL/PSDC/PSDB 3. **PMDB**/PST/PSC/PL/PPS/ PAN/PSB/PSD/PSDB	1. PT/PDT/PCdoB 2. PPR/PTB/PFL/PSDC/PSDB 3. PMDB/PST/PSC/PL/PPS/ PAN/PSB/PSD/PSDB
São Paulo	1990	1. **PPR**/PRN/PTB/PDC 2. **PMDB**/PFL/PL 3. **PSDB** 4. **PT**/PSB/PPS/PCdoB	1. PPR/PRN/PTB/PDC 2. PMDB 3. PFL/PL/PSD 4. PSDB 5. PT/PSB/PPS/PCdoB
	1994	1. **PP**/PPR 2. **PDSB**/PFL 3. **PDT**/PV/PRP 4. **PT**/PSTU/PPS/PMN/ PSB/PCdoB 5. **PMDB**/PL/PSD	1. PP/PPR 2. PSDB/PFL 3. PDT/PV/PRP 4. PT/PSTU/PPS/PMN/ PSB/PCdoB 5. PMDB/PL/PSD
	1998	1. **PPR**/PFL/PL 2. **PMDB** 3. **PSDB**/PTB/PSD 4. **PT**/PPS/PMN/PCdoB 5. **PDT**/PTN/PSN/PSB	1. PPR/PFL/PL 2. PMDB 3. PSDB/PTB/PSD 4. PT/PPS/PMN/PCdoB 5. PDT/PTN/PSN/PSB

Source: TSE (1991, 1995, 1999).

Table 5.3 also shows that alliance patterns vary within states over time. For example, in São Paulo, Brazil's largest and economically most important state, the gubernatorial and deputy alliances match for a given election, but they shift over time. In 1990 the PMDB, PFL, and PL allied in the gubernatorial race, opposing the PSDB, which ran its own candidate. In contrast, in 1994 the PFL allied with the PSDB, while the PMDB ran a candidate with two other parties, only one of which it had been allied with in 1990. In 1998, the PMDB ran a candidate, while the PSDB allied with two parties with which it had never allied, and the PFL ran on the PPR ticket along with the PL, which had been allied with the PMDB in the previous two elections.

This state-level confusion played havoc with the presidential alliances. For example, in São Paulo in 1998, neither Lula nor Cardoso could mobilize a unified following because of incongruent gubernatorial and deputy alliances. Despite allying with Cardoso's PSDB to elect São Paulo's governor in 1994 (Mario Covas), in 1996 the São Paulo PFL decided to switch its support to the candidate of Covas' archenemy (Paulo Maluf, of the PPB) for mayor of the city of São Paulo, instead of the PSDB's candidate (José Serra). Maluf's candidate won the election, and immediately thereafter Covas fired all PFL nominees in state government. As the 1998 gubernatorial election approached, Covas attempted a *rapprochement* with the PFL, to no avail. Maluf ran for governor against Covas' reelection bid, and PFL federal deputy Luis Carlos Santos ran for vice-governor with Maluf. Thus, the national PSDB-PFL alliance did not hold in 1998 in the home state of Brazil's president, due to local conditions.[95] On the other hand, gubernatorial and deputy alliances were congruent.

Likewise, the PT-PDT-PSB national alliance in 1998 did not hold in São Paulo, Lula's home state. Marta Suplicy of the PT competed for leftist voters in the gubernatorial race with Francisco Rossi of the PDT, who had deputy José Pinotti of the PSB as his running mate. Needless to say, relations in São Paulo between national "allies" the PSDB and PFL and the PT, PDT, and PSB are often not good. In short, while the gubernatorial race does drive the deputy race in each state at each election, alliance patterns have been inconsistent over space and time. This has allowed state-level parties extreme flexibility, but has limited the ability of presidential candidates to present a unified policy platform.

The case of São Paulo is illustrative and important, but how common is it? Many had hoped that the 1998 campaign would strengthen links between the presidential and legislative elections because of the repeat contest between Lula and Cardoso, because Cardoso's incumbent status scared off potential

[95] For details see *FSP* 5/8/97, p. 4; *OESP* 5/13/97, p. 6; *OESP* 5/14/97, p. 6; *OESP* 4/7/97, p. 7; *FSP* 4/4/97, p. 6; *GM* 10/11/96, p. 6; *FSP* 2/13/97, p. 5; *GM* 2/19/97, p. 12; *JB* 5/20/98, p. 5.

challengers, and because the elections were again concurrent. True, no viable challenger from the center or right of the political spectrum emerged, giving Cardoso a commanding national presence and attracting an even broader national partisan alliance than in 1994. However, despite the eventual emergence of a "two-horse" race, and despite concurrent *timing*, the elections failed to produce concurrent partisan *results*: state political arrangements still trumped national politics. As one analyst put it, in Brazil "the elections are married, but the results are divorced" (Figueiredo 1994, 22).

As the campaign began, Cardoso and his advisors attempted to line up gubernatorial and congressional alliances in the states. The president's advisors feared that competing pro-Cardoso gubernatorial candidates and incongruent congressional alliances supporting these competing gubernatorial candidates would damage Cardoso's campaign: his inability to endorse any of his "allies" would eliminate his capacity to form solid links to state-based political machines, and consequently endanger his candidacy.

To avoid these problems, Cardoso even attempted to suppress PSDB candidacies for governor in some states in favor of PFL, PPR, and PMDB candidates, as compensation for those parties' efforts on behalf of his reform proposals, and to avoid the PMDB and PPB running rival presidential candidates (*JB* 6/18/98, p. 5; *O Globo* 6/18/98, p. 2; *JB* 7/7/98, p. 2; *OESP* 7/16/98, p. 6). However, because state parties have the final word on nomination and alliances, these disputes proved irresolvable "from above," and Cardoso failed in his attempt to manipulate state party decisions (*JB* 6/17/98, p. 4; *OESP* 6/24/98, p. 6; *JB* 6/24/98, p. 2). This effort also soured relations with his own party, and the failure to limit competition meant that in July, with three full months to go, Cardoso concluded that he could only campaign in seven of Brazil's twenty-seven states without causing problems (*FSP* 7/8/98, p. 4).[96]

Newspapers noted that Cardoso's failure to coordinate national- and state-level alliances adversely affected his ability to campaign for his own party and for his allies (*O Globo* 7/20/98, p. 3; *JB* 7/23/98, p. 2; *JB* 7/10/98, p. 6; *OESP* 7/11/98, p. 4; *OESP* 8/10/98, p. 6). The media devoted considerable attention to Cardoso's coordination problems in the states of São Paulo, Minas Gerais, and Rio de Janeiro, which together hold 43 percent of the electorate and are thus crucial for the presidential election, and where gubernatorial (or vice-gubernatorial) candidates from the PSDB and PFL, Cardoso's main national alliance partner, competed against each other.[97] Several

---

[96] That same day Cardoso's team announced that the president would campaign in public as little as possible, "to avoid the danger to the president of bodily harm" (*OESP* 7/8/98, p. 4).

[97] Examples can be found in *O Globo* 6/24/98, p. 4; *JB* 6/25/98, p. 2; *FSP* 6/25/98, p. 4; *OESP* 7/4/98, p. 4; *FSP* 7/3/98, p. 4; *JB* 7/5/98, p. 4; *OESP* 7/6/98, p. 1; *JB* 7/11/98, p. 1; *O Globo* 7/11/98, p. 3; *FSP* 7/21/98, p. 1; *OESP* 7/22/98, p. 4; *OESP* 7/22/98, p. 4; *O Globo* 7/22/98, p. 5; *OESP* 7/26/98, p. 4; *O Globo* 7/26/98, p. 4; *JB* 7/31/98, p. 1; *OESP* 8/3/98, p. 4; *JB* 8/15/98, p. 6; *JB* 8/17/98, p. 2.

members of the PSDB even threatened the President with legal action if he stumped for candidates from other parties (*JB* 8/7/98, p. 2)! The party's exasperated secretary-general exclaimed that "it's just not acceptable that the president is virtually prohibited from entering Rio de Janeiro because of a dispute between the PFL and PSDB" (*JB* 7/10/98, p. 3). In general, when Cardoso hit the campaign trail, he took extreme care not to appear to be campaigning for gubernatorial or congressional candidates (*JB* 7/20/98, p. 6). Cardoso was even asked to stay away from several states because of cross-alliance tensions. In this very real sense, the leading candidate for president was physically unable to even attempt to generate coattails for allied candidates to other offices.

The same problems confronted the Lula-Brizola alliance. At one point, Brizola suggested that Lula avoid states with PDT gubernatorial candidates, while he would avoid states with PT gubernatorial candidates – even if they were not competing against each other (*OESP* 6/25/98, p. 7; *JB* 7/1/98, p. 6). The PT and PDT ran competing gubernatorial candidates in three states; in one state the PDT and PSB did as well. Lula admitted that "We're an alliance. If we brought all the state questions to the table, the national alliance wouldn't get off the ground" (*JB* 6/27/98, p. 6). Like Cardoso, this hurt Lula's campaign, for in some states PDT candidates refused to stump for votes for him (*FSP* 8/8/98, p. 1).

In sum, alliance patterns reveal that because the deputy race is intimately tied to the gubernatorial race, presidential candidates have thus far been unable to link their campaigns with the gubernatorial or deputy races in most states. Given this, Nicolau has concluded that the electoral process "unequivocally confirms the distance between the national party situation and partisan reality in the states . . . in truth, the central axis of the Brazilian political system derives from intra-elite state political disputes and not from national disputes" (1994, 19). A change in the electoral rules in 2002 may alter this dynamic, but at present it is too early to tell.

Gubernatorial Coattails: Two Statistical Tests

So far, I have provided solid theoretical reasons why we ought to expect strong gubernatorial coattails and weak presidential coattails in Brazil, and I provided evidence from interviews, newspapers, and alliance patterns that shows congressional candidates have coordinated their efforts around the gubernatorial race and not the presidential race. This evidence is strong but insufficient, however, because it doesn't demonstrate the existence of gubernatorial coattails in the technical sense. To demonstrate that gubernatorial coattails also affect the *outcome* of the congressional races, I will provide statistical evidence that in Brazil, coattail effects are more gubernatorial than presidential at both the "coalescence" phase and the "vote counting" phase of the election. First, I will show that the effective number of lists in the legislative election is a function of the effective number of gubernatorial candidates in each state, and not the number of presidential candidates. Second, I will show that the success of a deputy list depends on the strength of the gubernatorial candidates' coattails and not presidential coattails.

Gubernatorial Coattails and the Effective Number of Lists in Legislative Elections. I argued previously that following the nomination stage of the electoral process, candidates have strong incentives to line up behind candidates for governor. If this argument is true, then we ought to see a correlation, conditioned by the timing of the gubernatorial election, between the effective number of gubernatorial candidates and the effective number of congressional lists, above and beyond any effects due to presidential elections and district magnitude. Figure 5.1 represents the hypothesized causal model.

To test this model, I use pooled cross-sectional electoral data from Brazil's democratic periods, 1945–64 and 1989–98. The analysis focuses on five principal independent variables, four of which are interacted, and includes dummy variables for Brazil's states (to control for spatial fixed effects) and for each congressional election (to control for temporal fixed effects).

- ENEL$_{st}$, the dependent variable, is the effective number of electoral lists competing for seats in the Chamber of Deputies in state "s" at time "t," calculated as per Laakso and Taagepera (1979) using votes.
- PROXGOV$_{st}$ is the Proximity of the Gubernatorial Election to the legislative election in state "s," time "t." For an executive election to exert its greatest influence on a legislative election, the two must be proximal, as logic would suggest and as Shugart and Carey (1992), Shugart

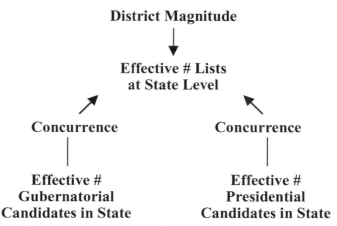

FIGURE 5.1. The Relationship between the Number of Competitors for Executive Elections, District Magnitude, and the Number of Lists in a Legislative Election.

(1995), Jones (1995), and Amorim Neto and Cox (1997) have demonstrated empirically. If executive and legislative elections are concurrent, they are maximally proximal, and PROXGOV takes a value of 1. In a separation-of-powers system, the least proximal elections are those held at the executive's midterm; in these cases PROXGOV takes a value of 0. If L_t equals the date of the legislative election, G_{t-1} signifies the date of the previous gubernatorial election, and G_{t+1} equals the date of the subsequent gubernatorial election, we calculate proximity in nonconcurrent cases as:

$$\text{PROXGOV} = 2 * |(L_T - G_{T-1})/(G_{T+1} - G_{T-1}) - 1/2|$$

This formula provides the time elapsed between the preceding executive election and the legislative election ($L_T - G_{t-1}$) as a fraction of the executive term ($G_{t+1} - G_{t-1}$). Subtracting one-half from this and then taking the absolute value shows how far away from the midterm the legislative election was held (Amorim Neto and Cox 1997). Then I interact this variable with ENGOV (see the following text). I hypothesize that candidates have greater incentives to coalesce around the gubernatorial field the closer they are to the subnational executive and national legislative elections: the closer the election, the fewer the lists.

- PROXPRES$_{st}$ is the Proximity of the Presidential Election to the legislative election in state "s," time "t." I use the same formula as mentioned previously for gubernatorial elections, and I interact this variable with ENPRES. However, I hypothesize that the proximity of the presidential election to the legislative election has no effect on the effective number of electoral lists in each district.
- ENGOV$_{st}$ is the Effective Number of Gubernatorial candidates, taken in votes, in state "s," time "t." I hypothesize that as ENGOV increases, so should ENEL. However, as per Cox (1997, 212–15) and as illustrated in the previous diagram, I hypothesize that the number of candidates only *indirectly* affects the dependent variable: its effect depends on the timing of the election, operationalized as PROXGOV.[98]
- ENPRES$_{st}$ is the Effective Number of Presidential candidates in state "s," time "t." I hypothesize that ENPRES is unrelated to the effective number of electoral lists in each district. As with ENGOV, ENPRES is interacted with PROXPRES.
- LogM$_{st}$ is the log of District Magnitude, the number of seats to be filled in the Chamber of Deputies from state "s," time "t." Typically, as per

[98] Suppose that in an election held at time "t," we have two presidential candidates. If the legislative election were held ten years later, we would have no reason to believe the number parties competing at that time ought to also be near two. On the other hand, if the legislative and executive elections were held concurrently, then we would suppose that executive election ought to influence the legislative election.

Taagepera and Shugart (1989), analysts enter logM into the equation instead of M in systems with large district magnitudes. Following established precedent, I hypothesize that as logM increases, so should the effective number of electoral lists in the state/district.

- $YEAR_x$ is a dummy variable for each legislative election year, to control for fixed temporal effects – events or circumstances in a given year that may boost or reduce ENEL – other than those captured by the other regressors.
- $STATE_x$ is a dummy variable for each of Brazil's states.

The precise specification of the equation is as follows:

$$\begin{aligned} ENEL_{st} &= \alpha + \beta_1 + \beta_2 PROXGOV_{st} + \beta_3(ENGOV_{st} * PROXGOV_{st}) \\ &+ \beta_4 PROXPRES_{st} + \beta_5(ENPRES_{st} * PROXPRES_{st}) \\ &+ \beta_3 logM_{st} + \beta_4 YEAR_x \cdots + \beta_{11} YEAR_x + \beta_{12} STATE_x \cdots \\ &+ \beta_{33} STATE_x + e \end{aligned}$$

PROXGOV and PROXPRES are included both independently and as interacted variables (the diagram indicates that the proximity of the election has a direct effect). The model focuses on the causal impact of the first five variables. The other variables are included as controls, and for space reasons I will not report their results.[99]

Table 5.4 relates the results for three models. In 1950, 1994, and 1998, presidential and gubernatorial elections were concurrent in all states. In these years, PROXGOV and PROXPRES would be perfectly collinear, and the computer will throw one variable out. To get around this problem, I ran three regressions, each one excluding one of the concurrent elections. The results from all three equations demonstrate that my key variables, those associated with the gubernatorial race, are significant. This suggests the findings are robust.

The exclusion of 1950, 1994, or 1998 hardly affects the results. Overall, these results confirm my expectations: the variables associated with the gubernatorial race are strongly significant in all three equations, while the variables associated with the presidential race exhibit no statistically significant impact at all. The state-specific fixed effects (not reported) wash out any effect district magnitude has.

To explain these results, consider a series of cases with concurrent gubernatorial elections (where $PROXGOV = 1$). If the effective number of gubernatorial candidates increases by one, the effective number of legislative lists in the state increases, on average, by about one-half. If we consider a series of cases where the legislative elections are halfway through the gubernatorial

---

[99] Excluding the fixed-effects variables does not affect the significance of the results. This model of course cannot account for variation in levels of multipartism during both the 1945–64 period and the post-1985 period.

TABLE 5.4 *Determinants of Effective Number of Lists in Brazilian Congressional Elections*

Independent Variable	Excluding 1950 Estimated Coefficient (S.E.)	Excluding 1994 Estimated Coefficient (S.E.)	Excluding 1998 Estimated Coefficient (S.E.)
LogM	.92	.92	.92
	(.53)	(.53)	(.53)
ProxGov	−1.17**	−1.17**	−1.17**
	(.38)	(.38)	(.38)
ProxGov*ENGov	.51***	.51***	.51***
	(.13)	(.13)	(.13)
ProxPres	−.53	−1.07	−.80
	(.73)	(.80)	(.81)
ProxPres*ENPres	.20	.20	.20
	(.14)	(.14)	(.14)
Constant	2.24	2.07	2.93
R-Square	.69	.69	.69
S.E.R.	.57	.57	.57
Degrees of Freedom	139	139	139

*$p < .05$, two-tailed test; **$p < .01$, two-tailed test; ***$p < .001$, two-tailed test.

term (PROXGOV = .5), then if the effective number of gubernatorial candidates increases by one, the effective number of legislative lists in the state would increase, on average, by about one-fourth. In sum, this statistical test confirms my hypothesis that all else being equal, gubernatorial elections exert a strong "coattails effect" influence on Brazilian congressional elections.[100]

Gubernatorial Coattails and Electoral Success in Recent Presidential Elections. The test in the previous section provides support for the hypothesis that the race for governor shapes the race for federal deputy. However, by using the "effective number of lists" as the dependent variable, this test cannot provide insight as to whether a strong gubernatorial (or presidential) candidate *actually helps elect members on that list.* This is the most common criticism of the use of an effective number of lists (or candidates) as a dependent variable. For example, if presidential candidate A gains 60 percent of the vote and presidential candidate B gains 40 percent of the vote, while their respective lists for legislative office gain 40 percent and 60 percent of the votes, then the effective number of candidates/lists are equal at both

---

[100] For additional methodological details, see Samuels (1999).

levels (~1.95), but the correlation between the relative success of presidential candidates and legislative lists is fairly low.

To test for an actual correlation between votes for executive-office candidates and legislative lists, I regress the percentage of the vote received by legislative lists on the percentage of votes received by presidential and gubernatorial candidates who head those lists. Given my argument, I hypothesize that the success of a deputy list depends on the strength of the gubernatorial candidates' coattails, and not the presidential coattails.

Ideally, I would pool all the data for presidential, gubernatorial, and deputy races at the district level. However, we face a serious methodological problem here not present when I explored the effective number of candidates and lists. Under the open-list PR system, if parties decide to run in an alliance, then their votes for deputy are pooled at the alliance (list) level and not the party level. Throughout Brazil's democratic periods, most candidates elected to the Chamber of Deputies have indeed won as members of multiparty alliances. The methodological problem is that in order to compare the potential impact of presidential versus gubernatorial alliances on deputy alliances, the alliances across levels of elections *must* be congruent. That is, the parties in each deputy alliance must support only one candidate for governor and only one for president. As shown, two problems exist: first, when the presidential elections are not concurrent, hardly any alliances in the subsequent deputy election match the presidential election alliances. Moreover, even when elections are concurrent, most alliances are still incongruent. Consequently, we cannot conduct a straightforward Ordinary Least Squares (OLS) regression to weigh the impact of each variable. Figure 5.2 illustrates the problem in most Brazilian states.

Each box represents the vote in a given district for the presidential, gubernatorial, or deputy alliance, and the arrows represent the hypothesized influence of presidential or gubernatorial coattails. As previously described, in most cases the alliances for deputy have matched the gubernatorial alliances but not the presidential alliances. In this hypothetical example, the presidential candidate finds that his allies are competing against each other

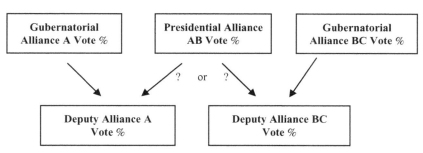

FIGURE 5.2. Presidential vs. Gubernatorial Coattails and "Incongruent" Alliances.

in the gubernatorial and deputy races. Under these conditions, we expect gubernatorial coattails, but it is impossible to accurately differentiate the impact of presidential versus gubernatorial coattails effects because we can't match cases of presidential and gubernatorial support.

I will concentrate on Brazil's two most recent presidential elections, both of which were concurrent. This simplifies the analysis without leaving much unexplained (e.g., it avoids the problem of comparing parties from the 1945–64 period to the 1989–present period, which I avoided when I used the effective number of candidates). Using these two elections, we can cull a (biased) sample of forty-two congruent alliances (26 percent of the total) that can be analyzed using OLS (I will explain the consequences of the sample bias following the analysis). I pooled the data and regressed the percentage of the vote received by federal deputy alliance A in state B (DEP%) on the following independent variables:

- The percentage of the vote received by the gubernatorial candidate (GOV%) supported by alliance A in state B. Given my argument, I expect a strongly positive relationship between GOV% and DEP%.
- The percentage of the vote received by presidential candidate (PRES%) supported by alliance A in state B. Given my argument, in general I expect a weakly positive or nonexistent relationship between PRES% and DEP%.
- A dummy variable indicating whether the alliance supports a leftist gubernatorial and presidential candidate (from the PT, PSB, PDT, PV, or PPS) (LEFTIST). This variable controls for the fact that leftist deputy alliances are often much smaller and less viable in many of Brazil's states, even though they may run popular gubernatorial candidates.
- The number of incumbents on deputy alliance A (NUMINCS). Following the U.S. literature on coattails effects (e.g., Campbell and Summers 1990), I include a variable to account for the advantages that incumbency provides to deputy candidates. I hypothesize that the more incumbents running on the list, the higher the likely vote percentage.
- A dummy variable for the 1998 election year (1998) to control for year-specific effects.

Table 5.5 presents the results.

The results provide evidence of both presidential *and* gubernatorial coattails: all else equal, a 10 percent increase in gubernatorial candidate A's vote total results in a 4.2 percent increase in the vote total for deputy list A, while a corresponding increase in presidential candidate A's vote total in a given state results in a 1.8 percent increase in the vote total for deputy list A. The results also show that for every additional incumbent, the list's vote total goes up by .72 percent. In addition, while leftism alone is not a significant reason for a list to receive a smaller vote total, the sign is in the expected direction.

TABLE 5.5 *Coattails Effects in Brazilian Elections – 1994–1998*

Independent Variables	Coefficient (S.E.)
GOV%	0.42***
	(0.09)
PRES%	0.18*
	(0.08)
LEFTIST	−4.48
	(3.17)
NUMINCS	0.72*
	(0.34)
1998	0.16
	(2.27)
Constant	5.88
	(3.85)
R^2	.77
S.E.R.	6.68
Degrees of Freedom	36

* $= p < .05$, two-tailed test; ** $= p < .01$, two-tailed test; *** $= p < .001$, two-tailed test.

The finding of both presidential and gubernatorial coattail effects may appear to contradict or at least complicate my argument, but it does not, for two reasons. First, the sample is highly biased toward finding evidence of presidential coattails, because the regression only includes those cases in which the presidential alliances match the gubernatorial and the deputy alliances. This regression says nothing about the other 74 percent of the cases, where we have good reasons to expect no presidential coattails because of the strong links between the gubernatorial and deputy alliances and because an incongruent presidential alliance means that the presidential candidate may be "supporting" ardent political enemies in many states and cannot, without risking his national alliance, attempt to generate coattails for one or the other alliance partner in each state without causing extreme displeasure among the other alliance partner(s). Presidential coattails have their only real chance in this sample of forty-two congruent alliances, yet we still find that gubernatorial coattails are more than twice as strong as presidential coattails. That is, even when presidential candidates manage to coordinate their alliances across states, the weight of state-level politics still minimizes their coattails.

Second, as previously noted, the sample is biased toward the PT candidate, Lula. The PT is widely regarded as the only large Brazilian party with a strong party organization and label, and thus we might expect the success of its congressional candidates to be a function of the success of its presidential candidate, who leads the national partisan charge during the election year. Twenty-eight of forty-two (67 percent) of the cases in the sample allied with Lula, while only seven cases (17 percent) lined up behind Cardoso. In other words, although Cardoso may have generated some weak coattails in the very few states where his alliances were congruent, the fact is that he was spectacularly unsuccessful in accomplishing this goal, and we can thus conclude that his coattails were very short.[101]

In sum, the evidence from interviews and an empirical analysis of Brazil's presidential elections demonstrates that gubernatorial coattail effects are quite strong, while presidential coattail effects are weak or nonexistent. The positive statistical finding of presidential coattails indicates that they are not an impossibility in Brazil, just an extremely uncommon phenomenon largely limited to the leftist presidential candidates, who have been relatively more successful in lining up congruent alliances. In any event, even in the few cases where alliances do match up across all three levels, gubernatorial coattails still outweigh the impact of presidential coattails. Relative to gubernatorial candidates, presidential candidates in Brazil simply do not possess the resources that congressional candidates need and require to win election.

CONCLUSION

In this chapter I demonstrated that because Brazilian politicians do not obtain the electoral resources they need from national parties or presidential candidates, but from state-level connections, they have few incentives to coordinate around national parties, or line up behind strong presidential candidates. Unlike in systems where elections for the national executive are an important influence on legislative elections, Brazilian coattails are more "gubernatorial" than "presidential" even in years when the presidential and legislative elections are held concurrently.

The "state centeredness" of legislative elections in Brazil plays itself out in executive-legislative relations, and explains how federalism affects the career ambitions, electoral strategies, and legislative behavior of both incumbents as well as candidates for federal deputy. In some countries, winning presidential candidates who can mobilize unified national partisan support may subsequently reap significant rewards in terms of executive-legislative relations. In contrast, an electorally weak president might face a more independent

---

[101] The regression also points to the counterintuitive result that even for leftist presidential candidates, the relationship between the gubernatorial candidate and the deputy list is much stronger than the relationship between the presidential candidate and the deputy candidates. Given the purported strength of the PT as a national organization relative to the other parties, this finding begs the question of why we see this result. Further research is required on the impact of party organization on electoral performance in Brazil and elsewhere.

legislature, even if his own party is nominally well represented, because legislators did not rely on the president to win office. Brazilian deputies know that no matter how strong a presidential candidate is, he has few tools to influence congressional elections.

Presidential candidates simply lack the resources necessary to help their allies win elections in Brazil – control over nominations and the organizational backing of well-developed clientelistic networks. In contrast, gubernatorial candidates typically control such resources, and as a result deputies look to them for support during the campaign. Consequently, results for the congressional race have tended not to follow the vote patterns in the presidential race. The evidence I provided – interviews with congressional candidates, a reconstruction of alliance patterns within and across states, and regression analysis – supports this contention.

Gubernatorial coattails have weakened the president's ability to construct a governing coalition. When elected deputies arrive in Brasilia to serve their term, they must continue to pay attention to the incumbent governor in their state, so as not to create a powerful political enemy. Incumbent deputies are also already strategically thinking about their own political futures. When pondering their futures, deputies weigh state-level political considerations heavily, because they know that the next statewide election may affect them personally.[102] In this way, gubernatorial coattails affect the nature of political ambition in Brazil. Although federal deputies do not simply ignore national partisan politics, they know that their own career success depends more on their state-level connections than their connections to their national party leader, the president, or a presidential candidate.

Weak presidential coattails means that there is a very limited connection between the electoral success of presidential candidates and that of individual deputies. As a result, the winning presidential candidate has limited ability to generate legislative support through electoral appeals.[103] This conclusion runs against some recent scholarship (e.g., Figueiredo and Limongi 2000a), but reinforces other work (e.g., Mainwaring 1999; Ames 2001). Weak presidential coattails imply that Brazil's president must seek to construct as broad a coalition as possible, because the president cannot even count on his own party's support. For example, at times Cardoso's "government coalition" comprised 80 percent of the Chamber of Deputies. With this level of support one might suppose any president could enact his full agenda, including

---

[102] As early as June 2001 this same dynamic was being cited as an important factor in the October 2002 general elections. See for example *FSP* 6/15/01, p. A4; *OESP* 6/21/01, p. A6.

[103] It may be the case that many deputy candidates strategically choose *not* to identify with their party's presidential candidate. This does not change the story: they can do this because there is little electoral cost to such a choice. In countries where the presidential election drives legislative elections, such a strategy could prove disastrous.

constitutional changes (which require a 60 percent majority in Brazil). Yet although Cardoso accomplished a great deal, key elements of his agenda (such as political reform and fiscal reform) never made it out of committee, and other parts were seriously watered down (e.g., administrative and pension reform).

Brazil's president only submits contentious legislation after extensive consultation with his and allied party leaders, doling out appointments and patronage (or threatening not to) in an attempt to raise legislative support (Ames 2001). In a system where incumbents could not be denied a place on the next election's ballot and party switching remains relatively easy (C. Melo 2000), party leaders and/or the president have relatively few tools with which to actually punish rebels. Given this, backbenchers simply don't show up for votes if they don't like the proposal, denying a quorum and thus impeding a vote.

When a floor vote finally takes place, the legislative cohesion that results is therefore somewhat illusory, because it arises more from a process of consensus building that must span across a complex multiparty coalition than from the president's or party leaders' ability to "whip" votes, as in the United Kingdom for example, by employing the threat of expulsion and denial of a place on the next election's ballot (Stepan 1999, 242; Palermo 2000, 539–40). And, in contrast to Figueiredo and Limongi's (1999, 2000a) arguments, even given the president's dominance of the legislative agenda and the drawn-out negotiations that precede floor votes that are designed to ensure passage by a broad margin, Carey (2001) has shown that Brazil's "government coalition" parties remain only moderately cohesive in comparative perspective. The main reason is because the president and national party leaders lack the resources to get their backbenchers to show up for votes or to punish them for defection.

Gubernatorial coattails affect the degree to which the president and national party leaders can drum up support in the Chamber of Deputies. Given their influence over members of Congress, governors can promise to support – or at least not interfere with – the president's agenda. Or, given that many important issues on the political agenda touch on federal relations – including fiscal reform, tax reform, decentralization in a wide variety of policy arenas, judicial reform, police reform, and administrative reform – Brazilian presidents may confront potentially fatal opposition from state governors. Governors can choose to pressure the deputies from their states if the president proposes a reform that would significantly reduce states' political autonomy (see Chapter 9).

President Fernando Henrique Cardoso assiduously cultivated links with state governors, perhaps learning from the mistakes of President Fernando Collor de Mello (1989–92), who did not. To cut down on the time and expense of dealing with the nearly 400 deputies in his potential coalition on each vote, from the start of his administration Cardoso has wooed state governors to lobby the deputies from their states on his behalf, with promises of federal pork going to the governors, not the deputies. This has aided Cardoso's efforts to pass proposals through Congress, but his task has still been made difficult by his and his party's weaknesses. Contrary to the optimistic expectations that concurrent elections and his two smashing victories generated, Cardoso was no more able than previous presidents to generate strong presidential coattails. This limited his ability to bring certain proposals to passage, and was a major factor in cutting his second honeymoon so short. That is to say, if Cardoso had stronger coattails, his successes would have been even greater.

In historical perspective, given Brazil's tradition of individually popular presidents who fail to muster consistent legislative support, this may appear unsurprising. Yet an answer to the question of *why* Brazil's presidential and legislative elections are so poorly linked that relies on the personalistic nature of presidential candidates is *ad hoc* and begs the question of what it is about Brazilian institutions in comparative perspective that *explains* this lack of linkage. Like Brazilian parties, political parties in the United States have been comparatively weak as organizations, and presidential candidates in the United States certainly do not emerge from within national party organizations. However, the coattails idea originated in the United States. In Brazil, the nature of federalism cuts presidential coattails short – or, to extend the metaphor, simply rips the president's coat off his back, cuts it up, and divides it among the governors. The root of this problem – and the reason why it remains so intractable – lies in the way in which the institutions of Brazilian federalism fragment the party system and limit the linkage between national-level executive and legislative elections.

Executive-legislative relations in Brazil involve a "Fourth Branch" of the presidential system: state governors. Because governors control resources that can influence other politicians' careers and national parties and the president lacks such resources, federal and intergovernmental disputes will continue to play a key role in defining executive-legislative relations.

INTRODUCTION

I n Section 1, I described the structure of political ambition in Brazil, and provided support for my hypothesis that Brazilian federal deputies do not typically aim to build a career within the legislature. Instead, they spend a relatively short time in the Chamber, and direct their energies toward continuing their careers at the subnational level. In Section 2 I showed how federalism influences legislative elections in Brazil, and how this also consequently affects executive-legislative relations. The combination of political ambition and federalism thus generates strong incentives for incumbent federal deputies to favor subnational interests while they serve in the legislature. In short, ambition and federalism powerfully shape the dynamics of congressional politics in Brazil. In Section 3, I demonstrate the utility of this interpretation of Brazilian politics for real-world events. I develop and play out several hypotheses that federalism and progressive ambition generate, and contrast the expectations of those hypothesis with what a reelection assumption might generate.

Chapter 6

On the Political (In)Efficacy of Pork-Barreling in the Chamber of Deputies

"The organization of Congress meets remarkably well the electoral needs of its members. To put it another way, if a group of planners sat down and tried to design a pair of American national assemblies with the goal of serving members' electoral needs year in and year out, they would be hard pressed to improve on what exists."

—David Mayhew, *Congress: The Electoral Connection*

INTRODUCTION

Does the organization of the Brazilian Chamber of Deputies meet the electoral needs of its members? In the United States, scholars argue that if House members act strategically to further their career goals, then form will follow function. If politicians are no more or less strategic outside the United States, then this claim ought to apply elsewhere as well. That is, we ought to be able to explain legislative institutions and processes in different democracies as a function of the nature of political ambition in each country.

In this chapter I begin to explain how political ambition helps explain legislative processes and structures in Brazil. If Brazilian Deputies behaved like their U.S. counterparts and sought a long-term legislative career, then the design of the Chamber might reflect that desire. However, the reelection assumption does not accurately depict political careerism in Brazil. Consequently, no stable majority of incumbency-minded deputies ever exists in Brazil's Chamber of Deputies. This impedes the institutionalization of legislative norms that would in turn enhance the status of incumbency.

However, the absence of a desire for a long-term career in the Chamber does not mean that deputies will not act to shape Chamber institutions to further their careers. Abandoning the Mayhewian motivational assumption does not mean we also have to abandon rational-choice tools to analyze the consequences of political ambition. On the contrary: deputies' extra-Chamber and mainly *subnational* ambition ought to distinctly shape critical aspects of legislative organization and policy output in Brazil. In this chapter and the next, I address the question of how these incentives shape the budget process. I focus in particular on Brazilian deputies' (in)famous "pork-barreling" behavior.

Why study budgeting? First, as in other countries, the Brazilian budget involves billions of dollars and is thus materially important to the millions of Brazilians who pay taxes and receive government benefits. Second, the budget process opens a window into how legislators' incentives can shape important political institutions in the period following a transition to democracy. Third, appropriations decisions – expressed in monetary terms – provide possibly the clearest statements of politicians' policy preferences and electoral or career strategies. Rational-choice theories of politics possess significant analytical leverage in this policy arena.

Few works have explored budgeting in Brazil, and existing studies have yet to consider the impact of deputies' extralegislative and subnational career incentives (cf. Longo 1991; Sanches 1993; Serra 1993, 1994; Pinheiro 1996; M. H. Santos et al. 1997; Figueiredo and Limongi 2000b). For example, Barry Ames (1987, 1995a, 2001) has suggested both that Brazilian deputies seek pork to gain votes in the next election and that access to pork helps deputies gain votes. Ames' argument seems plausible. Incumbents spend a great deal of time seeking pork-barrel funds, and the electoral rules appear to favor incumbency. Individual politicians make the decision to run for reelection largely independently of party leaders' desires, and unlimited reelection has been allowed and encouraged by the "birthright candidate" (*candidato nato*) rule that automatically places incumbents' names on the ballot. Moreover, a high degree of individualism characterizes legislative campaigns, and national party organization influence is minimal. In short, the institutional context favors incumbents and their individualistic "personal vote" – seeking strategies.

However, I argue that this view fails to explain the dynamic of pork-barreling in Brazil. The logic of progressive ambition gives us reason to question the link between pork-barreling and reelection. Although we know that deputies engage in extensive "personal-vote" seeking behavior and we know that reelection is both allowed and is institutionally encouraged, we also know that long-term careers in the Chamber are extremely rare. This creates a puzzle: if deputies are not primarily interested in solidifying a career in the Chamber, then why do they devote so much time and energy to pork-barreling?

In this chapter and the next, I challenge the conventional answer to this question, that deputies seek pork because doing so increases their chances of winning reelection. In this chapter, using data and methods similar to Ames, I conclude that pork-barreling does not help deputies win reelection. Ironically, however, in this way the design of the Brazilian Chamber of Deputies *does* meet the electoral needs of its members: deputies have not shaped the budget process to ensure reelection because their careers do not motivate them to do so. Of course, if pork provided no political return for them at all then we would be even more puzzled by the extensive pork-barreling in the Chamber. If my argument is correct, the obvious question is then "Why *do* deputies seek pork, if not to win reelection?" I answer that question in the next chapter.

THE RELATIONSHIP BETWEEN FORM AND FUNCTION IN THE CHAMBER: THREE HYPOTHESES

In this section I elaborate three hypotheses about the relationship between political ambition and the budget process in Brazil, focusing on deputies' efforts to influence the process by offering pork-barrel amendments to the yearly budget. Scholars have argued that deputies engage in this behavior because their reelection success depends on "bringing home the bacon." For example, Mainwaring (1999, 176) argued that politicians "use public resources and clientelistic practices to win votes." Similarly, Hagopian (1996, 152) claimed that "deputies appeal to electors on the basis of their ability to deliver state patronage." Finally, Ames (1995b, 406) hypothesized that "deputies will offer budget amendments to benefit target municipalities whose votes they seek in subsequent elections," and he found that amendments increased votes.[104]

I do not dispute that Brazilian deputies seek pork. However, we have good reason to expect a weak relationship between pork-barreling and reelection success in Brazil: the absence of congressional careerism implies that deputies have few incentives to focus their energies on constructing a budget process specifically designed to enhance incumbency. On the other hand, the importance of state- and municipal-level actors as well as state- and municipal-level directed careerism suggests that deputies might attempt to design the budget process to favor subnational interests as well as their own progressive ambition. Ironically, the pressures deputies face and the incentives that drive deputies' careers ought to leave them poorly positioned procedurally to secure pork for their own reelection. Specifically, I hypothesize that political ambition has three interrelated consequences for Brazilian budgetary politics:

- Hypothesis 1: Because Brazilian deputies do not build lengthy careers within the Chamber, they have few incentives to design a budget system that favors the use of pork to promote incumbency.
- Hypothesis 2: Because subnational actors play important roles in Brazilian the careers of deputies, deputies have strong incentives to promote the

---

[104] See also Geddes and Ribeiro Neto 1992; Avelino Filho 1994; Santos et al. 1997; Pereira and Rennó 2000.

interests of both state- and municipal-governments in the design of the budget process. State-based incentives ought to weigh particularly heavily.

• Hypothesis 3: Because many deputies continue their political careers outside the Chamber, as deputies they ought to act to enhance their future career prospects. Thus, "progressively ambitious" deputies ought to exhibit distinct pork-barreling strategies from those who seek reelection.

Playing out the consequences of progressive ambition paints a distinct picture of the purposes of pork-barreling in Brazil. Thus, in contrast to the conventional view, I argue that the relationship between pork-barreling and reelection ought to be fairly weak, while the relationship between pork-barreling and the forces that shape deputies' progressive ambition ought to be strong. In this chapter I discuss Hypothesis 1, and I defend Hypotheses 2 and 3 in Chapter 7.

ON THE INEFFICACY OF PORK-BARRELING TO SECURE INCUMBENCY

In general terms, the Brazilian legislature is at an extreme disadvantage in budgetary policy. The constitution states that the president controls the budgetary agenda, and with this power comes an information advantage: the executive branch controls the balance of the technical capacity to elaborate, implement, and oversee the budget (Serra 1994; Sanches 1996; Greggianin 1997). In addition, the president has both a line-item veto as well as the power to impound or transfer any revenue that the constitution does not require be spent. These powers significantly limit Congressional budgetary influence, "neutralize the oversight efforts of Congressional committees, . . . [and] facilitate retaliatory actions against deputies not aligned with [the president's] preferences" (Sanches 1995, 130). In addition, although the Chamber staff has developed greater budgetary expertise since the early 1990s, the Chamber's political institutions do not encourage deputies to develop budgetary expertise and oversight capacity. Although other Chamber committees turn over their membership every two years, the budget committee rotates its membership, including its leaders, every year. This gives more deputies a chance to serve on the budget committee, but it impedes the development of institutional memory and perpetuates the executive branch's overall dominance of the budgetary process.[105]

Deputies have never attempted to substantially reduce the president's budgetary authority and enhance the Chamber's control over the flow of budgetary resources. Would Mayhew be surprised at this situation? Does this institutional design serve the electoral needs of deputies? My first hypothesis

---

[105] This paragraph was based on interviews with Waldeck Ornellas, Luiz Tacca, Manoel Albuquerque, Antônio Carlos Pojo do Rêgo, Eugênio Greggianin, Oswaldo M. Sanches, Rita Maciel, José Vaz Bergalo, and Yeda Crusius.

supposes that deputies have few incentives to try to shape the budget process in order to enhance the probability of building a career in the Chamber. In the remainder of this section I describe the budgetary pork-barrel process and then explain how the system does not benefit incumbency-minded deputies. I argue that three "supply" problems plague deputies' efforts to "bring home the bacon" from the executive-branch butcher shop: they often can't get the butcher to "sell" them pork, they can't "buy enough bacon" to go around, and they cannot insulate themselves from competing breadwinners. Given these problems, pork-barreling ought to provide a low return for deputies interested in maintaining their seats. In Section 4 I confirm my argument through statistical tests of the impact of pork on deputy's reelection chances.

The Pork-Barreling Process in Brazil

Since 1988, Brazilian deputies (and senators) have had the right to submit pork-barrel amendments to the budget. Until 1993, only individual members of Congress (MCs) could submit amendments. Currently, state and regional delegations of MCs as well as permanent congressional committees can too (see Chapter 7). MCs can target these amendments to municipal-, state-, regional-, or national-level programs, or even for government expenditures abroad. In this chapter and the next I exclude from consideration amendments targeted to national and exterior programs (except when counting the total number of amendments submitted each year).[106] Examples of typical amendments include R$118,800 for rural electrification in the municipality of Solidão, Pernambuco; R$100,000 for basic sanitation in Santa Efigênia de Minas, Minas Gerais; and R$2.1 million for low-income housing in the state of Acre. Table 6.1 provides the total number of amendments submitted each year since 1988.

MCs initially submitted few amendments each, yet with the start of the 1991–4 legislature they began to submit dozens or even hundreds of amendments each per year. In 1992 MCs submitted an average of 126 amendments each, but since then these numbers have dropped off considerably. Although they could initially submit as many amendments as they wished, by 1996 MCs had limited themselves to a maximum of twenty submissions each per year.

The budget amendment process in Brazil proceeds as follows: in August of each year a joint Chamber-Senate budget committee (the *Comissão Mista*

---

[106] National and exterior amendments are often included in the budget at the executive's request to correct "technical" problems with its original proposal. Moreover, they are not typically "pork-barrel" proposals, as are regional-, state-, and municipal-targeted amendments. I also eliminated from all calculations in this and the subsequent chapter amendments that were signed by the President of the CMO and by the Chairs of the CMO's subcommittees, as well as by the directing committees of the Chamber and Senate. According to the Chief of the Chamber's Budget Committee Staff, these amendments are of a technical nature and are not typically pork-barrel proposals. Interview with Eugênio Greggianin.

TABLE 6.1 *Number of Budget Amendments Submitted per Year – 1988–2000*

Year	Amendments
1988	2,660
1989	11,180
1990	13,358
1991	71,543
1992	73,642
1993	22,613
1994	13,924
1995	23,251
1996	11,227
1997	11,664
1998	9,341
1999	8,205
2000	8,935

Source: Brasil, Senado Federal (1997–99); Brasil, Congresso Nacional (2000c, 2001a).

de Planos, Orçamentos Públicos e Fiscalização [Joint Committee on Planning, Public Budgets, and Oversight]) begins analyzing the president's proposed budget for the next fiscal year, which covers a normal calendar year. In September and October, the budget committee evaluates the president's proposal and incorporates deputies' and senators' amendments. The committee finishes its work in November, and then a joint session of Congress votes the entire proposal. During the fiscal year, the executive branch decides what parts and how much of the budget to implement, subject to a variety of restrictions.

I recognize that the yearly budget is not the only source of "pork" in Brazil. Some MCs may be able to claim credit for projects negotiated outside the amendment process, and others may work through a parastatal corporation, the Federal Savings Bank (*Caixa Econômica Federal*) or the National Economic and Social Development Bank (BNDES) to obtain funds, for example. These sources of particularistic goods may be important for deputies' careers. Yet we must keep the distinction clear between the access that members of Congress have attempted to insure for themselves as members of a collective body versus *ad hoc* deals that they may arrange individually. The issues are when, why, and to what extent ambitious, self-interested politicians would collectively organize to structure a set of legislative institutions to favor their career interests. Deputies have had several opportunities strengthen the Chamber's position in the budget process, but their inaction tellingly reflects the absence of individual-level incentives to organize to improve their own collective lot. Indeed, the current situation even constrains deputies' ability to "claim credit" for cajoling resources from the executive branch. In the following text, I describe three ways in which this is the case.

Supply Problem #1: Will the Butcher Sell to You?

The conventional wisdom holds that Brazilian deputies' reelection chances depend on the supply of "pork" they deliver to their vote bases. If this were true, we might suppose that deputies would have designed the budget process to ensure an adequate supply. However, they have not. Until 1995, MCs had not even institutionalized a guarantee that the budget committee would approve their submitted amendments. That year, Congress altered the budget process so that the budget committee automatically (given certain technical criteria) approves ten amendments that each MC prioritizes. Yet even with amendment approval now certain, deputies still have no guarantee that their pet projects will be funded because the president retains line-item and impoundment powers, which means that in some years virtually no "pork" is released at all. This was the case in 1995, when the Minister of Finance at the time, José Serra (PSDB-SP), simply vetoed almost all the amendments. In addition, deputies' amendments take last priority for the president, who has his own preferred pork-barrel projects. For example, President Cardoso devoted billions of *Reais* to his "Brazil in Action" infrastructure development program. Members of Congress rightfully feared that the president would fund only his projects and ignore theirs (*FSP* 2/2/97, p. A-5). They had reason to worry: Table 6.2 provides the average probabilities by party that the president released at least some portion of the value of a deputy's amendments from 1993–2000.[107]

Table 6.2 shows that amendment execution is uncertain from year to year, even for members of the president's coalition. In 1995, the President funded only 16 of the nearly 20,000 amendments deputies submitted. Even in relatively "good" years like 1993 and 1997 deputies have no guarantee that their amendments will be executed (and this table says nothing about whether 10 percent or 100 percent of the value of the amendment is released – see the following text). (Following a budget scandal, Congress approved the 1994 budget without amendments, so none were executed that year.)

Given executive control of the purse strings, deputies spend a good deal of time lobbying ministers and other executive-branch officials for their projects to be funded, but often with limited success. As one deputy put it, "You submit all these amendments, but you never know if the money will appear."[108] In fact, deputies have so little certainty that the executive will release funds that the President's threat to cut amendment allocations often sounds empty.

---

[107] Data on amendment execution prior to 1993 were unavailable.
[108] Interview with Jacques Wagner.

TABLE 6.2 *Deputies' Conditional Probability of Amendment Funding – by Party*

Party	1993	1994	1995	1996	1997	1998	1999	2000
PT	0.41	0.00	0.000	0.30	0.40	0.13	0.57	0.16
PDT	0.56	0.00	0.001	0.22	0.48	0.22	0.55	0.15
PSDB	0.62	0.00	0.003	0.46	0.74	0.37	0.51	0.28
PMDB	0.67	0.00	0.000	0.47	0.70	0.35	0.43	0.31
PTB	0.59	0.00	0.000	0.37	0.68	0.40	0.52	0.24
PFL	0.59	0.00	0.001	0.53	0.73	0.41	0.43	0.26
PPB	0.63	0.00	0.002	0.40	0.65	0.34	0.53	0.21
All	*0.62*	*0.00*	*0.001*	*0.42*	*0.62*	*0.34*	*0.49*	*0.25*

Source: Brasil, Senado Federal (1997–99); Brasil, Congresso Nacional (2000c, 2001a).

For example, in 1997, President Cardoso threatened to cut amendments from the budget if Congress did not extend his economic stabilization plan. Given that in the first six months of 1997 the central government released less than 2 percent of the value of all amendments, one deputy complained "How can the government threaten to cut amendments if it isn't releasing anything anyway?" (*OESP* 7/16/97, p. A-4). In brief, deputies spend a great deal of time seeking pork but have failed to create institutional guarantees to force the butcher to sell. Because the flow of funds is uncertain, deputies lack information to *plan* to take credit for pork-barreling. For a deputy who plans to rely on pork-barrel credit claiming for his or her reelection bid, this situation could prove deadly.

Supply Problem #2: Too Many Hungry Mouths to Feed

A deputy not only lacks a guarantee that his or her amendments will be funded, but even if the president deigns to release the funds the budget process pulverizes the amendments into relatively small amounts. Because their resources are scattered into many small, low-profile projects, amendments provide little political return. In the 1990s, deputies could submit up to twenty amendments for a total value of R$1.5 million. They could decide how to divide this sum up – any combination of between one amendment for the whole amount and ten R$150,000 amendments. Given that most deputies are under intense pressure from governors and mayors to submit amendments for the state and for particular municipalities, most deputies end up dividing their allotment into smaller slices. Table 6.3 provides the median size of each approved and executed amendment for 1995–2000[109] (comparisons

---

[109] Several amendments were not included in the analysis because they cover government administrative operations, for example amendments that fund the administration of the federal district of Brasília or the entire education system in Rio de Janeiro. See footnote 114 and Appendix 7.1 of Samuels (1998) for a details.

TABLE 6.3 *Median Approved and Executed Amendment Value – 1995–2000*

Year	Approved	Executed
1995	R$200,000	R$0
1996	R$120,000	R$123,700
1997	R$100,000	R$100,000
1998	R$90,000	R$60,000
1999	R$100,000	R$80,000
2000	R$80,000	R$80,000

Source: Brasil, Senado Federal (1997–99); Brasil, Congresso Nacional (2000c, 2001a).

with earlier years are difficult due to inflation distorting amendment values). This reveals that MCs tend to have relatively small amendments approved in committee, and also that the executive branch tends to release relatively small amounts for each amendment, when it does so.

Even the total value of deputies' funded amendments is relatively small. Table 6.4 presents the median total amount executed per deputy from 1995–2000 for those deputies who managed to get at least one project funded. Recall that no deputies received anything in 1994, and only sixteen amendments were executed in 1995. (Moreover, we should recall that the Brazilian currency was heavily devalued in 1999.)

In interviews, deputies recognize that pulverization and short supply mean that amendments provide little political return, even in "good" years. One deputy affirmed that amendments are "a drop in the bucket . . . and don't resolve anything. The sums are ridiculously small, insignificant in relationship to the budget overall."[110] Another deputy complained that,

It's fragmented. With a million and a half Reais, what can I do? What can any member of Congress do? I could put in half a mile of road [laughs]. A hospital? No way I can build a hospital with a million and a half. No one does. A dam? No way. I try to attend to the demands of the people the best I can.[111]

A third deputy confirmed that individual credit claiming is difficult because supply is short and the money fragmented into small projects. He affirmed that,

I got several amendments approved. I helped get a portion of the widening of the BR-101 highway approved, and I got a few other small things approved for some small municipalities. But, this provides you with no notoriety, no political return, because the amount is really small, the amendments in reality are very small.[112]

---

[110] Interview with Milton Mendes.   [111] Interview with Gonzaga Mota.
[112] Interview with César Souza.

TABLE 6.4 *Median Total Amount Executed per Deputy – 1995–2000*

Year	Value (in R$)
1995	R$0
1996	R$457,431
1997	R$1,121,784
1998	R$364,500
1999	R$750,000
2000	R$497,850

Source: Brasil, Senado Federal (1997–99); Brasil, Congresso Nacional (2000c, 2001a).

Brazil has tremendous infrastructural needs, but the pork-barreling process in the Chamber of Deputies forces deputies to spread their credit-claming activities very thinly across their constituencies. The amounts of pork that deputies typically can access is very small, especially relative to the resources the president and state governors control. Consequently, deputies agree that access to the pork-barrel typically provides scant direct electoral return.

Supply Problem #3: Competing Breadwinners

A final problem makes credit claiming difficult: if and when a deputy's amendments receives funding, he or she is not the only politician "bringing home the bacon" and attempting to claim credit. Municipal mayors and state-government officials may also claim a share of the credit. This is a function of the purpose of being a federal deputy in Brazil: deputies do not *implement* any projects at all. They are known as, and perceive themselves as, *despachantes de luxo*, or "luxury errand-boys" (and girls) who respond to the requests of governors and mayors. Their job is to expedite contact between government agencies. On the other hand, mayors, governors, and other state-government officers – that is, executive-branch politicians – are responsible for *implementing* public-works projects within their jurisdictions.

An example illustrates the deputies' problem: the president of the largest party in the Chamber in 1997–8, Deputy Antônio Paes de Andrade (PMDB), submitted an amendment for rural electrification to benefit his home town and principal bailiwick, Mombaça, in the state of Ceará. The town's mayor, Valdomiro Távora, from a more conservative party (the PPB), took half the credit for submitting the amendments, saying "Paes and I decided that these were the priority projects for Mombaça." For his part, Andrade defended the mayor's involvement and even gave the mayor his due, arguing that "he knows better than anyone the people's needs" (*FSP* 6/2/96, p. 1, 8). Yet deputies are not typically so generous, at least not in private: another deputy, deeply frustrated that the state government garnered most of the credit for public-works project implementation, stated that "Our participation is really reduced, very minor ... the state government takes care of this, on a much, much larger scale."[113]

In addition to having to share credit with state and local officials, who may or may not be political allies, deputies typically have to share credit with other deputies running for reelection in a given municipality. Ames (1995a) has shown that under Brazil's open-list electoral system, where states serve as the electoral districts, one can characterize the spatial distribution of deputies' votes along two scales: "concentration vs. dispersion," and "domination vs. sharing." A stereotypical clientelistic "local broker" deputy would exhibit a "concentrated and dominant" pattern, gaining most of his or her votes in one or a few contiguous municipalities ("concentrated"), and also gaining the most votes of all candidates in those municipalities ("dominant"). If this deputy were to bring pork home successfully, he or she might be the only deputy to claim credit for it justifiably.

On the other hand, another candidate might be well known across the state but might only win a few votes in every municipality ("dispersed") and also gain few votes relative to other deputies in those municipalities ("shared"). This deputy, if he or she targeted pork to a particular municipality, might face resentment and competition from other deputies who gained more votes in that municipality and who considered it their bailiwick. Moreover, those same competing deputies might also be targeting amendments to the same municipality. To get an amendment targeting a particular municipality funded, the deputy with the "dispersed-shared" vote distribution might also have to join with other deputies from the area to lobby the president. In the end, deputies with dispersed or shared vote distributions are more likely to have to share political credit.

Which type of deputy is most common? Figure 6.1 places the "concentration" and "domination" scales on the X and Y axes of a chart. For example, if we were to graph each deputy's spatial vote distribution, then a "concentrated-dominant" deputy would appear in the upper-right quadrant, with higher values on both measures.[114]

How many deputies actually fall in the upper-right quadrant? Figure 6.2 charts each winning deputy's degree of vote concentration versus his or her degree of vote dispersion in the 1990, 1994, and 1998 elections.[115]

---

[113] Interview with César Souza.
[114] My use of concentration and domination differs slightly from Ames'. See Ames (2001), Chapter 1.
[115] The sample size is 1,380. I did not include deputies from the Federal District of Brasília, which has no municipalities, thus making a calculation of "concentration" impossible. Also, the TSE never provided complete municipal-level returns for the 1990 elections, which reduced the "N" in this chart from a possible total of 1,505 (503 + 513 + 513 − 24 deputies from Brasília) to 1,380.

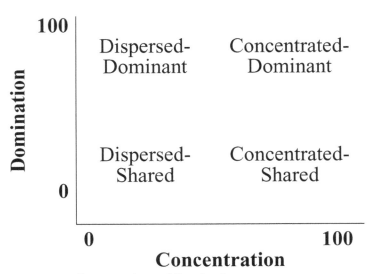

FIGURE 6.1. Concentration and Domination.

Concentration is defined as the percentage of a deputy's total vote obtained in the municipality where he or she received more votes than in any
other municipality. For example, if a deputy got 60,000 total votes and obtained 30,000 in municipality A, 20,000 in municipality B and 10,000 in

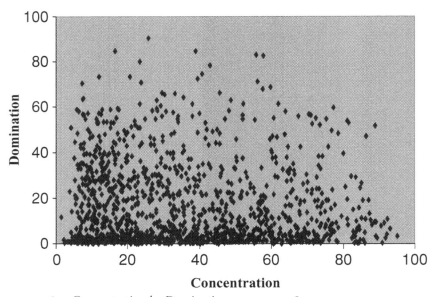

FIGURE 6.2. Concentration by Domination – 1990–1998.

municipality C, the concentration score would be 50 percent. Domination is defined as each deputy's percentage of all votes in the municipality where the deputy "concentrated" the most votes. Thus, if 120,000 total votes were cast in municipality A, our deputy would have a domination score of 25 percent to go with his concentration score of 50 percent.

As Figure 6.2 shows, the majority of deputies fall in the lower two quadrants: that is, whether they concentrate their vote or not, very few deputies dominate their vote bases. Instead, most deputies share their vote bases. Consider the deputies who concentrate just 20 percent or more of their vote in their top municipality. (This might not even be considered a "concentrated" pattern, but let us assume that it is.) Two-thirds of deputies achieve this level of concentration. However, only 30 percent of this group also obtains a domination score of 20 percent or higher in their top municipality. The remaining 70 percent of all deputies do not even obtain one out of every five votes cast in their own "bailiwick."

A deputy who concentrates 20 percent of his vote in one municipality must seek the remainder of his votes in at least four other municipalities, and more than likely in many more. Even if these municipalities were contiguous, this deputy is sharing the support of voters in his supposed bailiwick with several other candidates. In fact, a deputy could face different competitors, from different parties, in each municipality where he or she received votes. In short, most deputies are forced to "share" their municipalities with several other winning – or losing – candidates.[116]

Brazil's electoral system, which allows deputies to seek out votes in any corner of their state, is thus a two-edged sword: candidates for reelection can "invade" other bailiwicks to strategically seek out voters (Ames 1995a), but their own bailiwicks are also typically scenes of intense competition as well as subject to hostile invasion. In contrast to the Anglo-American single-member district system, Brazil's multimember at-large district system makes voter identification of "credit-worthy" candidates difficult. In many municipalities, several incumbents running for reelection may attempt to take credit for the same project.[117] Or, an incumbent may have to attempt to fend off attempts by the local mayor or some state-government official – now candidates for federal deputy – to take credit for public-works projects for which the deputy helped obtain funds, but which the mayor or state-government "executed." Because these deputies' bailiwicks' are so easily invaded, incumbents lack confidence that they can send clear "credit-claiming" cues to voters.

---

[116] Deputies might not dominate the same municipality where they concentrate most of their votes. But if this is the case, they are dominating a municipality that contributes relatively fewer votes to their overall total, reducing the importance of that municipality to their chances of winning election.

[117] Interview with César Souza.

In sum, three "supply problems" make individual credit-claiming based on access to pork from the national budget difficult for Brazilian federal deputies. First, deputies have no guarantee that the executive branch will fund their projects. Second, the amounts released for each project are too small to generate a substantial political payoff. Finally, deputies typically must share political credit with other deputies, state-government politicians, and mayors. For a reelection-minded deputy, the situation looks bleak. In the next section, I confirm this evaluation by statistically testing the relationship between pork and deputies' electoral success.

TESTING THE RELATIONSHIP BETWEEN PORK AND REELECTION

In the previous section I argued that deputies have uncertain access to pork at all stages of the budget process, and that this is likely to limit their ability to translate pork into an incumbency advantage. In this section I empirically investigate whether access to pork does or does not provide electoral benefits to reelection-minded deputies. I hypothesize that access to pork provides no benefit. To test this hypothesis I analyze the probability that pork improved the chances of deputies who ran for reelection in 1994 and 1998.

Comparison with Ames: Data and Methodological Issues

Before presenting and operationalizing my variables, I note a series of differences between my analysis and Ames (1995a, 2001). Like Ames, I use the deputies' budget amendments as the operational indicators of "pork." However, Ames explored the results of the 1990 election as compared against the 1986 election, whereas I explore the 1994 and 1998 elections. Analysis of two legislatures and two elections should strengthen the validity of my conclusions. I also operationalize the independent variable (pork) and the dependent variable (electoral success) differently, and I specify the relationship between pork and electoral success differently as well. These latter issues are important enough to merit discussion.[118]

---

[118] Pereira and Rennó (2000) also found that pork helps reelection. Their results are driven by their inclusion of *suplentes* in the sample. Their sample size is 446 for 1998, although by my count only 376 *titulares* ran for reelection that year. This creates substantial bias: *ceteris paribus*, *suplentes* as a group are much weaker candidates, since they, of course, failed to win election outright to begin with. *Suplentes*' initial relative weakness is exacerbated by the fact that they only enter the Chamber when a *titular* decides to take a leave of absence or is elected to another position. *Suplentes* thus typically do not have the same "access to pork" as incumbents do. The reelection rates of *titulares* versus *suplentes* illustrate the bias problem: *titulares* had a 69.4 percent chance of winning reelection in 1998 (261/376). Pereira and Rennó's figures provide a total of 446 candidates running and 288 winning reelection, meaning that they include 70 *suplentes*, only 27 of whom (38.6 percent) won reelection (Pereira and Rennó, pp. 20–1). It is therefore not surprising that Pereira and Rennó find that pork-barreling helps reelection – but the inclusion of *suplentes* may account for this

Ames operationalizes the independent variable as the *number* (logged) *of submitted amendments*. However, the number of *submitted* amendments deputies target is not the best option to test for pork's impact. Submitted amendments are two steps away from the end of the budget process; a better operational indicator would employ *"executed"* or funded amendments. As I argued in the preceding text, deputies have no guarantee that their submitted amendments will make it through the budget process. Conceivably, deputies could attempt to claim credit for submitted amendments, arguing that the approval and execution phases are beyond their control. However, this confounds the very logic of Brazil's electoral system that Ames (1995a) laid out. Given that many deputies face intense competition *within* their own bailiwicks, if one deputy attempted to claim credit for submitting an amendment to a municipality while another deputy claimed credit for not only submitting an amendment to that same municipality but for extracting the resources from the executive – actually "bringing home the bacon" – vote brokers and other hungry (and feckless?) clienteles might shift allegiance to the more successful deputy.

In short, only if the president releases funds could a deputy convincingly claim credit for mediating between federal and municipal governments. A deputy who had "gone shopping for pork" but who had failed to "bring home the bacon" would not reap any electoral benefits from closing a clientelistic deal. It would also be puzzling to find that submitted amendments influence vote totals and/or reelection success, because this would fail to explain why deputies spend so much time visiting ministers and pleading with the president to release the amendments' funds. If submission were all there were to credit claiming, deputies would turn to other activities after making their submissions.

In addition, the number of amendments – submitted or executed – may not be a good indicator. Instead, the *amount* of money involved is a better indicator. Using the number of executed amendments illogically supposes that the deputy whose amendment is executed for the amount of one Real gets as much "credit" as a second deputy, whose amendment in the same municipality might be executed in the amount of one million Reais.

We also have reason to believe that deputies themselves do not believe that the number of amendment submissions is related to their electoral prospects. If such a relationship existed, deputies would have resisted limiting the number of amendments they could submit each year, possibly instead limiting the amounts they could request. Yet since 1994 deputies have moved to limit the number of amendments they could each submit to twenty per year. This reduces the variation on the independent variable and largely eliminates the

result, because their inclusion strengthens the "performance" of *titulares* (in the absence of some control variable, relative to *suplentes* of course), who by definition have more access to pork.

possibility that the number of submissions could be related to vote swings, since most deputies submit close to twenty amendments. For these reasons, I operationalize pork as the *total value of all amendments for which each deputy obtained funding.*[119]

I also use a different measure of the dependent variable. Ames' dependent variable is the *swing in candidate C's vote in municipality M.* However, the Brazilian electoral system aggregates votes at the state, not the municipal level. Consequently, Ames' results do not tell us whether the reported increases in deputies' votes were enough to *win* reelection with a greater probability.[120] An example demonstrates the problem. Suppose Deputy Silva won his seat with 15,000 votes in election "t," obtaining 5,000 from municipality A, 5,000 from municipality B, and 5,000 from municipality C. During the legislative term, Deputy Silva submits amendments to benefit municipalities A and B, but not C. At election "t+1," Deputy Silva seeks reelection. He gains 15,000 votes again: 7,000 from municipality A, 7,000 from municipality B, but only 1,000 from municipality C. This result would confirm Ames' findings. However, suppose that because of intraparty competition Deputy Silva finishes lower on the list, and does not win reelection. Thus, a deputy who gains votes in a given municipality (because of pork or other factors) might still not gain enough votes to win reelection because he lost votes elsewhere, because competitors in the same municipality gained more votes, or because new entrants pushed him down the list.

It is therefore interesting but not sufficient to understand the relationship between pork and reelection to know whether on average, amendment submission means more votes in a given municipality. We need to know if amendment execution pays off overall: is pork an efficient *reelection* strategy? I thus measure the influence of pork on the probability of winning reelection, using a dummy dependent variable.

Finally, I also specify the relationship between pork and electoral success differently. Although I could include any number of potentially interesting and important variables that might be associated with a deputy's chances of winning reelection – such as a deputy's career background, important family ties, potential presidential or gubernatorial coattail effects – this chapter is not about the "factors associated with reelection in Brazil." It is about showing that one variable – pork – is *not* associated with reelection. I am not interested in finding the model with the "best" predictive power, and therefore limit the number of variables in the equation in order to focus on

[119] See Samuels (1998) Chapter 6 for other tests that confirm my hypotheses.
[120] In addition, Ames did not report the coefficients or t-statistics on any of the variables in his model, only the signs (positive or negative). Consequently, the reader has no way to know whether pork-barreling is more or less important (or to what degree) than any of the other variables.

the impact of pork. I should state that Ames (1995a) was concerned not only with the impact of pork, but more broadly with what determines electoral success, and tested for the impact of many variables.

I test for the impact of pork on a deputy's probability of reelection using LOGIT regression analysis. The sample populations in these equations are the 348 deputies elected in 1990 who ran for reelection in 1994 and the 376 deputies who won in 1994 and ran again in 1998.[121] I test several models for each legislature, progressively adding in independent variables to demonstrate that the results are stable. The independent variables are as follows:

- **Pork:** Each deputy's percentage of the total value of all pork-barrel amendments in his or her state, weighted by district magnitude.[122] I use percentage of pork in the district rather than absolute amounts of pork because we need a measure of deputies' success relative only to those they are competing against, not against all deputies running for reelection. For

---

[121] Regarding the changes in the sample sizes in the models: in 1994, the full sample is included in Model 1, and Pork does not come close to significance. For the other models, the first problem is calculating concentration and domination. The TSE never compiled complete municipal-level data for the 1990 election, making calculation of those variables impossible for candidates from Alagoas, Rio de Janeiro, and Rio Grande do Norte ($N = 49$), in addition to two other candidates for whom data are missing. This leaves 297 deputies for Model 2 for 1994. In addition, I exclude deputies from the Federal District of Brasília because there is no way to calculate concentration for them. Thus we have 291 deputies for Model 3. Models 4 through 6 all use campaign finance information, and in 1994 no candidates from Alagoas, Mato Grosso do Sul, or Rio de Janeiro sent campaign finance information ($N = 51$). In addition, another 47 of the 297 remaining candidates failed to send campaign finance information. In the regressions for 1998, 34 of the 376 candidates for reelection failed to send in campaign finance information, explaining the drop in the sample size from Models 1 and 2 to Models 4 and 5 that year. The other declines in Models 3 and 6 are from the exclusion of the deputies from Brasília because of the problem with calculating concentration as noted previously. For a discussion of the validity and reliability of the campaign finance data, see Samuels (2001a, 2001b).

[122] If the percentage were not weighted then the variable would be highly correlated with state size, simply because the number of competitors varies as a function of state size. (The correlation between a deputy's percentage of the pork and district magnitude is $-.37$, for example.) Consequently, an unweighted percentage regressed on reelection success might measure the relationship between state size and reelection as opposed to the relationship between pork and reelection; there is no way to distinguish this effect. Therefore, state size must be controlled for across these values (along with campaign finance, see following text), and the issue then becomes how to weight each deputy's percentage: by district magnitude or number of voters. Magnitude is better: the number of competitors in each state is determined by district magnitude more than by the number of voters, because there is both a minimum and a maximum district magnitude, both of which are independent of state population. Thus, I weighted by district magnitude. (I ran the same regressions weighting "pork-barrel" by the number of eligible voters in each state; the results do not change.) This eliminates this potential bias problem.

the 1991–4 legislature, I use 1993 data: the 1991 budget was prepared under the previous legislature, data are unavailable for the 1992 budget, no amendments were executed in 1994, and amendments executed in 1995 could not have aided a 1994 reelection bid. For the 1995–8 legislature, I used the value of amendments (corrected for inflation) executed in 1996–8 (that is, submitted in 1995–7). I expect no relationship between pork and reelection. Sources: Brasil, Senado Federal (1997–9) and Brasil, Congresso Nacional (2000b).

- **Domination:** Ames (1995b) suggested that deputies who "dominate" a municipality would have a relatively easier time winning reelection. To test this, I use each deputy's vote in his or her top municipality as a percentage of all votes in that municipality. Deputies who dominate the municipality will have a higher percentage, while deputies who share their votes will have a lower percentage. Sources: Brasil, Tribunal Superior Eleitoral (1991, 1995).

- **Domination*Pork:** This interacts the value of a deputy's budget amendments with his or her degree of domination. Like the previous variable, we might hypothesize that a deputy who we could readily identify as *the* boss of the area might be more able to claim credit for obtaining funds for public-works projects that benefit his bailiwick. Thus, I interact each deputy's degree of domination with his or her pork success. I expect no relationship between this variable and reelection success.

- **Concentration:** We also might suppose that deputies who concentrate their votes might have safer seats. To test this hypothesis I use the percentage of each deputy's total vote obtained in that deputy's top municipality. Sources: Brasil, Tribunal Superior Eleitoral (1991, 1995).

- **Concentration*Pork:** This variable interacts the value of a deputy's budget amendments with his or her degree of vote concentration. As with domination, we could hypothesize that the typical "local broker" deputy – one who concentrates his or her vote in a limited area – might also reap relatively greater rewards from bringing home the bacon, because voters would be more likely to observe the fruits of the deputy's labor. In contrast, a deputy who has a dispersed vote pattern might have a harder time advertising his or her pork success. However, I expect no relationship between this variable and reelection.

- **Cash:** This measures each deputy's percentage of all campaign finance in his or her district, weighted by district magnitude. As I have found in other work (Samuels 2001a, 2001b, 2001c), I expect this variable to be positive and significant. Sources: Brasil, Tribunal Superior Eleitoral (1997, 2000).

- **Cash^2:** The deputy's percentage of all campaign finance squared, weighted by district magnitude. It is standard practice in the campaign finance literature to control for the potential that money provides diminishing returns. This variable should return a negative coefficient.

I also include several control variables:

- **Switch:** Indicates whether the deputy switched parties during the legislature or not. This variable is included to test whether, as scholars have hypothesized, deputies who switch parties are generally weaker candidates for reelection (Schmitt 1999; Desposato n.d.). Thus I expect a negative coefficient. Source: Brasil, Câmara dos Deputados (1991–2001).
- **Quality:** A nonpartisan nongovernmental organization's (NGO) qualitative evaluation of a candidate's chances of winning election. This takes a value between zero and three and is based on each candidate's background and legislative prominence. Theoretically, we suppose that deputies who stand out because of their legislative expertise or because of their more extensive connections back home might be more likely to win reelection independently of their pork-barrel success, which was not included in the NGO's measure. Source: INESC (1994, 1998).[123]
- **ListQuality:** Controls for the quality of the candidates on each deputy's list, and thus controls for any list-specific effects. This is the average of the INESC "Quality" score for all candidates on the list. The theoretical expectation here is unclear. A higher-quality list both helps and harms each candidate's prospects, because higher-quality candidates both have better chances of winning *ceteris paribus* and a higher-quality list means that competition for the last seat on the list is relatively more fierce, *ceteris paribus*.[124]
- **#Terms:** The total number of terms each candidate has served. This measures the degree of a candidate's seniority. We might suppose that more experienced deputies have better chances of winning reelection, independently of other variables. However, given my argument in chapters 1 and 2 I have no *a priori* reason to believe that this variable should have any particular impact. Source: author's compilation, from Tribunal Superior Eleitoral sources.
- **Vote^{t-1}:** Is the percentage of the vote in the district each incumbent received in the previous election. It is standard practice to control for a candidate's performance in the last election. Source: Brasil, Tribunal Superior Eleitoral (1991, 1995).

---

[123] For more information on this variable, see Samuels (2000b or 2001a).

[124] There is an independence problem in any analysis of reelection in Brazil, because Brazil's electoral rules create a situation where deputies' reelection depends on both their own performance and on their list-mates' performance. The only way to truly solve this problem is to create a dummy variable for each list in each state. Unfortunately, doing so creates eighty-three dummy variables (for 1994), and forces much of the data out of the equations because there are many "lists" that include only one incumbent candidate, which means the dummy is perfectly correlated with that list. Instead of sacrificing this many degrees of freedom by using a dummy for every list, I use the "ListQuality" variable to control for list-specific effects. I thank Scott Desposato for bringing this problem to my attention, although he cannot be blamed for the solution.

- **Party Dummies:** A dummy variable was included for each candidate's party, to control for any potential national-level party-specific effects. Source: Brasil, Tribunal Superior Eleitoral (1995, 1999). (The results for the party dummy variables are not shown in tables 6.5 and 6.6.[125])

If my argument is correct, pork should have no effect, nor should any of the variables interacted with pork. Tables 6.5 and 6.6 display the results for six models for each year.[126] The models are the same for both election years, and all the models contain all the control variables. Model 1 is the simplest test for a direct relationship between pork and reelection. Models 2 and 5 also include the "Domination" and "Domination*Pork" variables, while Models 3 and 6 include the "Concentration" and "Concentration*Pork" variables. Models 4 through 6 also include the campaign finance variables.

The results for both years are consistent, and fully substantiate my argument: pork does not help a deputy win reelection. Even when we control for "likelihood of benefiting from pork," pork never demonstrates a positive and significant relationship with reelection success (i.e., the p-values are never below .05). For example, the Domination*Pork variable supposes that pork helps only those deputies who are both good pork-barrelers and who dominate their vote bases. As previously explained, in reality very few deputies are able to do so, but in any case the variable is insignificant. Pork comes close to significance only in Model 5 for 1998, as does Domination*Pork, but in the opposite direction as one might suppose. And in this case, when we compare Model 2 with Model 5, we see that the introduction of the campaign finance variables has dramatically affected the pork variables, suggesting that the results on the Pork variables are not stable. (And of course, they are not significant in any of the other eleven models.) In contrast, campaign finance is quite strongly associated with reelection success in both years, and the results on that variable are robust to the inclusion of the different specifications of Pork. As for the control variables, I only had strong expectations for the directions of the Switch, Quality, and $Vote^{t-1}$ variables. These always come up in the predicted direction, and are often significant. Because none of the pork-associated variables came up significant, I dispense with further analysis of the coefficients.

These findings contradict the view that budgetary pork helps Brazilian deputies win reelection. Instead, they confirm my first hypothesis, that pork-barreling provides little direct political payoff for reelection-minded deputies. The analysis here improves upon previous research by using a more direct

---

[125] The party dummies control for any independent effect that party membership might have on one's reelection chances relative to membership in the "controlled-for" party. The choice of dummy is always somewhat arbitrary. In both years I used the PDT as the "control" dummy. The choice of party dummy does not affect the results on the other variables substantively.

[126] I ran these regressions in STATA 6.0, using the "robust" command to correct for heteroskedasticity. None of these variables are collinear with each other at a level above .60.

TABLE 6.5 *Factors Associated with Reelection in Brazil – 1994 (logit regressions)*

Independent Variable	Model 1 Coefficient (s.e.)	Model 1 p	Model 2 Coefficient (s.e.)	Model 2 p	Model 3 Coefficient (s.e.)	Model 3 p	Model 4 Coefficient (s.e.)	Model 4 p	Model 5 Coefficient (s.e.)	Model 5 p	Model 6 Coefficient (s.e.)	Model 6 p
Pork	.001 (.001)	.258	.00001 (.001)	.992	.003 (.002)	.159	-.0006 (.001)	.662	-.001 (.002)	.489	.002 (.003)	.417
Domination	—	—	-.008 (.008)	.327	—	—	—	—	-.007 (.011)	.503	—	—
Domination*Pork	—	—	.0004 (.0001)	.439	—	—	—	—	.0001 (.0001)	.449	—	—
Concentration	—	—	—	—	-.006 (.007)	.466	—	—	—	—	-.004 (.009)	.660
Concentration*Pork	—	—	—	—	-.00005 (.00005)	.353	—	—	—	—	-.00005 (.00006)	.396
Cash	—	—	—	—	—	—	.021 (.007)	.002	.020 (.007)	.002	.019 (.007)	.006
Cash²	—	—	—	—	—	—	-.0006 (.0003)	.038	-.0003 (.0005)	.458	-.0002 (.0005)	.665
Switch	-.822 (.299)	.006	-.659 (.324)	.042	-.783 (.334)	.019	-.630 (.390)	.107	-.629 (.407)	.123	-.773 (.429)	.072
Quality	.493 (.132)	.000	.468 (.148)	.001	.449 (.148)	.002	.442 (.165)	.007	.446 (.171)	.009	.459 (.171)	.007
ListQuality	.084 (.417)	.841	.361 (.441)	.413	.067 (.461)	.884	-.029 (.564)	.959	-.193 (.567)	.734	-.277 (.591)	.640
# Terms	.142 (.106)	.182	.022 (.121)	.853	.028 (.118)	.814	-.048 (.123)	.696	-.038 (.122)	.756	-.023 (.121)	.849
Vote1990	.015 (.005)	.001	.016 (.005)	.004	.016 (.005)	.002	.012 (.006)	.058	.014 (.007)	.040	.015 (.007)	.030
Constant	-2.23 (.613)	.000	-2.36 (.756)	.002	-2.04 (.853)	.017	-2.31 (.883)	.009	-2.20 (.910)	.015	-2.07 (1.04)	.046
Log-likelihood	-201.967		-172.544		-168.587		-134.449		-129.151		-128.739	
N	348		297		291		250		243		243	
% Predicted Correctly	69.54		71.38		68.04		72.40		75.72		76.13	

Dependent Variable: win/lose.

TABLE 6.6 *Factors Associated with Reelection in Brazil – 1998 (logit regressions)*

Independent Variable	Model 1 Coefficient (s.e.)	p	Model 2 Coefficient (s.e.)	p	Model 3 Coefficient (s.e.)	p	Model 4 Coefficient (s.e.)	p	Model 5 Coefficient (s.e.)	p	Model 6 Coefficient (s.e.)	p
Pork	-.00004 (.0009)	.962	.0007 (.002)	.693	.0001 (.002)	.975	.0008 (.0009)	.405	.005 (.003)	.078	.001 (.002)	.528
Domination	—	—	-.007 (.008)	.391	—	—	—	—	.001 (.012)	.938	—	—
Domination*Pork	—	—	-.00007 (.0001)	.476	—	—	—	—	-.0003 (.0002)	.063	—	—
Concentration	—	—	—	—	-.011 (.006)	.074	—	—	—	—	-.007 (.007)	.301
Concentration*Pork	—	—	—	—	2.47E-06 (.00003)	.939	—	—	—	—	-2.8E-06 (.00003)	.925
Cash	—	—	—	—	—	—	.017 (.004)	.000	.016 (.004)	.000	.016 (.004)	.000
Cash²	—	—	—	—	—	—	-.0003 (.0001)	.000	-.0004 (.0001)	.000	-.0003 (.0001)	.000
Switch	-.480 (.269)	.07	-.509 (.267)	.056	-.559 (.276)	.043	-.601 (.307)	.051	-.642 (.311)	.039	-.623 (.310)	.045
Quality	.797 (.156)	.000	.802 (.154)	.000	.822 (.156)	.000	.630 (.158)	.000	.646 (.165)	.000	.647 (.159)	.000
ListQuality	.359 (.278)	.196	.412 (.284)	.146	.182 (.285)	.523	.077 (.307)	.803	.157 (.324)	.628	-.021 (.309)	.945
# Terms	-.050 (.088)	.575	-.062 (.091)	.493	.099 (.091)	.271	-.105 (.101)	.300	-.113 (.106)	.296	-.131 (.103)	.204
Vote1990	.009 (.005)	.111	.011 (.006)	.062	.008 (.005)	.120	.013 (.006)	.041	.016 (.007)	.014	.011 (.006)	.059
Constant	-1.48 (.74)	.045	-1.60 (.728)	.028	-.759 (.775)	.327	-1.32 (.92)	.149	-1.77 (.91)	.053	-.836 (.945)	.376
Log-likelihood	-200.782		-198.870		-191.961		-162.226		-157.231		-158.582	
N	376		376		371		342		342		340	
% Predicted Correctly	73.40		74.20		74.39		76.90		78.07		77.06	

indicator of pork – executed amendments – and by operationalizing the dependent variable to test for whether pork actually helps win reelection. The consistent, nonsignificant results on the pork variables suggest that the findings are robust.

CONCLUSION

This chapter began with a puzzle: despite pervasive pork-barreling, personalistic campaigns, institutional incentives to develop a congressional career, and scholarly claims that Brazilian deputies seek pork to win reelection, congressional careers are extremely rare in Brazil. When deputies do not seek to build long-term careers in the Chamber, we have good reason to believe that they may not have designed legislative institutions to help them win reelection. Brazilian deputies have not collectively implemented a pork-barreling system that enhances incumbency. They lack significant control over the budget. This leaves them vulnerable to executive caprice, because the president controls the purse strings. Even when their projects are funded, deputies lament that small project sizes means that pork-barreling provides little electoral return. In addition, deputies must compete for credit with other deputies, further diluting the potential impact that pork might have on their reelection chances. Finally, because credit for "federal" pork does not necessarily accrue to a deputy but often goes to a state or municipal officeholder, with the deputy gaining credit for *mediating* but not *executing* the deal, voters consequently may have a less clear notion that the federal deputy is in some way worthy of receiving political credit for the amendment's execution. Given these credit-claiming problems, most deputies are poorly positioned to take credit for pork, and we therefore have good reason to suspect that pork provides reelection-minded deputies with little electoral return. I provided statistical verification of the deputies' predicament, finding no relationship between pork-barreling and the deputies' probability of winning reelection.[127]

I end this chapter with another puzzle: if pork provides no return to incumbency-minded deputies, why do deputies spend so much time pork-barreling? The solution comes through an exploration of Hypotheses 2 and 3: because subnational political forces shape and direct deputies' careers, deputies have strong incentives to favor subnational governments in the budget process and to use the pork-barrel as part of a *progressive* ambition strategy. I turn to these issues in the next chapter.

---

[127] I should reiterate that I did not specifically contest Ames' (1995a) finding, which was that deputies target specific municipalities and gain votes *in those municipalities*. This might indeed be true, but it does not provide a clear answer to the question of whether pork improves deputies' overall probability of winning reelection.

Chapter 7

Progressive Ambition, Federalism, and Pork-Barreling in Brazil

INTRODUCTION

The last chapter ended with, and this chapter begins with, a puzzle: if pork-barreling in Brazil provides no clear incumbency advantage, why do so many deputies seek pork? In this chapter I solve the puzzle by returning to my arguments about political ambition and the way in which federalism pushes deputies to favor state-based political interests. As I demonstrated in chapters 1 through 4, while very few Brazilian deputies develop long congressional careers, many attempt to jump from Congress to a position in state or municipal government. In Chapter 5 I also demonstrated that a state-based dynamic drives deputy elections.

In what way are deputies' relatively short time horizons in Congress and the strength of subnational political forces related to the structure and process of pork-barreling in Brazil? In the last chapter I hypothesized that pork-barreling is related to the incentives driving deputies' careers in two ways. First, pressure from subnational actors pushes deputies to favor subnational interests in the budget process. Deputies react to these pressures because these actors affect their careers. As I will describe, state-based forces weigh particularly heavily, and deputies have responded by shaping the pork-barreling process to favor state-level interests. Second, although pork-barreling does not appear to help deputies interested in maintaining their seats, the pork-barrel process does allow deputies to pursue their *progressive* ambition strategies, and progressively ambitious deputies ought to exhibit distinct pork-barreling strategies from those who seek reelection. Thus, political ambition in Brazil has not driven the creation of a pork-barreling process that enhances incumbency. Instead, pork-barreling indirectly and directly reflects the incentives and pressures driving deputies' progressive ambitions.

This chapter is organized as follows: in the next two sections, I provide evidence supporting Hypothesis 2, that subnational forces have pushed deputies to reshape the budget process. First I explain how deputies have structured the budget committee and the budget process to reflect state-level interests in particular. Subsequently, I support Hypothesis 3 by demonstrating how progressive ambition directly shapes deputies' pork-barreling strategies.

STATE-LEVEL INTERESTS IN THE BUDGET COMMITTEE AND
BUDGET PROCESS

Although access to the budget does not appear to help deputies individually develop long-term congressional careers, MCs do spend a good deal of time seeking pork. In this section I discuss how state-level pressures have pushed MCs to structure the budget committee (Comissão Mista do Orçamento [CMO]) and the pork-barreling process.

Structure: State "Representation" on the Budget Committee

The CMO was first created after the promulgation of Brazil's new constitution in 1988. The way in which members of Congress set up the CMO reflects both their desire to limit national partisan influence in budget policy and their strong ties to subnational political institutions and actors. Thus, although party representation in Congress proportionally determines the initial distribution of seats on the CMO (as it does with all committees), parties as such have no role in the formulation of budget priorities or in the negotiation of budget amendments. Instead, the structure and process of the CMO privilege state-level political interests. The CMO privileges all states because it is a joint committee of Congress, and it privileges certain states over others by overrepresenting Brazil's poorer states, which comprise a majority of both houses of Congress and where the weight of state-level political actors and interests is particularly strong.

Jointness. The CMO is a joint committee of Brazil's National Congress; deputies and senators serve as coequals. The presidency of the CMO switches from a deputy to a senator each year. Neither the Senate nor the Chamber has an independent budget committee – only the CMO analyzes, modifies, amends, and votes on the executive's proposal before the final vote in a joint session of Congress. The CMO's jointness favors state interests because as the budget is being prepared and analyzed, deputies and senators do not meet in partisan groups, but as state delegations. Jointness thus transforms deputies into "mini-senators," because deputies and senators work together as a state delegation to defend both the individual amendments of all MCs from their state as well as defend their state's delegation amendments, which the entire delegation submits as a group (see the following text).[128]

---

[128] Interviews with Lidia Quinan, Waldeck Ornellas, and Antônio Carlos Pojo do Rêgo.

TABLE 7.1 *Malapportionment in the Brazilian Congress – 1998*

Region	% Chamber	% Senate	% Population
Center-West	8.0	14.8	6.4
Northeast	29.4	33.3	29.2
North	12.7	25.9	6.8
Southeast	34.9	14.8	42.5
South	15.0	11.1	15.1

Source: Nicolau (1996); Mainwaring and Samuels (1999).

Malapportionment. Malapportionment in the CMO also tends to favor state-level interests in the budget, because it tends to favor the states where state-level political forces have historically been particularly strong. As Table 7.1 shows, Brazil's Congress overrepresents the poor, less-populated states of the country's Center-West, North, and Northeast regions.

Table 7.1 provides the percentage of seats the states in each region have in each chamber of Congress, and the percentage of the country's population in each region. If the percentage of seats in either chamber exceeds the percentage of the population, the region is overrepresented. Table 7.1 reveals that the three less-developed regions had 50.1 percent of the Chamber seats, 74 percent of the Senate seats, and 54.3 percent of the seats overall in the 1995–8 legislature. Because the Chamber and Senate vote jointly on the budget, we might suppose that the CMO would reflect the division of seats in the joint plenary session: that is, the poorer regions would get 54.3 percent of the seats. However, the CMO exacerbates the extant overrepresentation of poorer states. Table 7.2 breaks the membership of the CMO down according to whether the senators and deputies on the budget committee were from the "poor" regions or the "rich" regions and reveals that on average, Brazil's three poorer regions send about 81 percent of the senators and about 58 percent of the deputies to the CMO, for an overall average (% Poor Total) of 64 percent of the budget committee seats. This means that the budget committee is about 20 percent more malapportioned than the Chamber.

The three poorer regions dominate the CMO because they can. As noted, the states in these regions already possess an absolute majority of the joint session of Congress. The reason that MCs from these regions desire to dominate the budget committee is because the states in these regions have historically been relatively more dependent on federal-government support than states in the South and Southeast, and because municipal-level interests are less prominent and less well articulated in contrast to state-level political interests in these states. Consequently, MCs from these regions are likely receive more intense pressure from their state governments to obtain resources. In addition, because relatively fewer deputies from the poorer regions turn to municipal-level politics upon leaving the Chamber, their own career ambitions tend to favor state-based political interests. In short, the

TABLE 7.2 *Malapportionment and CMO Membership*

	1992	1993	1994	1995	1996	1997	1998	1999	*Average*
% "Poor" Senators	83.3	80.0	71.4	85.0	78.3	82.1	85.7	90.4	*82.0*
% "Rich" Senators	16.7	20.0	28.6	15.0	21.7	17.9	14.3	9.6	*18.0*
% "Poor" Deputies	57.8	63.3	58.7	54.1	48.1	62.2	60.0	55.6	*57.5*
% "Rich" Deputies	42.2	36.7	41.3	45.9	51.9	37.8	40.0	44.4	*42.5*
% "Poor" Total on CMO	64.2	67.5	63.4	61.7	57.8	67.6	66.7	64.2	*64.1*
% "Rich" Total on CMO	35.8	32.5	36.6	38.3	42.2	32.4	33.3	35.8	*35.9*

Sources: Author's compilation from Brasil. Senado Federal, Secretaria-Geral da Mesa, 1991–99.

weight of state-based interests is relatively greater for deputies from the three poorer regions. Along with jointness, overrepresentation of poorer states tends to increase the weight of state-level interests in the budget process.

Process: How and Where Congress Targets Pork

Not only does the structure of the CMO privilege state-level interests – certain state-level interests in particular – but the process of pork-barreling does so as well, in two ways. First, MCs have come to organize at the state level to submit and approve budget amendments, instead of simply submitting them as individuals. Second, whether as individuals or organized as a state delegation, MCs have also come to target a good portion of budgetary pork to state governments, as opposed to only municipal governments.

How MCs Target Pork. Ames (1995b, 2001) highlighted the MCs' capacity to present budget amendments as individuals, and when Congress set up the budget-amendment process in 1988, only individual MCs could submit amendments. However, MCs have altered the amendment submission and approval process several times over the last decade, limiting their own individual involvement and increasing their activities as members of organized groups, in particular as state delegations. Table 7.3 relates the *number* of amendments (not their relative amounts) submitted by since 1992 by agent.

Since 1991 the number of amendments MCs have submitted as individuals has declined, while several types of groups of MCs have been allowed to submit amendments: state and regional delegations, congressional committees, political parties, executive-branch agencies, and supra-partisan groups

TABLE 7.3 *Budget Amendments by Agent*

Agent	Number of Amendments Submitted per Year								
	1992	1993	1994	1995	1996	1997	1998	1999	2000
Individual MC	73,642	20,826	13,915	22,664	10,403	10,348	8,533	7,572	8,334
Congressional Committee	—	257	9	28	517	1,018	537	361	112
Executive Agency	—	—	—	84	—	—	—	—	—
Party	—	—	—	7	—	—	—	—	—
Regional Delegation	—	—	—	—	28	27	26	—	24
State Delegation	—	1,407	—	468	279	271	245	272	275
Group of >30 MCs	—	108	—	—	—	—	—	—	—

Source: Author's compilation from Brasil. Senado Federal, 1997–99; Brasil, Congresso Nacional (2000c, 2001a).

TABLE 7.4 *Percent Value of all Submitted Amendments – by Submitting Agent*

Agent	1992	1993	1994	1995	1996	1997	1998	1999	2000
Individual MC	100	64.0	99.8	90.1	68.8	57.6	27.8	26.3	35.2
State Delegation	—	34.0	—	8.9	21.9	32.7	69.5	70.9	59.6
Congressional Committee	—	0.4	0.2	0.1	5.4	4.5	1.1	2.8	1.6
Party	—	0.0	—	0.1	—	—	—	—	—
Regional Delegation	—	0.0	—	—	3.8	5.2	1.5	0.0	3.6
>30 MCs	—	1.6	—	—	—	—	—	—	—
Executive Agency	—	—	—	0.9	—	—	—	—	—

Source: Author's compilation from Brasil. Senado Federal, 1997–99; Brasil, Congresso Nacional (2000b, 2000c, 2001a).

of more than thirty MCs. Currently, in addition to individual MCs, state and regional delegations; permanent congressional committees; and the president of the CMO and the presidents of its subcommittees can submit amendments. Tellingly, despite giving parties the right to submit amendments in two years, parties submitted a total of only seven amendments, all in 1995.

The raw numbers of submitted amendments do not relate the relative *amounts* of money these actors target. Tables 7.4 and 7.5 present this information for both submitted and approved amendments as a percentage of the total value of all amendments, providing strong evidence of the increasing weight of state delegation amendments in recent years.

Tables 7.4 and 7.5 show that while individual MCs initially accounted for 100 percent of both submissions and approvals, by 2000 individual

TABLE 7.5 *Percent Value of all Approved Amendments – by Submitting Agent*

Agent	1992	1993	1994	1995	1996	1997	1998	1999	2000
Individual MC	100	71.0	X	41.6	30.5	32.5	33.5	58.5	44.7
State Delegation	—	25.6	X	46.2	58.9	60.6	48.8	32.1	50.2
Congressional Committee	—	2.4	X	0.5	1.3	2.3	15.0	5.9	2.3
Party	—	0.0	X	0.0	—	—	—	—	—
Regional Delegation	—	0.0	X	—	9.4	4.6	2.7	—	2.7
>30 MCs	—	1.1	X	—	—	—	—	—	—
Executive Agency	—	—	X	11.7	—	—	—	—	—

X = no approved amendments.

Source: Author's compilation from Brasil. Senado Federal, 1997–99; Brasil, Congresso Nacional (2000b, 2000c, 2001a).

TABLE 7.6 *Percent Value of Submitted Amendments – by Level of Government*

Target	1992	1993	1994	1995	1996	1997	1998	1999	2000
% to Region	0.7	15.0	3.3	1.6	7.5	6.3	1.9	2.6	2.8
% to States	7.4	38.6	22.3	39.4	43.8	38.8	59.5	40.7	71.5
% to Municipalities	91.8	46.4	74.4	59.0	48.7	54.9	38.5	56.7	25.7

Source: Author's compilation from Brasil. Senado Federal, 1997–99; Brasil; Congresso Nacional (2000b, 2000c, 2001a).

amendments accounted for only about a third of all submissions, and less than half of the value of all approved amendments (moreover, this number obscures *where* individual deputies target their amendments). On the other hand, the amounts that state delegations have submitted and approved has increased dramatically. I explain this transformation in the following text.

Where MCs Target Pork. Where do MCs target their pork, whether as individuals, members of a state delegation or congressional committee? Ames and others have focused on the deputies' propensity to target municipalities, highlighting their "localistic" and individualistic behavior. Do members of Congress only target municipalities? Amendments can target municipal, state, regional, national, or "exterior" governments or agencies. Table 7.6 demonstrates that over the last ten years the portion of submitted amendments targeted at municipalities has declined, while the portion targeted to states (and regions) has increased. That is, regardless of *how* MCs target pork – whether individually or in groups – MCs have attempted to direct ever-larger amounts of pork to state governments over the 1990s.

The trend to favor state programs becomes even more pronounced when we consider not only what MCs submit to the CMO, but what the CMO actually approves. Table 7.7 shows that currently, most of the value of approved amendments funds state-level projects (no amendments were approved for the 1994 budget).

TABLE 7.7 *Percent Value of Approved Amendments – by Level of Government*

Target	1992	1993	1994	1995	1996	1997	1998	1999	2000
% to Regions	13.3	8.2	X	1.6	7.9	3.8	1.0	0.6	2.7
% to States	46.9	42.4	X	45.0	47.5	46.9	68.4	75.3	72.7
% to Municipalities	39.8	49.5	X	53.4	44.6	49.3	30.5	24.0	24.6

X = no approved amendments.
Source: Author's compilation from Brasil. Senado Federal, 1997–99; Brasil, Congresso Nacional (2000b, 2000c, 2001a).

TABLE 7.8 *Percent Value of Executed Amendments – by Level of Government*

Target	1993	1994	1995	1996	1997	1998	1999	2000
% to Regions	2.3	X	0.0	7.4	1.5	0.6	0.3	2.5
% to States	71.1	X	92.3	58.1	68.6	75.2	82.7	81.9
% to Municipalities	26.7	X	7.7	34.4	29.8	24.2	17.0	15.6

X = no executed amendments.

Source: Author's compilation from Brasil. Senado Federal, 1997–99; Brasil, Congresso Nacional (2000b, 2000c, 2001a).

Finally, at the most important and final stage of the budget process, the "execution" stage, when the executive branch releases funds, states are also highly favored over municipalities. Information on funded amendments for 1993–2000 is provided in Table 7.8 (no amendments were funded in 1994 and only thirty-nine were funded in 1995).

Although MCs do target municipalities, most of the money that the executive branch releases ends up funding state-level projects. MCs and executive-branch officials affirmed that this has historically been the case.[129] Thus, although deputies may spend considerable time and effort targeting municipalities – as Ames argues, for example – the big money, and thus the big political payoff, comes with funding state-level pork-barrel projects. In sum, the current budget-amendment process limits deputies' ability to see their own amendments, often targeted at their municipal vote bases, approved and funded, thus limiting their credit-claiming ability. On the other hand, amendments directed at states tend to have a better chance of approval and execution.[130]

The Forces Favoring State Interests in the Amendment Process

Why have MCs limited their individual involvement in the amendment process? Why have state delegation amendments gained in relative importance? By the early 1990s, a series of factors created a context for a reform of the budget-amendment process. First, continued high individual demand for pork caused administrative chaos. When the number of amendments submitted in 1991 and 1992 swamped the CMO and impeded its ability to finish its work on time, the final budgets for those years were delivered late (Sanches 1993). The executive used this delay to its advantage, manipulating funds at will while Congress dallied.

---

[129] Interviews with Waldeck Ornellas, Antônio C. Pojo do Rêgo, Manuel Albuquerque, Luiz Tacca, and Aglas Barrera.

[130] As noted, this analysis does not include a discussion of pork-barrel projects that do not enter the budget as amendments, such as President Cardoso's *Brasil em Ação* ("Brazil in Action") programs.

Second, submission of over 70,000 amendments a year pulverized the resources available for pork-barrel projects. Many projects require multiyear funding. However, with no multiyear guarantees, MCs' submissions resulted in literally thousands of small, unfinished projects dotting the Brazilian landscape (*FSP* 6/2/96, pp. 1, 8). Because many individual amendments went uncompleted, they provided deputies with little political return.

Third, a lack of legislative leadership control over the budget committee, combined with most MCs' complete lack of knowledge of budgetary techniques allowed a small clique of MCs to grab control over the pork supply. In the absence of peer oversight, these "Cardinals" of the budget committee began to hog larger pieces of pork and took bribes to direct pork a certain way. However, following Congress' impeachment of President Fernando Collor in the Fall of 1992, deputies and senators turned their investigative spotlights upon themselves and exposed a scandal in the budget committee that resulted in the expulsion of seven deputies in Spring of 1993, with five more resigning before expulsion votes could be taken (INESC 1993a, 1993b).

Fearing another scandal, Congress passed the 1994 budget without amendments and in 1995 implemented parts of an investigative committee's recommendations (the recommendations included eliminating individual amendments altogether, but MCs did not accept this). MCs institutionalized and prioritized collective amendments, reduced the weight of individual amendments, and reduced the power of the CMO's president and subcommittee presidents.[131] They also reduced the maximum number of amendments each MC could submit to twenty (a 1993 resolution had set the limit at fifty) and forced themselves to prioritize ten of these, and they required that three-quarters of a state delegation sign each state-delegation amendment (*FSP* 12/6/96 p. A-9; *OESP* 12/15/96, p. A-4; Sanches 1996; Greggianin 1997).

Given the administrative chaos and corruption, one might suppose that eventually some kind of crisis would push MCs to reform the budget-amendment process. However, nothing mentioned previously predicts any particular modification. Why not simply continue with an individualized process, although with fewer amendments and greater self-policing? Or, why not let the president's party coalition decide pork-barreling priorities, for example? Why did state interests win out? One can understand individual MCs' desire to target municipalities, because the municipality is the unit of government closest to the voters and most deputies maintain ties to local vote brokers or have their own local organizations. Yet individualized pork-barreling, targeted mainly at municipalities, provides no clear political return for deputies interested in reelection (Chapter 6). MCs ultimately chose

---

[131] Interviews with Waldeck Ornelas, Lidia Quinan, João Henrique, Onofre Quinan, Milton Mendes, Jacques Wagner, and Antônio Carlos Pojo do Rêgo.

to limit their individual ability to submit amendments (typically targeted at municipalities), and the CMO now also approves far fewer amendments that target municipalities (see Table 7.7).

To understand why MCs ended up privileging state delegations and reducing individual involvement, I return to my argument about the relationship between political careerism (chapters 1–4) and the pressures legislators face from state-level political actors (Chapter 5). One reason many deputies support state-government interests is that many come from and will continue their careers at the state level. Deputies' progressive ambition does not favor a congressional-centric process, nor does it favor a purely municipal-oriented pork-barreling process. A substantial number of deputies have developed and desire to maintain clienteles within the state bureaucracy, and thus tend to favor state interests in the national budget.

A more important factor that affects a greater proportion of deputies is what is called *governismo* in Brazil, a tendency for politicians to support whomever is in government once an election has been decided. At the state level, *governismo* has historically been particularly strong (Abrucio 1998). After a gubernatorial election, politicians seek to distance themselves from the losing candidates and strengthen their ties to the winner, because he or she will control the state-government budget and access to jobs in the state bureaucracy, with very few checks and balances. This provides governors with considerable power over both mayors and federal deputies. Mayors need the support of the governors because they lack their own resources to fund primary and secondary education; health care; and infrastructural investment. Deputies depend on close ties to state-government officials for their own political survival because they need "their" mayors to be on good terms with the governor, because much federal pork is channeled through the governor's hands, and because they also often seek state-government pork or state-level jobs for their cronies.

As noted in Table 7.7, over two-thirds of all federal-government pork is typically sent to state governments. Once in a state government's hands, the federal government loses influence over the ultimate destination of the funds; the governor can distribute the funds according to his or her own (political) criteria.[132] Governors can also access their own coffers to distribute pork-barrel goods, and can decide which municipalities and which politicians to benefit with the political credit. On the other hand, nearly all mayors lack such capacity, and depend instead on state and federal funds. Deputies in all of Brazil's regions recognize that these resources provide the governor with powerful tools that can be used as political "carrots" or "sticks." One deputy from the poor northeastern state of Piauí lamented that "In my first

---

[132] Interviews with Aglas Watson Barrera, João Henrique, Virgílio Guimarães, Waldeck Ornellas, Gonzaga Mota, Onofre Quinan, Antônio Carlos Pojo do Rêgo, Sandro Scodro, and Mara José de Macedo.

term, the governor was my political opponent. So, I was practically impeded from realizing my goals."[133] A deputy from Pernambuco, another poor northeastern state, stated that "The governor controls important political resources. For example, the current governor has really emphasized rural electrification. The impact that this has is incredible for people who live on a farm in the interior, where when it gets dark, it gets dark. For someone who didn't previously have access to these things, it has incredible significance."[134] Deputies from relatively wealthier states also recognize the governor's influence. One deputy from the southern state of Rio Grande do Sul claimed that "In order for a deputy to have visibility in his state, either he's allied with the governor, or he's in the [leftist] opposition and is extremely clever. Because if he has nothing to offer, the mayors say 'this town is off-limits to you, don't come here'."[135]

We might suppose that deputies with municipal-level electoral bases would feel relatively free of state-government pressures. However, one deputy from the state of São Paulo, which has several relatively wealthy and thus relatively politically autonomous municipalities, affirmed that his state's governor still controls resources that ambitious politicians desire:

A deputy often needs the governor for his own reelection. In areas such as health care, public security, roadbuilding, education, the power of the governor is considerable. He can make or break somebody's election. He'll put a road in the deputy's region that the deputy wants, or let the deputy nominate the head of education in the area, or the health post. Or not – he could turn against someone. He's got a lot of strength.[136]

As a practical matter, economies of scale and the municipalities' lack of technical know-how limit the amounts that could be earmarked for municipal pork.[137] As one senator put it, "Municipalities are not viable agents for infrastructural investment. States are the agents that can operate in these areas, they have better technical capacity."[138] As in the United States, the state and federal governments in Brazil take responsibility for infrastructural investment in such politically credit-worthy activities as road building; dam construction; bridge building; and construction and upkeep of schools and hospitals.[139] Thus, although MCs can only direct small-scale projects to their municipal bases, state governments undertake higher-impact projects.

---

[133] Interview with João Henrique.   [134] Interview with Sílvio Pessoa.
[135] This interview with Yeda Crusius was conducted before the PT won the statehouse in Rio Grande do Sul.
[136] Interview with Alberto Goldman.
[137] Interviews with Aglas W. Barreira, Luiz Tacca, Manoel de Albuquerque, and Waldeck Ornelas.
[138] Interview with Waldeck Ornellas.
[139] Even when the federal government sponsors an infrastructure project and does not technically "send" the funds to a state government, the state government often plays an important political role through counterpart funds. For example, this is the case with many of the projects in President Cardoso's "Brazil in Action" program, which the President has employed to demonstrate his government's commitment to infrastructural investment. In

Knowledge of this reality shapes MCs' behavior. They know that to bring home the really valuable political bacon, they must have good relationships with those in power at the state level.[140]

Deputies recognize that state politics affects their careers. No deputy wants to be on the governor's "bad side," as the governor could shut off access to political career-sustaining jobs and pork-barrel funds, or direct such resources to a deputy's rival. While governors or their emissaries are often seen patroling the halls of Congress and the Executive-branch ministries lobbying for pet projects, their efforts need not always be so overt. Because many deputies' careers are intimately linked to state-level politics and because all deputies face pressures to support the incumbent governor, regardless of their or the governor's partisan affiliation, they have strong incentives to support state-level interests in the budget. In the next subsection I describe a major innovation: the state delegation amendment, whereby all deputies and senators from each state come together to propose pork-barrel amendments on behalf of their state.

Submission and Approval of State Delegation Amendments

In the 1990s the state delegation amendment has gained a larger share of the available budgetary pork. At all stages of the budget process, the state-delegation amendment impedes individual credit claiming. Instead, the governor plays a key role and MCs must share credit. Each state delegation may submit twenty amendments. In a series of meetings the states' deputies negotiate and prioritize ten amendments, which the CMO subsequently approves. While in theory delegation members could divide up these amendments and submit them individually,[141] the entire delegation (deputies and senators) meets to determine which amendments to submit, and a state-based "Government and Opposition" logic determines which amendments are prioritized (and not a national "government and opposition" logic). For example, in Bahia, one Workers' Party deputy (in opposition to the governor) explained that "The group that supports the current governor is in the majority, so they proposed seven amendments, and the opposition in the

---

one instance, Cardoso's Minister of Mines and Energy, Eliseu Padilha, traveled to São Paulo to publicize the President's efforts on behalf of the state. Instead of returning to Brasília confident that his boss had received the greater part of the political credit, Padilha had to sit through a speech by São Paulo governor Mario Covas, who noted that in all the projects Padilha cited, including a major rail bridge, the widening of an important highway, and a "beltway" project to ease traffic congestion in the city of São Paulo, the state government would spend *more* money than the federal government (*OESP* 9/5/97, p. 6). Fortunately for Padilha, Cardoso and Covas were close allies. In other states the governor's capacity to spend and thus claim credit for infrastructural development could create even more awkward situations for the President.

[140] Interviews Yeda Crusius, Waldeck Ornelas, Mussa Demes, and César Souza.

[141] Although this would not be feasible for states with more than ten deputies.

state proposed three amendments."[142] Since the amendments ultimately fund
state-level projects, even the opposition amendments may end up benefiting
the governor, who will be "executing" the project.

The state governor also typically plays a direct role in the delegation
amendment process. The governor might be seeking counterpart funds for a
pet project or simply additional pork-barrel funds to use for his own benefit.
Depending on his or her degree of domination of the state's politics (which
is usually quite great, see Abrucio [1998]), the governor can set the priorities
for his state. In Goiás, one progovernment deputy stated that

> The delegation amendments are super-party amendments. We all meet, and the gov-
> ernor presents his proposal. Those of us in the governor's party agree to prioritize
> whatever amendments the governor sends.[143]

The chief technical advisor to the Chamber on budgetary matters affirmed
that

> The state delegation amendments, because they must be approved by three-fourths of
> the deputies and senators of each state, end up highly influenced by the governors be-
> cause of their natural capacity to form a super-majority. As a rule, this translates into
> funds for projects in the interest of the state government or of the large metropolitan
> regions (Greggianin 1997, 15).

Given the governor's involvement and the need to negotiate as a group,
deputies and senators confirmed that state delegation amendments limit individual credit claiming and force all MCs to take responsibility for the state's
budget success.[144] One PT deputy stated that delegation amendments are

> A form of self-control, tying our own hands. We start with thirty suggested amend-
> ments. Then we say, for example, 'Hey, this one is really to benefit that construction
> firm.' So that one gets thrown out, it's not approved. The delegation amendment not
> only promotes the general idea that the state brings benefits to the population, but it
> also reduces the kind of things that only benefit this or that particular group.[145]

A PFL deputy added that

> More and more we are realizing that because of the dispersion of resources, these
> amendment projects often never get finished. So nothing gets built, and you have no
> dam, no road, or no electricity. So, we've united to make our demands as a bloc,
> even though the political benefits of the project might be inevitably divided among
> members of the delegation.[146]

MCs devote a good amount of energy to the submission and approval process of state-delegation amendments. However, this kind of pork-barreling

---

[142] Interview with Jacques Wagner.   [143] Interview with Lidia Quinan.
[144] Interviews with Onofre Quinan, Gonzaga Mota, Antônio Carlos Pojo do Rêgo, and
Waldeck Ornellas.
[145] Interview with Milton Mendes.   [146] Interview with João Henrique.

impedes individual credit claiming. When state delegation amendments obtain funding, MCs must share credit both with the "executor" of the amendment, the governor, as well as with other deputies and senators. As noted, when federal money goes to a state, the state government executes the project not the federal government. Governors, not deputies or senators, can then decide where to spend the money. One deputy described the situation: "The state delegation submits an amendment, for example, for 'sanitation improvements in the state of Goiás,' but the governor determines which municipalities will be included in this program."[147]

It should come as no surprise that state-level politics "matters" here. As one official in the Ministry of Planning put it, "You have some states where the governor exerts almost complete control over the delegation amendments. The governor's group is politically hegemonic, and he divides up the pie ... typically, there will be some kind of 'agreement' on where to distribute these funds."[148] That is, mayors and deputies allied with the governor obtain preferential treatment. Deputies rely on mayors to maintain their local support networks, but because the state governor controls resources that mayors need, he consequently influences federal deputies as well. One deputy explained the governor's influence this way:

How do you take credit? Normally, with public works projects. And who undertakes public works projects? The executive branch. The executive branch initiates projects to benefit its friends, that's how it obtains political support. So normally the executive branch at the state level controls the majority of the state's congressional delegation.[149]

In some cases, the governor's involvement in the submission and execution phases of state-delegation amendments leads to friction between the governor and "his" state delegation. For example, in 1996, deputies from the state of Minas Gerais threatened to retract the power they had delegated to the governor to decide the state's delegation amendments. One deputy complained that after giving the governor essentially a blank check, with the understanding that the funds would be distributed evenly across the state, the governor had instead used the amendments to further his electoral goals by distributing money only to municipalities run by his allies (*Estado de Minas* 10/22/96, p. A-3).

Despite the obvious tension in the relationship, since 1988 MCs have not overhauled the pork-barrel system to their individual benefit. Instead, they have increased governors' influence in the pork-barreling process. This appears puzzling: if the governor is so powerful, and has so many tools to use against deputies, why have deputies allowed such a situation to develop? Why have they given state delegation amendments more weight in

---

[147] Interview with Sandro Scodro.　　[148] Interview with Antônio Carlos Pojo do Rêgo.
[149] Interview with Virgílio Guimarães.

the pork-barrel process than their individual amendments? Despite the difficulty in claiming credit individually, they do so in their own interest: as one ex vice-governor and senator explained, "Governors influence deputies, because deputies need the governor to bring resources to their municipalities. The deputy needs both state funds and federal funds. And the governors now command more and more of these funds."[150] With their governor's help, deputies hope to build up a political clientele that will help them continue their careers, something they cannot do on their own (cf. Ames 1995a).

The changes in the pork-barreling process since 1988, specifically the institutionalization of the state-delegation amendment, have tended to favor state-government interests. Deputies have not reformed the budget process in a way that would enhance their individual prospects for reelection. However, they have strengthened "federal" interests in the budget process in their own career interests. Today, to benefit politically from budgetary pork, a deputy must be close to state-government officials, primarily the governor, and must cooperate with other MCs from his or her state, including deputies from other parties. This holds for *all* deputies, now that opposition parties such as the PT, PDT, and PSB have won several statehouses. Still, deputies might differ in the degree to which they support state and/or municipal governments with pork, depending on their personal career motivations. I explore this possibility in the next two sections.

PORK AND PROGRESSIVE AMBITION: RUNNING FOR STATEWIDE OFFICE

I have argued that Brazilian deputies do not use pork for "static" ambition, that is, to hold onto a seat in Congress. Instead, pork serves deputies' "progressive" ambition: deputies use pork to pave their future noncongressional career paths, at the state or municipal level. In this section, I demonstrate that deputies who seek *state-level* elected positions strategically employ pork differently than do deputies who do not seek such positions, and that political variables also influence pork strategy *within* the group of state-office–seeking deputies.

Hypotheses: The Links between Pork and State-Level Progressive Ambition

What would we expect to see if those deputies who choose to run for statewide office (governor, vice-governor, or senator) attempt to use the pork-barrel to improve their chances of electoral success? Two ways to distinguish this type of progressive ambition through analysis of pork-barreling strategy exist, both of which compare where deputies who run for statewide office target pork against where deputies who do not run for statewide office target

---

[150] Interview with Onofre Quinan.

pork. Deputies can submit amendments to benefit the state government, or to benefit municipal governments.[151] Given their previous job experience, for example as State Secretary of Public Works, a deputy might already exercise some influence within the state bureaucracy, and directing pork to the state government could thus serve as a strategy to maintain support. On the other hand, a deputy might target the state government in an attempt to *build* support within the state bureaucracy. Thus, first, I hypothesize that deputies who run for statewide office ought to 'pave their way' by submitting more pork to state-government agencies in the election year.

Second, we can explore the degree to which deputies spread their pork around. As Ames (1995b) has described, because the entire state serves as the electoral district in Brazil, deputies can "concentrate" their votes in just one municipality, or obtain a "dispersed" vote pattern, even getting votes in every municipality in their state. Ames argued that deputies use pork to seek out new voters in their rivals' bailiwicks in order to win reelection. However, that finding may be a function of progressive, not static ambition: let us suppose that Deputy X and Deputy Y each win election at time "t" by concentrating their votes equally in ten municipalities. At time 't + 1,' Deputy X runs for reelection, and Deputy Y runs for governor. What kind of pork-barreling strategy might we see for each politician? An "Amesian" hypothesis might hold that Deputy X would submit amendments to twelve municipalities – his or her original ten plus two others where votes might be found. Ames implies nothing about what Deputy Y would do.[152]

I hypothesize that Deputy Y's best strategy for a run for statewide office is to spread pork around to a much greater extent than a deputy who runs for reelection. A deputy who runs for statewide office must construct a much broader clientelistic base of support than a deputy running for reelection, because winning executive office requires winning a plurality race, while winning reelection requires winning only a PR race in large multimember districts. Mayors and other local bigwigs serve as vote brokers, so a deputy running for statewide office ought to attempt to broker more pork and develop relatively more ties to local officials than a deputy running for reelection.

Testing the Hypotheses

To test these two hypotheses, I used the budget amendments from the 1991–4 and 1995–8 legislatures. At the end of the 1994 term, forty-seven deputies ran for governor, vice-governor, or senator. At the end of the 1998 term,

---

[151] Here I ignore amendments targeted to regional as well as exterior and national entities.
[152] I recognize that deputies who run for statewide office would not be counted in the same group as deputies who run for reelection, and thus one would not include the former set of deputies in analysis of incumbency-minded deputies' pork strategies. However, the point remains: even deputies running for reelection may be planning a longer-term investment in developing statewide contacts, in the hope that a statewide career opportunity opens up.

TABLE 7.9 *Average Portion of Amendment Value Submitted to Benefit State Government Per Deputy – 1991–1998*

	1991	1992	1993	1994	1995	1996	1997	1998
Overall Average %	19.3	14.1	20.9	23.4	13.6	6.0	3.6	5.6
Standard Deviation	26.2	21.2	24.5	26.8	23.7	17.3	14.0	18.3
Average if Run State	20.9	16.9	22.1	30.0	10.8	4.9	1.5	5.3
Standard Deviation	24.4	24.3	26.5	25.1	20.3	12.2	4.6	19.5
N	37	37	44	37	30	30	31	33
Minimum %	.06	0	0	0	0	0	0	0
Maximum %	88.6	98.5	89.4	78.6	82.7	48.8	23.3	100.0
Average if Not Run State	19.1	13.8	20.7	22.7	13.9	6.1	3.7	5.3
Standard Deviation	26.4	21.0	24.2	26.9	23.9	17.6	14.5	17.8
N	430	425	392	351	444	439	450	480
Minimum %	0	0	0	0	89.5	95.2	100	100
Maximum %	100	95.32	97.44	100	0	0	0	0

Source: Author's compilation from Brasil. Senado Federal, 1997–99.

thirty-two ran for statewide office. I first hypothesized that deputies who run for statewide office ought to attempt to "pave their road" to statewide electoral success with pork by submitting relatively more pork to the state government, in particular during the election year. Table 7.9 provides, for deputies who submitted amendments, the average percentage of *all* deputies' pork submissions to benefit the state government, and also separates *deputies who ran* for statewide office from those who *did not run* for statewide office and provides the same averages.[153]

While there is good evidence that deputies in the 1991–4 legislature who ran for statewide office did target their state government, and that the difference was most pronounced during the election year, the evidence does not support this contention for the 1995–8 legislature. Why is this the case? Two factors explain the difference.

First, the changes in the budget amendment process since 1994 that increased the weight of state-delegation amendments parallel the decrease in *all* deputies' individual submissions to their states. Fewer deputies targeted their state government in the 1995–8 legislature than did previously because all MCs were working harder as members of state "teams" to deliver pork

[153] N.B.: The percentages in this table do not equal the Total % of Pork given to the state in Table 7.5 because this table does not include state delegation amendment submissions.

to their state. For example, in 1995, 194 of the 513 deputies targeted some portion of their amendments at the state level. This number dropped to 111 in 1996, 71 in 1997, and remained at 73 in 1998. Deputies now are less likely to individually submit amendments to their state because a collective system is now employed. This explains why individual deputies now target a much lower percentage of their pork to states.

The second factor is that fewer deputies ran for statewide office in 1998, and those who did had relatively fewer incentives to target the state. The number of deputies running for statewide office in 1998 declined for two reasons: because state governors could run for reelection (incumbents ran for reelection in twenty-one of twenty-seven states) and because the senate election was for only one seat in each state as opposed to two in 1994. Allowing reelection at the state level made it less likely that politicians would want to challenge the incumbent (Abrucio and Samuels 1997) (in the end, fifteen of the twenty-one incumbents who ran won).

The presence of incumbent governors on the ticket eliminated "favorite son (or daughter)" deputies who were candidates for statewide office. Prior to 1998, if a deputy running for statewide office was of the governor's party (or coalition), he or she might have been considered the "favorite child" candidate, and exhibited a different pork-barreling strategy. For example, all deputies who ran for statewide office in 1994 submitted on average 30 percent of their pork to benefit state government. However, "favorite children" candidates for statewide office sent 40 percent of their pork to the state, hoping to benefit from their tighter connections to the incumbent government.

Favorite children candidates attempted to play on the advantage of incumbency: not their own, but that of their political group. They sent more money to the state government because their allies controlled state government, in the belief that their allies' control over the state machine would help them win statewide office. On the other hand, candidates on the "outs" at the state level attempted to go "under" or "around" the state machine relatively more, by attempting to rely relatively more on municipal contacts to construct a statewide political coalition. The "favorite child" strategy became less feasible in 1998. That year, only two of the thirty-two candidates for governor were "favorite children." The rest ran as opposition to the incumbent governor. Given this, fewer deputies had strong incentives to target pork to their state government.

My second hypothesis about the relationship between state-level progressive ambition and deputies' pork-barreling strategies suggests that deputies who run for statewide office will spread their pork around in an attempt to construct alliances with local brokers such as mayors. If my argument is correct, then we ought to see deputies who run for statewide office strategically submitting pork to benefit relatively more municipalities in their state, regardless of the extent to which their own vote base is concentrated or dispersed. Table 7.10 provides, for deputies who submitted amendments to

TABLE 7.10 *Average Percentage of Municipalities to which Deputies Submitted Amendments as a Percentage of All Municipalities in the State – 1991–1998*

	1991	1992	1993	1994	1995	1996	1997	1998
Overall Average %	14.8	10.1	10.8	14.2	8.5	9.4	8.8	6.1
Standard Deviation	19.1	13.3	14.7	18.0	12.9	13.8	13.5	9.0
Average if Run State	18.9	12.8	10.3	19.7	9.6	11.1	10.4	6.6
Standard Deviation	24.6	8.4	11.7	19.9	13.3	12.5	11.6	4.7
N	37	37	44	37	28	27	32	28
Minimum %	0.5	0.8	0.5	0.2	0	0	0	0
Maximum %	98.6	33.9	66.7	93.3	63.6	54.5	54.5	16.5
Average if Not Run State	14.4	10.1	10.9	13.6	8.1	9.2	8.7	6.1
Standard Deviation	18.5	13.7	15.0	17.8	11.5	13.8	13.6	9.2
N	407	416	387	340	423	418	434	430
Minimum %	0.02	0.1	0.3	0.4	0.2	0	0	0
Maximum %	100	100	100	100	100	100	100	100

Source: Author's compilation from Brasil. Senado Federal, 1997–99.

municipalities,[154] the average percentage of the municipalities in a state to which deputies targeted pork for each year of the two legislatures analyzed.

In three of the four years in the 1991–4 legislature, deputies who ran for statewide office in 1994 targeted more municipalities. This difference is statistically significant at the .01 level in 1994, when deputies who ran for statewide office targeted almost 50 percent more municipalities on average than did deputies who did not run for statewide office. In the 1995–8 legislature, deputies who eventually ran for statewide office target only a slightly higher percentage of their states' municipalities. As with my previous measure, the transformations in the budget process since 1995 that tend to benefit the state government have conversely tended to limit the MCs' ability to target large numbers of municipalities. Prior to 1995, deputies could submit fifty amendments each, but starting that year they could only submit twenty each. This reduction necessarily restricts the number of municipalities to which MCs can submit amendments. Thus, on our second measure, we find some confirmation that deputies who run for statewide office strategically attempt to employ pork differently than deputies who do not run for

---

[154] This thus excludes all eight deputies from the Brasília, which has no municipalities. I also excluded one deputy from 1995–8 (Haroldo Sabóia) due to contradictory information.

statewide office,[155] particularly for the 1991–4 legislature, prior to the MCs' institutionalization of a budget process that favored states relatively more.

Summary

I hypothesize that in general, progressive ambition ought to shape deputies' pork-barreling strategies. In this section, I hypothesized that deputies who run for statewide office ought to exhibit different pork-barreling behavior from deputies who do not run for statewide office. Prior to 1995, I showed this to be clearly the case: deputies who ran for statewide office attempted to direct more pork to the state government as opposed to municipal governments, in an attempt to build up support within the state bureaucracy. They also tended to attempt to "spread" their pork around to a greater number of municipalities, in an attempt to build a wide coalition of local-level political bosses in preparation for the statewide plurality election. However, once MCs deliberately changed the amendment process to favor state-based interests, their strategic behavior as individuals no longer appeared to favor states as much. (Future research might reveal how certain deputies attempt to "claim credit" for state-delegation amendments together with their state's governor on the campaign trail.)

PORK AND PROGRESSIVE AMBITION: RUNNING FOR MAYOR

In this section, I demonstrate that deputies who seek *municipal* posts adopt a distinct pork-barreling strategy.

Hypotheses: The Link between Pork and Municipal-Level Ambition

What would we expect to observe if those deputies who run for mayor attempt to use the pork-barrel to improve their chances of winning? All deputies can submit amendments to benefit municipalities. However, deputies may choose which municipalities to target, and how much to submit to each municipality. Let us suppose that Deputy X and Deputy Y both obtained 4,000 votes in municipality 1, and 1,000 votes in municipality 2, at election "t." Deputy X decides to run for mayor in municipality 1, whereas Deputy Y seeks only to maintain her current vote base in municipality 1. If both deputies have ten amendments to submit, we might see Deputy X "concentrate" his pork and submit all his amendments to municipality 1, whereas Deputy Y might divide her amendments up proportionally according to where she obtained votes, that is, eight in municipality 1 and two in municipality 2. Deputy X seeks to use pork to maximize his vote totals in

---

[155] I do not control for the number of municipalities in each state in this test. I also have said nothing about whether such a strategy is successful; I will address this issue in future work.

municipality 1 because he needs to win a plurality race for mayor, whereas Deputy Y only seeks to maintain her level of support in each municipality. This example is deliberately simple: we might in fact see Deputy Y also submit ten amendments to municipality 1, because she felt her vote base was shaky there. However, I hypothesize that *ceteris paribus*, deputies who run for mayor ought to "concentrate" their amendments in the municipality where they run for mayor.

Due to Brazil's electoral cycle, we can posit a corollary hypothesis. Municipal elections are held at the mid-term of the legislative term: legislative elections were held in 1990 and 1994, municipal elections in 1992 and 1996. I hypothesize that deputies who run for mayor should exhibit the "concentration" strategy hypothesized previously *only during the municipal election year*. Deputies who win the mayoral race do not continue to submit amendments following the election because they must vacate their congressional seat. Deputies who *lose* the mayoral race, however, should continue to submit amendments, but after the mayoral election year they will do so either to run for reelection as deputy, to switch to statewide office, or seek some other political position. Thus, while during the municipal election year these deputies should "concentrate" their amendments on one municipality, after the municipal election I hypothesize that they would "de-concentrate" their amendment-submission strategy to reestablish clienteles they had ignored, or to strategically seek out electoral support elsewhere.

Testing the Hypotheses

To test these two hypotheses, we can use amendment-submission data from 1991–8. For each deputy who ran for mayor in each year, I tracked the amount of money sent to the municipality where the deputy ran for mayor as a percentage of the total amount that deputy submitted. If my hypotheses are correct, we ought to see a jump in the amount sent to this municipality during the election year, and a subsequent decline, as deputies "de-concentrate" their amendment submissions in an attempt at political survival by other means. Table 7.11 provides the findings.

Table 7.11 shows unequivocally that deputies who run for mayor exhibit a clear strategy: during the municipal election year, they direct pork where they are campaigning. For example, in 1992, for the 1993 budget (which would be in effect during the subsequent mayoral term), deputies running for mayor attempted to direct almost four times as much pork to the municipality where they wanted to serve as mayor as they had the previous year. Following the election, deputies who lost then clearly changed strategies and "de-concentrated" their amendment submissions.

A similar pattern holds for deputies in the 1995–8 legislature who ran and lost in the 1996 election. Although 1996 also exhibits an increase over 1995, the difference is not so stark (and is not statistically significant). The

TABLE 7.11 *Value of Amendments Submitted to "Their" City as a Percent of the Total by Deputies Running for Mayor – 1991–1998 (municipal election years 1992 and 1996)*

YEAR	1991	1992	1993	1994	1995	1996	1997	1998
% To City	10.1	38.0	17.6	16.3	32.6	38.5	17.6	17.0
Minimum	0	0	0	0	0	0	0	0
Maximum	100	100	77.0	60.7	100	100	100	73.3
Std. Dev.	27.5	35.2	21.6	15.0	27.3	30.9	20.7	20.4
N	75	78	51	45	101	96	73	73

Source: Author's compilation from Brasil. Senado Federal, 1997–99.

explanation for this is that deputies were already "concentrating" their submissions in 1995, because of changes in the amendment submission process in 1994 (see previous text), which limited deputies to twenty amendments each. Given this limitation, deputies had less leeway to spread their amendments around their state in the first year of the legislature. Thus, deputies who planned to run for mayor in 1996 had to begin their strategy earlier. If they lost, the data again clearly show that deputies "de-concentrated" their amendment submissions in 1997 and 1998 to adopt a different strategy.

Deputies who run for mayor ought to use the pork barrel to further their goals. They ought to concentrate their pork submissions more heavily in the city where they run for mayor, and we ought to observe this phenomenon during the second year of the legislature. Through an examination of deputies' amendment-submission strategies, I confirmed these two hypotheses. This provides additional confirmation that progressively ambitious members of the Brazilian Congress have designed the budgetary process to further their goals.[156]

CONCLUSION

In this chapter, I answered the question raised at the conclusion of Chapter 6: if deputies cannot effectively use budgetary pork to secure a congressional career, why do they spend so much time seeking access to the budget? I argued that we can explain much of the structure and process of pork-barreling in Brazil by focusing on the factors that drive deputies'

---

[156] Moreover, in contrast to the apparent lack of impact that pork has on a deputy ability's to win reelection, deputies who pursue the "concentration" strategy for a mayoral run tend to be more likely to win. The simple correlation between the degree that a deputy concentrates his or her submissions from the first year of the legislature to the second and whether he or she wins election as mayor was .53 for those deputies who ran in 1992 and .40 for those deputies who ran in 1996. This finding is obviously preliminary; in other work I investigate more fully the degree to which deputies can successfully employ the pork-barrel to pursue an extralegislative position at either the state or municipal level.

extralegislative ambition. Specifically, I hypothesized that progressive ambition has two particular consequences. First, although deputies are often portrayed as favoring local or purely municipal interests, the nature of political careers in Brazil strongly encourages representation of states' interests in the Brazilian budget. As such, deputies have incentives to organize collectively along state lines to favor state governments as recipients of pork-barrel projects, and they have altered the pork-barreling process over the 1990s to reflect these incentives. This does not mean, however, that deputies have stopped targeting their municipal vote bases. They continue to do so, but without much hope that such a strategy will help them win re-election. On the other, hand, the pork-barreling process does permit deputies to pursue their extralegislative goals. I also hypothesized that deputies who seek state- and/or municipal-level office ought to exhibit different pork-barreling strategies from deputies who choose not to make such a move. Through an examination of the structure and process of pork-barreling in Brazil, I confirmed these hypotheses. This finding has broad implications for how we understand the link between pork-barrel politics and the "electoral connection" not only in Brazil but also in comparative perspective. Without careful attention to legislators' career goals, we may arrive at erroneous explanations for their activities and policy choices.

Chapter 8

Institutions of Their Own Design? Democratization and Fiscal Decentralization in Brazil, 1975–1995

INTRODUCTION

A dramatic transformation of political institutions and processes gained momentum in Latin America in the 1980s and 1990s: decentralization of policy authority and fiscal resources to subnational governments (World Bank 1997; Willis, Haggard and Garman 1999; Montero and Samuels [eds.] n.d.). In historical perspective, decentralization marks a major shift away from a central-government dominance at all stages of the policy process – initiation, funding, and implementation. Both empirically and theoretically, decentralization raises a number of questions. What explains the move away from centralization? Is the shift more apparent than real? What are the consequences of decentralization in terms of policy performance, political accountability, and democratic governance? By shifting power and resources to regional or local levels does decentralization "boomerang" back into national politics and subsequently affect the party system and executive-legislative relations? These and other questions have gained prominence in recent studies of Latin American politics.

Continuing my focus on the policy consequences of political ambition in Brazil, in this chapter I ask "What explains the process of fiscal decentralization in Brazil since 1975?" I argue that ideology and party-system variables are largely useless to explain decentralization in Brazil, and also that although several potentially important factors such as democratization, federalism, or interest-group pressure may be necessary conditions, they are not sufficient. Strategic, ambitious politicians decided how to decentralize, and therefore any explanation of this policy choice must thus incorporate these politicians' incentives. I suggest that given the context of democratization and federalism, career-minded members of the Brazilian Congress chose to decentralize fiscal resources to states and municipalities to further two interrelated goals: to provide resources to their supporters, and to further their own ambitions.

The focus on fiscal decentralization in Brazil is merited for three reasons. First, empirically it was extensive. From 1980 to 1995 the state governments' share of total government expenditures increased 17 percent, and municipalities' share increased 93 percent (Varsano 1997, 38).[157] During that period, some taxing authority was shifted to states and municipalities, but the most dramatic change was the 113 percent increase in central-government transfers to subnational governments, nearly all of which were made automatic and not subject to national-government political manipulation (Nogueira 1995, Table 23). Decentralization also had an important effect on national macroeconomic health: because it so restricted the central-government's budgetary leeway, fiscal decentralization limited the central government's ability to use macroeconomic policy as a stabilization tool (L. Graham 1990; Bonfim and Shah 1991; Abranches 1993; Velloso 1993; Affonso 1994; Werneck 1995; Abrucio and Costa 1998). One need not look far to observe the painful consequences of fiscal decentralization for the central government, as President Cardoso has spent the large part of his two terms administering what seems to be a permanent central-government revenue shortfall (see Chapter 9).

Second, exploring fiscal decentralization allows me to demonstrate the usefulness of the rational choice approach I have adopted in an important area of policy reform. Geddes (1995, 198) has argued that the "explicit inclusion of intra-governmental interests motivated by the desire to remain in office in theories about how the political world operates can yield a coherent explanation of the weak relationship between societal interests and government policies." My argument provides such an explanation for this important policy change, which had little apparent input from civil-society or business interests.

Finally, fiscal decentralization merits scrutiny because it reflects and reinforces the renewed importance of federalism after Brazil's transition to democracy. Fiscal decentralization increased the power of governors and mayors at the expense of the president and the central government (Souza 1996; Abrucio and Samuels 1997; Abrucio 1998), and the process thus serves as an excellent case study of how legislators' and other actors' incentives operate during a democratic transition to shape political institutions in their own interests.

In the next section I describe fiscal centralization under Brazil's military regime from 1965 to 1975, and the subsequent decentralization of resources up through 1995. I then argue that we must include politicians' career incentives to understand the process of fiscal decentralization. Subsequently, I hypothesize about the preferences and strategies of the actors interested

---

[157] These figures are in terms of percentage of GDP that each level of government can spend, and includes subtractions for intergovernmental transfers, but do *not* include consideration of governments' indebtedness.

TABLE 8.1 *Share of Revenue and Expenditure by Level of Government in Selected Latin American Countries*

	Share of Total Government *Revenue* Collected by Level of Government			Share of Total Government *Expenditure* by Level of Government		
	Central	Intermediate	Local	Central	Intermediate	Local
Chile, 1992	100.0	0.0	0.0	87.3	0.0	12.7
Venezuela, 1989	96.9	0.1	3.1	77.7	15.7	6.5
Mexico, 1992	82.7	13.4	3.9	87.8	9.5	2.8
Colombia, 1991	81.6	11.1	7.3	67.0	15.7	17.3
Argentina, 1992	80.0	15.4	4.6	51.9	39.5	8.6
Brazil, 1995	67.2	28.0	4.8	56.3	27.5	16.2

in fiscal policy, and then I explain the outcome by exploring each relevant actor's actions during the study's time frame.

FISCAL CENTRALIZATION AND DECENTRALIZATION IN BRAZIL

Empirically, fiscal decentralization dramatically transformed the distribution of government revenue and expenditure across Brazil's three levels of government. In this section I describe the process of fiscal centralization and decentralization in Brazil from 1965 to 1995. Tables 8.1 and 8.2 demonstrate that cross-nationally, both revenue and expenditures in Brazil are highly decentralized to state and municipal governments.

Subnational governments have historically controlled a substantial portion of expenditures in Brazil (Mahar 1971; Mahar and Rezende 1975).[158] Still, revenue distribution has not remained constant, but has fluctuated with changes in Brazil's political regimes (Varsano 1996). Decentralization characterized the oligarchic and highly federalized First Republic (1889–1930) and the competitive Second Republic (1945–64), while centralization characterized Getúlio Vargas' dictatorial reign (1930–45) and the 1964–85 military regime.

I concentrate on the shift from the relatively centralized system that the military junta implemented in the late 1960s to the relatively decentralized system in place up through the mid-1990s. Table 8.3 shows the shifts since 1960 in the balance of fiscal federalism in Brazil.

---

[158] Brazil's system of intergovernmental revenue transfer and distribution has its roots in the 1934 Constitution, which centralized most tax receipts and divided up resources to states and municipalities. The 1946 Constitution largely maintained this system, but decentralized spending authority somewhat, mostly to states (Mahar 1971). See Samuels (2000a) on the political evolution of Brazil's municipalities.

TABLE 8.2 *Share of Expenditure by Level of Government in Selected Federal Countries*[a]

	Level of Government		
	Central	Intermediate	Local
Austria, 1987	70.4	13.7	16.9
United States, 1987	60.3	17.3	22.4
Germany, 1983	58.7	21.5	17.9
Brazil, 1995	56.3	27.5	16.2
Australia, 1987	52.9	40.4	6.8
Switzerland, 1987	47.5	28.3	24.2
Canada, 1987	41.3	40.3	18.4

[a] Following all intergovernmental transfers.
Sources: Levin (1991); Willis, Haggard, and Garman (1998).

The central government's share of both revenue and expenditures be-gan to increase soon after the 1964 military coup.[159] In 1966 the military created two funds, one for states (the *Fundo de Participação dos Estados*, FPE) and one for municipalities (the *Fundo de Participação dos Municípios*, FPM), through which the central government would automatically transfer a portion of the federal income tax (*Imposto de Renda*, IR) and manu-factured products tax (*Imposto sobre Produtos Industrializados*, IPI). Yet in 1968 the government simply halved (from 10 percent to 5 percent) the share of the IR and IPI it had initially designated to the FPE and FPM, and also transferred some state taxes to central-government control (Oliveira 1995a).

Table 8.3 shows that these centralizing changes affected subnational gov-ernments' finances. From 1965 to 1975, for example, state governments' share of total expenditures declined by 33.6 percent, and municipalities' share declined by 14 percent. Because the military not only reduced trans-fers but also placed tight restrictions on how state and municipal govern-ments could spend transferred funds (Oliveira 1995a, 22), this period saw a substantial reduction in subnational governments' political autonomy. The story of fiscal decentralization in Brazil involves explaining how and to what extent states and municipalities regained tax authority, a larger share of rev-enue transfers, and thus greater political autonomy. This would not occur until the 1980s. In the next section I begin to explain this shift.

---

[159] The military government's goal was not "only" to centralize control over fiscal policy. The regime wanted first to increase the government's ability to raise revenue in absolute terms, and wanted to streamline the country's tax collection system, which had not been reformed in a major way since the 1930s (see Oliveira 1995a, Chapter 1).

TABLE 8.3 *Division of the Fiscal Pie in Brazil – 1960–2000*

	Share of Total Revenue			Share of Total Expenditures		
Year	Central	State	Municipal	Central	State	Municipal
1960	63.9	31.3	4.7	59.5	34.1	6.4
1965	63.8	30.9	5.9	54.8	35.1	10.1
1970	66.7	30.6	2.7	60.8	29.2	10.0
1975	73.7	23.5	2.8	68.0	23.3	8.7
1980	74.7	21.7	3.7	68.2	23.3	8.6
1985	72.8	24.9	2.4	62.7	26.2	11.1
1990	67.3	29.6	3.1	57.1	28.0	14.9
1995	67.2	28.0	4.8	56.3	27.5	16.2
2000	69.2	26.2	4.6	59.9	25.1	15.0

Source: For 1960–85: Rezende (1995). For 1990–2000: Brasil, Ministério da Fazenda, Secretaria da Receita Federal (2001b).

Institutions of Their Own Design? Careerism and the *Choice* to Decentralize

Regime change and fiscal decentralization are somehow related in recent Brazil. However, "democratization" is too broad conceptually to explain the specifics of decentralization in any country or across cases (cf. Souza 1996). Democratization cannot be a sufficient cause of decentralization. In addition, although democratization and decentralization appear to go hand in hand in nearly all Latin American countries (Willis et al. 1998), in a broader and longer historical perspective, it is not even clear that democratization is a *necessary* cause of decentralization (Eaton n.d.). Historically, democratization has also been associated with political centralization, as in the emergence of the national state in France and England.

To understand the link between democratization and decentralization in Brazil, we must place democratization in the context of the military government's initial fiscal centralization as well as in the context of the emergence of municipalities as important institutions in Brazilian politics. Democratization cannot be a sufficient explanation for decentralization because Brazil had a prior experience with mass democracy (from 1945–64). However, fiscal decentralization took a very different form during that period. The military's policies and the increasing importance of municipalities created the different "democratic" context within which Brazilian politicians would act in the 1980s. Thus, we must specify how and why politicians had different incentives in the 1980s, under the same general regime type, to understand why decentralization took the particular form that it did.

Given the return of democracy, we could also consider interest groups' influences in the process of decentralization. Although interest groups played important roles in shaping Brazil's democratic transition, they played a minor role in the process of fiscal decentralization. This raises an important question: if we cannot map interest group demands directly onto policy output, then what factors or actors play the important roles? While the contextual factors I mentioned previously are important, they do not provide a sufficient explanation. Politicians' career motives provide the final ingredient. Given the broader context of democratization and federalism, fiscal decentralization occurred in Brazil because career-minded deputies shaped the institutions of fiscal revenue sharing for two intimately related reasons: to provide resources to those who support their career goals, and to further their own ambitions.

Career incentives are necessary to understanding the process of fiscal decentralization during Brazil's transition. Without including politicians' incentives, the outcome may be underdetermined. Consider the following counterfactual: in countries A and B, the president can impound budgetary funds, but in both countries a majority of legislators have decided to organize to reduce the president's relative power in budgetary affairs. These legislators could adopt any number of strategies to achieve this goal. For simplicity's sake, let us limit their choices to [decentralize, balance] – where *decentralize* means automatically transferring resources to subnational governments, and *balance* means increasing the legislature's power in budgetary affairs relative to the executive branch, as was the case in the Congressional Budget and Impoundment Control Act of 1974 in the United States (Kiewiet and McCubbins 1991).

Whether legislators would choose decentralize or balance depends importantly on their career incentives. All else equal, if legislators desire a long career in the legislature, they ought to have a greater propensity to choose 'balance.' If on the other hand they do not desire long-term careers in the legislature but instead desire offices in subnational government, then they ought to favor 'decentralize,' aiming to both appease their future supporters as well as increase the attractiveness of the offices they themselves hope to hold in the future, but not endowing the legislature with greater fiscal authority either in the present or in the future.

This point implies that pressure from subnational governments to decentralize is also insufficient to explain the particular form fiscal decentralization took in Brazil. If state and municipal actors lobbied deputies for additional funds, but deputies had long careers in the Chamber, then deputies might be more disposed to choose balance as opposed to decentralize, in order to build legislative control over the budget, as opposed to granting subnational governments control over budgetary resources. Note also that similar party, constituency, or interest-group pressures might confront legislators in both countries, but the outcome could still differ based on the different career structures in each country. Thus, in the absence of the specific incentives that political careerism generates for Brazilian legislators, fiscal decentralization might have taken a different form.

In sum, given the important background elements, military centralization, the emerging democratic transition, and the increasing importance of Brazil's municipalities (Samuels 2000a), we can explain the adopted policy of fiscal decentralization and put Brazil in comparative perspective. To explain how career-minded politicians got their preferred outcome, I must relate their preferences to other actors' preferences. In the next section, I hypothesize what actors' preferences are and then narrate the story of fiscal decentralization in Brazil.

FISCAL DECENTRALIZATION IN BRAZIL: THE PLAYERS AND THEIR PREFERENCES

Fiscal decentralization involves a series of policy choices. Dramatically simplifying, the first is *whether* to decentralize or not, the second is *to what extent* to decentralize, and the third is *how* to decentralize. Let us assume that a system of intergovernmental transfers exists. If politicians choose to decentralize, they could choose to increase *automatic* transfers from the central government to subnational governments, or increase *discretionary* transfers from the central government. Both choices could result in similar degrees of decentralization, but both imply distinct political logics: automatic transfers imply subnational autonomy, while discretionary transfers imply central-government authority. On the other hand, politicians could leave the system of intergovernmental transfers alone and decentralize through the transfer of taxing authority to subnational governments.

In this section I evaluate whether a set of political actors might favor or oppose fiscal decentralization generally, and whether each actor might support automatic transfers, politically conditioned transfers, or transfer of taxing authority to subnational governments. I also ask whether these actors would favor policy decentralization concomitantly with fiscal decentralization. Understanding actors' preferences provides the framework for explaining the process of decentralization.

The Military High Command

In the years after it took power in 1964, the Brazilian military centralized fiscal decision-making authority and reduced subnational governments' influence over spending decisions (Oliveira 1995a; Varsano 1996). When pressures for fiscal decentralization first emerged in the mid-1970s, the military could still resist governors' and mayors' entreaties. However, as part of the process of controlled democratization that began under President Ernesto Geisel (1974–9), the military began to strategically attempt to bolster its conservative allies in Congress. To accomplish this goal, it gradually and slowly began to decentralize fiscal resources (Oliveira 1995a, 56–62; Leme 1992). In exchange for providing increased resources to subnational governments, the military demanded that conservative local power brokers provide support for the regime (Ames 1987; Affonso 1994). Given this, as the transition began military leaders ought to have favored limited decentralization, particularly to the more conservative and poorer regions of Brazil. They would also oppose automatic resource transfers, instead favoring conditional transfers that the government could manipulate politically.

The President

While up through 1989 Brazil's presidents faced no electoral incentives (as they were either appointed military officers or an indirectly elected civilian), the President's job is to ensure the economic health and political stability of the central government, and his or her historical legacy or future career depends on maintaining that health. As such, while presidents might advocate decentralization to promote economic efficiency, they ought to oppose decentralization of resources without concomitant policy decentralization. Decentralizing resources without policy responsibilities reduces the government's pool of resources and tends to increase budget deficits in the absence of tax increases. In addition, because presidents typically exchange resources for legislative support, presidents ought to oppose *automatic* decentralization that would reduce their ability to manipulate the budget. Thus, I hypothesize that the President ought to prefer no decentralization first, fiscal decentralization with concomitant policy decentralization second, and fiscal decentralization with no policy decentralization last, and ought to prefer increases in *conditional* revenue transfers over increases in *automatic* revenue transfers.

High-Level Central-Government Bureaucrats

Central-government bureaucrats ought to oppose fiscal decentralization, because it would reduce their power and their ministries' power. As one economist who worked on fiscal decentralization during the Constitutional Convention affirmed,

Resistance to decentralization comes from within the government. Explicit resistance. In the Ministries, the groups of bureaucrats that oppose it see the state and municipal governments as inferior entities that ought to await decisions taken at the central level.[160]

If faced with the inevitability of fiscal decentralization, central-government bureaucrats would prefer conditional transfers over automatic transfers, to maintain greater political control over subnational governments.

---

[160] Interview with Thereza Lobo.

National Party Leaders

National party leaders in a given country might oppose or favor decentralization, either as a function of their electoral platform or of holding positions in national and/or subnational government (Willis et al. 1998; O'Neill n.d.). Yet in Brazil national party leaders did not take up the issue of the distribution of fiscal resources as an electoral appeal. Politicians generally advocated decentralization as part of the democratization process, but national party leaders did not direct or lead the process of negotiating the actual policy choices. Fiscal decentralization was not a high-profile public issue relative to other hot-button items. As Oliveira (1995b, 86) notes, "the debates in the Constitutional Congress about public finance were not marked by confrontation between progressives and conservatives, between left and right." National partisan commitments played little role in the outcome; instead, the importance of federalism and subnational career incentives proved more important.

Members of Congress

As I have demonstrated, Brazilian deputies typically spend one or two terms in Brasilia and then often attempt to return to state and/or local politics. As such, their behavior is directed toward furthering their own extralegislative career goals, even while they are serving as federal deputy. Did such incentives motivate fiscal decentralization? I have argued that careerist motivations drive Brazilian deputies to strategically attempt to shape their own political futures, and I have every reason to suppose that during a crucial period of institutional transformation such as the transition to democracy in the 1980s, these incentives would be particularly strong. In fact, they were: a survey in the Brazilian newsweekly *Veja* found that "95% of deputies desire to bring home a larger piece of the tax pie" (*Veja* 2/4/87, p. 26).

Political careerism, which gained renewed momentum in the late 1970s as the military withdrew from politics and politicians could once again freely seek positions at both the state and municipal levels, helps us understand the incentives that shaped the fiscal decentralization process. When interviewed, politicians supported this hypothesis. One deputy who served on the committee that rewrote the revenue-sharing system in the Constitutional Congress declared without hesitation that careerism of the sort I have described dominated politicians' motivations regarding fiscal decentralization:

This is an undeniable aspect of politics. Those with ideological positions were a tiny minority. When there are no other conditioning factors, [careerism] is something you just know, and don't need to prove.[161]

[161] Interview with Virgílio Guimarães.

Another deputy who had served as Minister in the military government declared that in his view,

> During the Constitutional Convention, principally in relation to the fiscal policy chapter, the two main authors of the proposal [Deputies José Serra and Francisco Dornelles] were candidates for governor. Without a doubt. They were already thinking about what they could do when they were governor, thinking, "As soon as I can make my bed, I can sleep in it..."[162]

Admittedly, these quotes provide only anecdotal evidence that careerism drove deputies' decisions to decentralize. Unfortunately, I cannot return in time to interview deputies at the constitutional convention about what factors were motivating their decisions. Nevertheless, the evidence from previous chapters clearly suggests that Brazilian politicians focus their energies while in the Chamber on their future careers, which are largely built at the subnational levels of government. These incentives were already present by the 1980s. The structure of political careers in Brazil thus provides a useful heuristic to understand why members of Congress implemented the policies they did.

Thus, we have some evidence that deputies would support decentralization and that few if any would defend the status quo. This is important, but insufficient to understand the particular choices that they made. I also suggested that most deputies would support automatic versus *discretionary* transfers, aiming to ensure subnational political autonomy from national-government political manipulation. However, deputies' preferences will diverge based on regional lines. Deputies from the relatively richer South and Southeast regions, in particular from the state of São Paulo, ought to favor a combination of automatic transfers and increases in state and municipal tax bases, because the states in these regions can generate their own wealth. In contrast, deputies from the relatively poorer North, Northeast, and Center-West regions ought to focus more on increasing automatic transfers from the central government relatively more than raising state and/or municipal tax bases, because governments in these regions can not generate much wealth.

Business Community and Civil Society

Potentially, private-sector representatives might express great interest in the efficiency consequences of substantially altering a country's tax and revenue system. However, Brazilian politicians seem to have fought the battle over the division of billions of dollars in revenue without significant input from the business community. (Business played a more active role in the 1990s, see Chapter 9.) Likewise, although the president of the Constitutional Congress,

---

[162] Interview with Antonio Delfim Netto.

Deputy Ulysses Guimarães (PMDB-SP) baptized the *magna carta* as the "Citizens' Constitution" because so many organized civil society groups provided input (e.g., labor unions, women's groups, and representatives of indigenous peoples), no civil-society organizations lobbied the committee specifically charged with restructuring Brazil's fiscal system.[163] As one deputy who served on this committee stated,

> This is a very arid area. Very few people understand it. So there weren't many groups pressuring the committee. No private-sector groups. It was very different from the other issues at stake in the constitutional convention.[164]

The absence of business and civil-society groups from the debate on fiscal decentralization means that politicians' own incentives became more important for the final outcome than they might otherwise have been.

Subnational Politicians

Although no civil-society or business-community organizations lobbied prominently for (or against) fiscal decentralization, subnational politicians and their supporters did heavily lobby Congress throughout the 1980s. As I have emphasized, incumbent deputies have strong incentives to pay close attention to these actors' demands.

Subnational politicians' preferences became clear long before democratization began in earnest. By the late 1970s, even though they had been nominated by the military, state governors began to protest fiscal centralization (Oliveira 1995a, 62). Moreover, as democratization slowly advanced, "Representatives of states and municipalities ... organized, held meetings, produced innumerable letters, and generated complaints [about fiscal centralization] that were sent to and heard throughout the Congress" (ibid., 65).

Following the 1982 elections, which brought to power democratically elected governors, mayors, and members of Congress, subnational politicians' pressures to decentralize increased. In interviews, several governors elected at that time affirmed that lobbying Congress for fiscal decentralization numbered among their top priorities.[165] The vice-governor of São Paulo at the time, Orestes Quércia, also emerged as a leader of the national "municipalist" movement, which organized mayors to pressure Congress for fiscal decentralization to municipalities.

Given their revenue losses due to the military's centralization policy and the limited decentralization in the late 1970s, it should come as little surprise that once democratic elections had resumed elected subnational officials would pressure Congress to speedily decentralize resources. These recently elected subnational officials needed additional resources to fulfill

---

[163] Interview with Thereza Lobo.   [164] Interview with José Maria Eymael.
[165] Interviews with Gonzaga Mota, Franco Montoro, Gerson Camata, and Orestes Quércia.

their campaign pledges. Governors, mayors, and politicians linked to state and municipal governments thus ought to favor decentralization, and favor automatic decentralization over presidentially dominated discretionary transfers.

Like their representatives in Congress, whether governors and mayors would favor fiscal transfers over increasing states' and municipalities' own taxation authority depends on whether the state or municipality can generate tax revenue. Thus, politicians from wealthier states favored transferring taxes to state control, while politicians from poorer states favored increases in transfers. Since most municipalities lack the ability to generate their own revenue, regardless of region I hypothesize that representatives of municipalities would favor increased automatic transfers.

Section Summary

National party leaders, civil-society groups, and the business community were largely absent from the fiscal decentralization process. I expect the president and the upper echelons of the bureaucracy to oppose fiscal decentralization without policy decentralization, while I expect representatives of subnational governments to lobby Congress for extensive automatic fiscal decentralization, without policy decentralization, and I expect members of Congress to respond positively to this pressure. In the next section, I describe the process of fiscal decentralization in Brazil. This supports my claim that members of Congress, pressured by subnational representatives, decentralized resources with their own careers in mind.

THE PROCESS OF FISCAL DECENTRALIZATION IN BRAZIL

By the late 1960s the military had centralized revenue and dramatically reduced subnational governments' fiscal autonomy. Starting in 1975, however, subnational governments began to win back some lost ground. Through the early 1970s, criticism of fiscal decentralization was muted by the overall health of the Brazilian economy. However, when the economy took a downturn and the military's civilian allies suffered a defeat at the polls in 1974, these same allies began to pressure the central government to decentralize. Oliveira (1995a, 61) cites subnational governments' pressure on the military as responsible for pushing the initial, limited steps toward decentralization.

The military responded slowly to these incipient pressures, submitting and then obtaining passage for a constitutional amendment in June 1975 that slightly increased the revenue destined to the FPE and FPM.[166] In 1977, the central government agreed to pay the entire manufactured exports subsidy,

---

[166] *Emenda Constitucional* #5 increased the percentage of the IR and IPI destined for the FPM and FPE 1 percent per year through 1979, so that by 1979 9 percent of both taxes went to the Participation Funds.

whereas previously state governments had paid half the subsidy (Oliveira 1995a, 62). In 1979 the military agreed to eliminate the restrictions it had imposed on how states and municipalities could spend their FPE and FPM allocations, except for requiring that municipalities spend 20 percent of their funds on education (Decree 83.556 of 7/7/79) (ibid., 54, 112). This change "restored [states' and municipalities'] autonomy to decide how to best spend their resources" (ibid.). At that time the military also increased the rate of the main state tax, the value-added tax, which ought to have increased state revenue (Resolution 129 of 11/28/79). Still, as Table 8.3 demonstrates, these measures did not immediately affect the relative distribution of resources.

Large-scale changes in the distribution of resources would only come after the return of democratic elections in 1982. Up through 1982 military President Figueiredo had managed to rebuff pressures for extensive fiscal decentralization (see e.g., JB 9/28/83, p. A-4), but the return of democratic elections implied a dramatic change in executive-legislative relations (even though a military president remained in office until 1985). Free and fair legislative elections reduced the military's sway over Congress while simultaneously reinvigorating the importance of subnational politics for national legislators, because mayoral and gubernatorial elections were held concurrently with the legislative elections. The new governors and mayors confronted a more active civil society that was demanding better public services, as well as declining tax revenue and rising unemployment. They thus immediately began pressing "their" deputies and senators for additional decentralization.

In stark contrast to the often lugubrious pace of political reform in Brazil, within months of taking office members of Congress passed two constitutional amendments that accelerated fiscal decentralization, over vocal opposition from the military president and central-government bureaucrats, who feared that decentralization would destroy Brazil's capacity to fulfill its obligations to the IMF (Oliveira 1995a, 148, 177). Both constitutional amendments increased the automatic revenue transfers through the FPE and the FPM. (From 1980 to 1986, the shares of the income and industrial products taxes devoted to the FPM increased from 9 percent to 17 percent, and for the FPE from 9 percent to 14 percent [Abrucio 1998, 108].)

Regardless of his preferences, President Figueiredo could no longer oppose legislators' efforts to decentralize because the military regime was clearly – if slowly – relinquishing power and he needed to negotiate congressional support for other proposals. Given the process of democratization, the military's veto power essentially vanished after 1982. The government's Minister of Planning at the time, Antônio Delfim Netto, who was responsible for responding to congressional pressure for fiscal decentralization after the 1982 elections, acknowledged that at that time,

There was enormous pressure for decentralization. We ceded in 1983 ... right after the 1982 elections, when the authoritarian period really ended. The newly elected governors pressured the government, and while the government anticipated this, it could no longer resist their pressure. It was a question of power – the authoritarian regime was finished in 1982.[167]

Congress would decentralize even further during the 1987–8 Constitutional Convention. Let us explore the pressures on members of Congress at the time in order to better understand the specific outcome. At that time, the most intense pressures came from subnational governments, while the president – and thus the central government – remained particularly weak. Deputies and other officials involved with the process affirmed that mayors and in particular governors lobbied the Constitutional Congress for additional decentralization, directing their efforts to the subcommittee that prepared the decentralization proposal for the new constitution. For example, in interviews, deputies stated that:

During the Constitutional Congress, there was no public pressure, but the governors articulated behind the scenes to encourage their deputies to give more to the states.[168]

State governments had extensive participation in this process.[169]

I received appeals from the governor. One feels very conscious of this, that one represents a state in the congress.[170]

One deputy elaborated on the type of pressure he and his colleagues felt:

What influenced the subcommittee and the plenary was the "Politics of the Governors." State finance secretaries had a decisive influence in sealing the deals. The governors also influenced their state delegations, they had great influence. The state finance secretaries were even holding parallel meetings to Congress' subcommittee meetings, to come to agreements on the points that were in the interest of the states, particularly in relation to the issue of their participation in and share of the FPE revenue. In this instance one sees the influence, the control, of the [state] executive branch in Congress.[171]

State-government pressure was not simply behind the scenes, but quite overt. In January 1987, just after the Constitutional Congress was installed, twenty-one of the twenty-two governors from the dominant PMDB party (Brazil had twenty-three states at the time) met with the president's ministers and urged an "emergency" fiscal decentralization (*GM* 1/15/87, p. 1; *OESP* 1/15/87, p. 1). Newspapers reported meetings between the governors and the several states' congressional delegations to organize support for fiscal decentralization (*JB* 5/10/87, p. A-2; *OESP* 5/10/87, p. A-2; *FSP* 9/5/87, p. A-1; *FSP* 9/9/87, p. A-6; *GM* 9/29/87, p. A-6). The governor of the state of Rio Grande do Sul argued that fiscal decentralization "is a matter of life

---

[167] Interview with Antônio Delfim Netto.   [168] Interview with Alberto Goldman.
[169] Interview with Ivo Wanderlinde.   [170] Interview with José Maria Eymael.
[171] Interview with Virgílio Guimarães.

or death for us governors" (*FSP* 4/13/88, p. A-4; *GM* 4/13/88, p. A-3; *OESP* 4/13/88, p. A-2).

Municipal mayors also pressured for fiscal decentralization, in particular for increases in automatic transfers through the FPM. Throughout the 1980s a nationwide "municipalist" movement organized protests for decentralization, including marches on Brasilia of thousands of mayors, city council members, and their political supporters. For example, in September 1983, over one thousand people participated in a "National Pro-Tax Reform Meeting," lobbying military President Figueiredo for fiscal decentralization (Oliveira 1986, 29; *JB* 9/28/83, p. A-4). Municipal supporters held other protest marches and meetings closer to the Constitutional Congress. On March 24, 1987, nearly two thousand mayors demonstrated in Brasilia for fiscal decentralization (*FSP* 3/23/87, p. A-10; *GM* 3/26/87, p. A-7; *JB* 3/26/87, p. A-20; *OESP* 3/26/87, p. A-4). These lobbying efforts translated into pressure on deputies, who rely on municipal-level contacts to advance their political careers (Ames 1995a, 1995b).

Given this pressure from subnational governments, how and why did members of the constitutional convention respond? Members of Congress mostly increased automatic transfers as opposed to decentralizing states' and municipalities' tax base (Leme 1992, 81). The most important effort to decentralize included substantial increases in the percentages of the IR and IPI automatically transferred to the FPE and FPM, so that by 1993 each fund received 21.5 percent and 22.5 percent respectively of the income and industrial products taxes. In 1968 only 5 percent of each tax was transferred to states and municipalities. The volume of automatic transfers as a percentage of the central government's budget increased approximately 200 percent from 1978 to 1993 (Nogueira 1995, 28) and represented about 25 percent of the central government's expenditures by 1997.[172]

Why did Congress concentrate on increasing transfers as opposed to decentralizing tax authority? Governors from the less-developed regions pressed for increases in automatic transfers, while governors from the more-developed regions, particularly the governor of São Paulo, pressed for decentralization of tax authority to states (Oliveira 1995a, 1995b). However, the states in the less-developed regions acted more cohesively than the states in the more-developed regions, holding numerous meetings and even organizing a movement favoring the interests of the poorer states (Leme 1992, 143–59; Universidade Federal do Ceará 1995). This organized action resulted

---

[172] Members of Congress introduced few changes into the decentralization proposal from its emergence from the subcommittee to its final passage on the plenary floor (Brazil 1987; Leme 1992; Oliveira 1995a). The final vote on the sections in the constitution on fiscal decentralization gained the votes of all members except those from leftist parties (about 10 percent of the Congress), which by that point had decided to vote against the majority's proposals on principle, regardless of the topic (Leme 1992, 175).

TABLE 8.4 *Average Percentage of*
States' Revenue from Own Taxes

Region	% of Revenue
North	33.7
Northeast	44.7
Center-West	51.9
South	67.7
Southeast	74.3

Source: Author's compilation.

in particularly acute pressure on deputies from these regions. One senator stated that

The pressure of mayors and governors was already great, but in the Northeast the state governments pressure their deputies much more.[173]

And an economist working with the fiscal policy subcommittee noted that

The states in the Southeast region don't have much in the way of "representation" [*representividade*] in Congress, but this is not the case for the states from the North, Northeast, and Center-West regions. These states have a great deal of "representation" in the Congress.[174]

Gubernatorial pressure helped maintain the cohesion of the delegations of deputies and senators from the less-developed states. These states favored automatic transfers over a transfer of tax authority to subnational governments because they have a relatively weak tax base and rely on revenue transfers from the central government, as shown in Table 8.4 (Nogueira 1995, Table 21).

The Constitutional Congress concentrated on automatic transfers because deputies and senators from the states that generate relatively less revenue on their own controlled an absolute majority of the seats. These states' representatives successfully dominated the drafting and passage of the fiscal decentralization aspects of the new constitution, from the early stages in the subcommittee to the final votes in the plenary (Leme 1992). Representatives from the relatively poorer states wanted to assure that important taxes would continue to be administered at the federal level. Keeping revenue administration at the federal level meant those who controlled the constitutional convention could also decide how and how much revenue to transfer, and to *which* states and municipalities. Representatives from the poorer regions thus decided not only to augment revenue transfers in general, but also to increase their share of those transfers, to the detriment of the states in the wealthier regions. For example, prior to the Constitutional Congress, the

[173] Interview with Gerson Camata.   [174] Interview with Clóvis Panzarini.

seven states in the two wealthier regions received approximately 23 percent of the FPE transfers, although they contain about 60 percent of the national population (IESP 1992, Table A.2.9). Afterward, they received only 15 percent (Barrera 1994, 118). The state of São Paulo (which has about 20 percent of Brazil's population) received a 4 percent share of the FPE proceeds under the old system, but currently receives only 1 percent of the FPE proceeds.[175] In short, state-based pressures decisively shaped the fiscal decentralization process during the Constitutional Convention.

Explaining Municipalities' Success

Both states and municipalities had also lobbied the 1945 constitutional congress for fiscal decentralization (Samuels 2000a), but at that time, municipalities failed to gain substantial additional resources. We can understand the success of state governments in both 1945 and 1988 because during both periods members of Congress faced similar political pressures from the state level. As I demonstrated in earlier chapters, state-level electoral dynamics drive elections in the current democratic period much as they did from 1945–64. State-level political networks never lost importance for deputies' careers during the dictatorship (see especially Hagopian 1996). In addition, as in 1945, in 1988 many incumbent legislators had developed their careers through experience in state government and many hoped to return to state government following a stint in Congress. Even deputies without formal connections to or a desire for a career in state politics confront the reality that state-level political pressures heavily influence their own political trajectory. Thus, all members of Congress have strong incentives to respond to state-government pressures.[176]

---

[175] Reflecting São Paulo's lack of influence in this decision, in an interview, São Paulo's representative to the group that decided how to divide up the FPE proceeds described the process:

> When we had the meeting to define the criteria, the representatives of the Northeast came with a proposal in hand: "the states from the North, Northeast and Center-West shall receive 85%, and the states from the South and Southeast shall receive 15%." São Paulo will receive 1% of the total. And so I asked, "What is the criteria for this decision?" "Criteria?" They said. "There is none." I said, "You're going to cut our share by 75% without any reason?" "Yes," they said, "And if you complain you'll get zero." So I said "Oh, OK, one percent is good, great, that's fine."

Interview with Clóvis Panzarini.

[176] One might ask why members of Congress would decentralize if they cannot be certain they themselves will reap the benefits in the future. I have argued that deputies regard access to state-level clientelistic resources as more effective politically than access to federal-government resources; that electoral dynamics in Brazil revolve around state-level politics and not national-level politics; and that many deputies continue their careers at the state

Thus, state-level pressures worked in similar ways in the 1940s and the 1980s, demonstrating the persistent importance of state-level politics for national-level politics in Brazil. Still, how can we explain the different outcomes for municipalities? "Municipal autonomy" has been a political rallying cry in Brazil for almost a century, but Congress decentralized very little to municipalities during the 1945 Constitutional Convention, while states gained a great deal of new resources. Indeed, municipalities remained politically dependent on states and the federal government, which maintained significant discretionary power to distribute resources to municipalities during the 1945–64 period (Mahar 1971; Varsano 1996). In 1988, municipalities won substantial autonomy, gaining huge increases in automatic transfers. What explains the different outcome in these two experiences with democratization?

To explain the increase in municipal autonomy one must understand the change in the nature of the connection between municipalities and deputies' careers. As they do today, during the 1945–64 period deputies also depended heavily on their municipal bases of support (see e.g., Ames 1987). However, as I explained in Chapter 3, the relative political attractiveness of a municipality *as part of deputies' careers* began to increase during the military period. Only when municipalities became attractive political prizes in their own right did politicians respond by decentralizing revenue to them. Previously, the weight of state-based political and career interests had been paramount. Given political rise of municipalities, when democracy returned again in 1988 federal deputies had strong incentives to favor municipalities as well as states when deciding to decentralize resources.

Explaining the Failure of the Central Government to Protect its Interests

What was the role of the president and the executive branch given the pressures from states and municipalities and members of Congress' intentions to decentralize? As noted, the military president had opposed Congress' 1983 initiatives without success. Could the first civilian president exercise authority to get what he wanted? During times of normal politics, presidents typically possess some kind of veto power. Yet although the President might not have preferred to decentralize, or might have preferred to increase discretionary over automatic transfers, during Brazil's 1987–8 Constitutional Congress the President did not possess a veto – in fact, the President's

---

level. These forces generate what is called *governismo* at the state level in Brazil. Because politicians make or break their careers at the state and not the national level, they face strong incentives to favor *whoever* is in power at the state level. For any individual deputy, the danger of being "on the outs" at the state level is much greater than the danger of being "on the outs" at the national level. Thus members of Congress have strong incentives to support their state government in the national legislature, regardless of who controls the state government at the time.

approval was not even required for the constitution's passage. Given this, Brazil's first civilian president, like the last military president, had a relatively limited ability to influence Congress. (This is in great contrast to the post-1994 situation. See Chapter 9.)

Although an interministerial working group had elaborated a proposal for the 1988 constitutional convention that decentralized both resources and policy responsibility (Oliveira 1995a, 119–20), during the Constitutional Congress President Sarney offered no positive *or* negative input into the draft chapter of the constitution dealing with fiscal decentralization. (Sarney concentrated his lobbying efforts in only two areas: extending the length of his term by one year, and maintaining a presidential form of government.) Congress' decentralization proposal ultimately ignored the working group's suggestions and included only decentralization of resources, not of policy responsibilities.[177]

When Sarney and his economic advisors realized the extent and form of Congress' proposed decentralization, they belatedly united to oppose passage of the draft chapter on fiscal policy. Luis Carlos Bresser Pereira, Minister of Finance at the time, declared that the decentralization proposal would bankrupt the central government in a short time (*OESP* 9/20/87, pp. A-1, 5). The President's Chief of Staff feared that "the central government will become unviable if this is approved as is" (*FSP* 4/5/88, p. A-8), and the Secretary-General of the Finance Ministry twice warned of Brazil's "impending financial collapse" if the fiscal decentralization proposal passed (*GM* 9/19/87, p. A-5; *JB* 9/19/87, p. A-14; *OESP* 8/19/87, p. A-20). Congress ignored these alarmist pleas (although they would later turn out to be partly true). Brazil's presidents behaved as expected in opposing fiscal decentralization, but both the last military and first civilian president's relative political weakness during the 1980s meant that they could do little do oppose the movement.

CONCLUSION

From 1975 to 1995, Brazilian state governments' share of total national expenditures increased 17 percent, and municipalities' share increased by 93 percent. Already quite decentralized in comparative perspective, fiscal decentralization transformed Brazil into one of the world's most fiscally decentralized systems. A close exploration of this process reveals that while existing accounts (e.g., Souza 1994, 1996) focus on federalism and democratization, these variables cannot provide a sufficient explanation.

The process of fiscal decentralization in Brazil followed the incentives and pressures driving legislators' careers. Societal and business pressures were largely from this policy arena, and pressure from the executive branch

---

[177] Interview with Thereza Lobo.

proved ineffectual. Ambitious politicians in the legislature, pressured by representatives of subnational governments, chose the extent and form of fiscal decentralization. Any explanation of these policy choices must therefore include an understanding of these politicians' incentives. Members of Congress could have chosen to retain authority over fiscal resource allocation at the national level, in the legislature. However, they chose *not* to strengthen Congress' budgetary authority but instead to implement automatic transfers to states and municipalities, permanently codifying increased political autonomy and strength for Brazil's subnational governments. Fiscal decentralization in Brazil thus provides an excellent example of how politicians can shape institutions according to their own desires during democratic transitions. Fiscal decentralization was the first major reform passed following the resumption of democratic elections in Brazil, and was the *only* reform actually *implemented* immediately following the 1987–8 Constitutional Convention.[178]

Fiscal decentralization also highlights how the particulars of the Brazilian transition appear to both contradict and confirm the theoretical expectations of the democratization literature, which predicts that actors will work cautiously and seek to limit uncertainty. On the one hand, the dramatic degree of decentralization reduced the central-government's budgetary leeway, impeded the ability of the central government to stabilize Brazil's economy (e.g., Bonfim and Shah 1991), and pushed the central government to attempt to recentralize in the 1990s. In this way, political reform also impeded political stability; this counters the expectations in the literature.

On the other hand, the democratization literature also teaches us (e.g., Hagopian 1996) that actors in a transition will seek to preserve their own political survival (Ames 1987). In Brazil, career incentives and federal institutions pushed politicians to focus more on political survival than on limiting uncertainty. Fiscal decentralization can be seen as a policy success from the point of view of those who voted for its passage, but by the early 1990s its very success proved deleterious to Brazil's overall macroeconomic health. This in turn provoked a reaction by the central government, principally during President Fernando Henrique Cardoso's administration (1995–2002). I explore this reaction to fiscal decentralization and its implications for Brazilian federalism in the next chapter.

---

[178] Newspapers noted this intention to implement decentralization as rapidly as possible (see e.g., *Gazeta Mercantil* 4/16/88, pp. 1, 7).

Chapter 9

The Cardoso Administration and Changes in Brazilian Federalism

INTRODUCTION

In this chapter I explore the evolution of federalism during the administration of President Fernando Henrique Cardoso (1995–2002). In general terms, the differences between the pre- and post-1994 periods are clear: presidential weakness and governability problems characterized the 1982–94 period, but Cardoso's administration marked the emergence of a more coherent executive branch in Brazilian politics, which enhanced governability. Cardoso controlled inflation and brought relative economic stability, articulated broad congressional support, and passed several important political and economic reforms. In terms of federalism, some have concluded that the Cardoso administration has reversed the decentralizing trend that began toward the end of the military regime (e.g., Abrucio 1998, 231; Abrucio and Ferreira Costa 1998, 77; Affonso 1998; Kugelmas and Sola n.d., 10; Afonso and Mello 2000, 17; Montero 2001; cf. Weyland 2000). If true, this rapid change in policy direction demands explanation, given this book's emphasis on the weight of federalism in Brazilian politics. To what extent is this argument correct?

I explore this question through the concept of "predatory federalism" (Abrucio 1996). Federalism gained increasing importance during Brazil's redemocratization because the presidency lost power while subnational governments gained autonomy (Abrucio and Samuels 1997). As the party system entered a period of high volatility and rapid fragmentation and members of Congress increasingly responded to subnational electoral politics (which preceded national electoral competition by almost a decade), the central government came to depend more and more on state governors to obtain support in Congress. Thus, redemocratization increased the power of subnational actors in national politics, especially state governors.

Federalism became "predatory" after redemocratization because its institutions generate incentives for intergovernmental conflict (both within and across levels) far more than cooperation. Predatory federalism has both vertical and horizontal elements. The vertical dynamic expresses subnational actors' influence within national politics, and is characterized by states and municipalities "preying" on the central government's coffers. During the 1980s and early 1990s, states and some municipalities began spending far beyond their means and accumulating large debts. Until the Cardoso administration, subnational governments never truly assumed the costs of these decisions, because through Congress they would force the central government to cover their debts. By July 2000, the national government had assumed over U.S.$100 billion in subnational debt (Afonso and Mello 2000, 17n). Soft budget constraints are the roots of the vertical face of predatory Brazilian federalism.

The horizontal dynamic of predatory federalism is characterized by presence of strong incentives toward competition rather than cooperation between subnational units. For example, states (and municipalities) "prey" on each other by renouncing tax revenue to attract investment, and as a result all governments lose revenue. This has come to be known as the "fiscal war" (Arbix 2000; Silva Fernandes and Wanderlei 2000; L. Oliveira 2000). Politicians largely failed to develop horizontal cooperative institutions during Brazil's redemocratization, and the absence of such mechanisms affects Brazilian national politics far beyond the fiscal war, in areas such as negotiations over the degree of social-policy decentralization (Abrucio and Ferreira Costa 1998, 38; Arretche 2000).

Predatory federalism provides a useful lens through which we can explore changes in both the vertical and horizontal elements of Brazilian federalism during the Cardoso administration. The *Plano Real* is the starting point for such an analysis, because it provided Cardoso's government with advantages to leverage concessions from Congress and thus from subnational governments. The *Plano Real* did allow Cardoso's government to gain enhanced regulatory capacity over subnational governments and tame some of the worst excesses of *vertical* predatory federalism. In particular, by ending inflation the *Plano Real* closed an era of "fictional budgeting" in Brazil, which gave the central government leverage to force state governments to privatize their banks and other parastatal agencies and otherwise commit themselves to meeting their debt obligations. Prior to the Cardoso administration, subnational governments' fiscal profligacy had reached the point of affecting national macroeconomic health. Thus, Cardoso's successes are both real and important.

Nevertheless, in this chapter I argue that what many regard as Cardoso administration victories over subnational governments were qualified at best. For one, these victories were not simply imposed; intergovernmental relations in Brazil evolved during the Cardoso years more as a result of bargaining and negotiation. Second, the victories were not complete, and were costly. Governors, mayors, and members of Congress forced the president to alter or even abandon parts of his core reform agenda and pay a tremendous price to achieve his goals. Finally, horizontal predatory federalism continued largely unabated, also obstructing important aspects of Cardoso's reform agenda.

The reforms that the Cardoso administration achieved following the implementation of the *Plano Real* reflect a supreme preoccupation with putting Brazil's fiscal house in order. Whether or not this effort will succeed in the long run remains to be seen, but the effort was certainly necessary. Still, this "fiscal tunnel vision" ignored broader political reforms and has not at all altered the fundamentally decentralized nature of electoral and partisan politics in Brazil. Cardoso's policies have not changed the fact that Brazil remains one of the most decentralized federations in the world. Most importantly, Cardoso's reforms have not changed the social and political organization of the political elite, and thus not altered the way in which subnational governments achieve representation in the national legislature. Consequently, federalism and intergovernmental relations remain a critical variable in determining the flow of national executive-legislative relations. In this way, Brazilian federalism has retained its vitality despite the transformations of the late 1990s.

To illustrate how federalism continued to shape the national political agenda during the Cardoso years, in this chapter I explore the main issues surrounding intergovernmental fiscal relations: the *Plano Real* and its consequences; the proposals for fiscal reform; and the much-praised "Fiscal Responsibility Law." I explain how subnational political interests, through their "ambassadors" in Congress, have limited the central government's capacity to alter federal relationships in each of these areas, and how some of the government's successes may be temporary or even illusory. This analysis serves to support my contention that subnational interests remained critical under Cardoso, who many consider Brazil's most successfully "centralizing" democratically elected president.

FEDERALISM AND THE *PLANO REAL*

The *Plano Real*, the stabilization plan Cardoso introduced in 1993 while serving as Finance Minister, underlies many of the later changes in intergovernmental relations.[179] By 1993, after a series of failed stabilization plans, hyperinflation had returned and economic growth was faltering. The political situation was also chaotic: Brazil's first democratically elected president in nearly three decades (Fernando Collor de Mello) had been impeached in September 1992, and many saw the new president, Itamar Franco, as weak and/or unprepared for the job. Franco had appointed Cardoso (who had served as Senator from São Paulo since 1982) as Minister of Foreign Relations, and after another series of failed attempts to bring order to the

---

[179] A useful review of the details of the *Plano Real* is Filgueiras (2000).

economy, in May of 1993 Franco asked Cardoso to assume the Ministry of Finance.

Cardoso and his team of advisors concluded that previous stabilization plans had failed because they did not address the root cause of macro-economic instability: fiscal imbalance at all levels of government (A. Souza 1999). At the national level, fiscal decentralization had cut the central government's share of revenue while leaving it with largely the same spending responsibilities (see Chapter 8), contributing to budget deficits. At the sub-national level, government debt more than doubled between 1983 and 1993 (Abrucio 1998, 197) because democratically elected governors and mayors employed deficit spending to fulfill campaign pledges and win new support. Most state governments also owned one or more banks, which governors employed to obtain money for political purposes, driving their governments deeper into the red.

A serious moral hazard problem further encouraged debt growth at the subnational level: no governor ever paid a price for deficit spending because Brazilian federal institutions permitted soft budget constraints. Time and again, the federal government would assume state debts, creating the norm that the federal government guaranteed subnational debts, no matter how large. For example, in 1989 the federal government assumed states' debts to foreign lending agencies and banks, but failed to force state governments to comply with the conditions that would have avoided another debt crises. Thus, in 1993 the federal government assumed another U.S.$28 billion in state debt. States were given lengthy repayment periods and below-market interest rates for repayment.

As long as inflation persisted, budget deficits at either level of government caused few immediate political problems because governments could reduce real expenditures by delaying disbursements for salaries and government contracts long enough for inflation to have eroded their value (the "Tanzi effect"). But mounting debts contributed to inflationary pressures, creating a vicious circle. Cardoso's team was the first to take the relationship between inflation and fiscal profligacy seriously, and thus the *Plano Real* aimed to generate budget surpluses at the national level and eliminate soft budget constraints at the subnational level.

To control inflation in the short term, the *Real* was to be pegged to the U.S. dollar. This overvalued the currency, causing an increase in imports and thus a current-account deficit. To finance this deficit, maintain the value of the currency, and thus control inflation in the long term, the government had to attract dollars. To do so, the plan required high domestic interest rates. This in turn would increase the debt burden of anyone holding debt in domestic currency. However, Brazil could only attract foreign investment (and fulfill IMF obligations) if it also reduced public debt. If public debt levels could not be controlled, the plan would lose credibility (A. Souza 1999, 54). Thus, fiscal austerity was required at all levels of government.

To generate surpluses at the national level, the economic team created the "Social Emergency Fund" (*Fundo Social de Emergência*, FSE), which gave the central government more budgetary leeway by disconnecting 20 percent of all central-government revenue from any constitutionally mandated spending. Because the FSE would alter the distribution of federal tax revenue, it required a constitutional amendment to pass. Constitutional amendments need a 60 percent majority of all members of both houses of Congress, and thus Cardoso had to drum up Congressional support for this core component of the Real Plan. At the same time (Fall 1993), the horse race for the October 1994 presidential elections had already begun. Because it would not be fully implemented until mid-1995, the Real Plan was therefore necessarily linked with a presidential candidate who would be committed to the plan through the next administration. As the person responsible for the plan's success or failure, Cardoso's name quickly entered the list of likely presidential candidates.

The process of articulating congressional support for the FSE and for Cardoso's presidential candidacy are thus inseparable. The difficulties of getting the FSE through Congress led Cardoso, a leader of the center-left PSDB party, to court the leaders of the PFL, a large center-right party in late 1993. Along with Cardoso, PFL members realized that if the plan succeeded it could propel an alternative to the PT's presidential candidate Lula, who at that point led every poll by a substantial margin (Dimenstein and Souza 1994, 130). Thus, PFL members agreed to support the FSE in exchange for the right to nominate the vice-presidential candidate on Cardoso's slate. The FSE was approved on February 8, 1994, for a two-year period. Weeks later, as required by law, Cardoso resigned as Minister to launch his presidential candidacy. As the election neared and the FSE and other aspects of the *Plano Real* went into effect, inflation declined and Cardoso inexorably moved up in the polls. In the end, he won handily, even avoiding a second-round runoff.

Gaining the tools to control subnational spending resulted from the political consequences of the plan's implementation. By stopping inflation, the plan eliminated the Tanzi effect. Governors could no longer reduce their bills using inflation, and some found themselves with payrolls of 80 percent to 90 percent of revenues, little money to pay their debts and even less money for public-works investment. To add insult to injury, the high interest rates that the Real Plan caused increased states' interest payments, further exposing the fragility of subnational finances (Afonso and Mello 2000, 16). After the implementation of the plan, states found themselves in an untenable fiscal position for the first time (Abrucio and Ferreira Costa 1998, 80). This gave the federal government leverage to convince subnational governments to change their behavior. Using this leverage, Cardoso sought to tighten restrictions on subnational debt and to push state governments to sell or restructure their publicly owned banks (Garman et al. 2001).

The *Plano Real* has proved remarkably durable, and has successfully controlled inflation for the duration of Cardoso's two presidential terms. Its success also propelled Cardoso to an easy reelection victory in 1998. In terms of intergovernmental relations, a diverse audience has interpreted the *Plano Real* and especially the FSE as a central-government "victory" over subnational governments (e.g., Bernardo 1997; Kugelmas 2001, 38). Ames (2001, 260) suggested that as a result of the FSE, "the losers would be the states and municipalities, which would find their receipts reduced sharply." To what extent is this true? Did the *Plano Real* reverse the decentralizing trend explored in Chapter 8?

The implementation of the *Plano Real* did alter the rules of the game in favor of the central government, which finally gained effective control over Brazil's money supply. The consequences of the *Plano Real* also gave the central government leverage it had never before possessed to force subnational governments to commit to a deep fiscal restructuring. These developments are important advances for Brazil's macroeconomic health. However, for our purposes the key question is not simply what the central government "gained" or subnational governments "lost" after the Real Plan was implemented, but whether the plan was unilaterally imposed, what price the central government paid to establish a new degree of coordination, whether the situation is permanent, and most importantly whether the consequences of the plan have changed the strength of subnational "representation" in national politics.

An exploration of the approval and maintenance of the FSE reveals that the plan was not unilaterally imposed but resulted from extensive negotiations between the central government, Congress, and subnational governments; that subnational interests have forced the central government to pay a high cost for its policies; and that the arrangements giving the central government greater budgetary leeway are actually temporary. The give and take of the *Plano Real* illustrates how subnational interests continued to shape national policy even where the central government most demanded political autonomy.

The Great Log Roll: the Fund for States' Debts

The central government paid an extraordinarily high price to win initial support for and maintain the *Plano Real*. In return for governors' support, which helped assure passage of the FSE in Congress, the central government agreed to refinance state banks and purchase state debts once again, on a much larger scale than ever (Abrucio and Ferreira Costa 1998, 47). In the first six months of 1994, the central government spent R$5 billion to help state banks, twice what had been spent in the previous six years (Abrucio 1998, 216), and by the end of 1996 the federal government had assumed a total of R$123 billion in state debt (Dillinger and Webb 1999, 25). States did not have to assume the full value of their debts, because the central government granted them below-market interest rates for repayment. The direct central-government subsidy to states for this bailout has been estimated at between R$32 and R$46 billion (in 1997 values) (Rigolon and Giambiagi 1998, 15). Although the central government forced subnational governments to commit a portion of their revenue to paying their debts,[180] this direct subsidy reduced states' debt burden and dwarfs any potential revenue losses that the FSE may have caused. Moreover, the subsidy increased the central government's debt level, restricting its own budgetary leeway.

The Details of the Deal: No Revenue Losses for Subnational Governments

The debt subsidy proved insufficient to win the support of state governors for the FSE. To win passage for the fund, the central government also had to agree that states and municipalities would not receive any *less* revenue in transfers from the FPE and FPM than in 1993 (*FSP* 1/18/94, p. A-8). Cardoso had initially proposed reducing transfers to states and municipalities by 15 percent, or about U.S.$2 billion, but backed off this proposal owing to lobbying from governors and resistance from legislators (*FSP* 1/31/94, p. A-5; *FSP* 2/3/94, p. A-3).[181] The president was forced to settle for the following: to gain the FSE's approval, Cardoso decreed an income-tax rate increase in the last week of 1993, much of which Congress subsequently passed into law (*FSP* 1/4/94, p. A-4; *FSP* 1/27/94, p. A-5).[182] Prior to the FSE, states and municipalities received approximately 45 percent of all revenue from the corporate and individual income taxes (see Chapter 8). The final FSE proposal stipulated that all revenue generated from federal-government employees' personal income tax plus revenue generated from the income-tax rate *increase* (charged on all Brazilians) would henceforth *not* be divided with states and municipalities.[183]

However, this in no way implied that the central government would reduce transfers to subnational governments by 20 percent. The FSE amendment also stipulated that the central government could only increase its share of corporate and personal income tax revenue by a maximum of 5.6 percent, in contrast to the 20 percent of all other taxes and contributions that the FSE

---

[180] The government can withhold constitutionally mandated FPE and FPM transfers if a subnational government refuses to pay.

[181] Cardoso implied as much in his television pronouncement explaining the FSE to the general population, stating that "I agreed to maintain the resources destined for the states and municipalities, because they need them" (cited in *FSP* 2/9/94, p. 8).

[182] Congress approved an increase in the personal income tax rate but not the corporate tax rate.

[183] In terms of taxes divided with subnational governments, the FSE also included a portion of the Rural Property Tax, but revenue from this tax is so small that I ignore its effect (see Varsano et al. 1998).

permitted the central government to "de-link" (see Brasil, Senado Federal 2001, 262). This percentage (5.6 percent) was the estimated amount by which income-tax revenue would rise given the tax-rate increase Cardoso had just decreed (Motta 1998). This element of the FSE assured subnational governments that their constitutionally mandated transfers would at least stay constant after the FSE was promulgated. It also assured that Cardoso would obtain about two-thirds *less* than the amount he originally wanted by reducing transfers to subnational governments.[184]

In short, to obtain passage of the FSE the central government only managed to get subnational governments to forego receipt of an expected *increase* in federal transfers. And even given this concession, federal transfers to subnational governments actually increased in real terms after the implementation of the *Real*. Although it is true that between 1991 and 2000 the central government's share of total government spending increased 8.1 percent (from 55.4 percent to 59.9 percent of the total) while the states' share declined by 10.8 percent and the municipalities' share by 8.9 percent (Brasil, Ministério da Fazenda, Secretaria da Receita Federal 2001a, 2001b), this tells us only about relative levels of revenue, not absolute levels. In fact, states and municipalities gained revenue in absolute terms during the 1990s, only not as fast as the central government. Revenue at all levels of government as a percentage of GDP increased from 25.2 percent in 1991 to 33.2 percent in 2000 (an all-time high). Central government revenue as a portion of GDP increased by 37.4 percent, states' portion by 19.2 percent, and municipalities' by 25.6 percent (Brasil, Ministério da Fazenda, Secretaria da Receita Federal 2001b).[185]

Under the 1988 constitution, if federal-government tax revenue increases, so must transfers to subnational governments. A constitutional loophole explains why the central government's revenue has increased relatively faster than the subnational governments' revenue, thus creating the impression of fiscal recentralization. Central-government revenue can come from "taxes," "contributions," or assorted other tariffs and fines.[186] In contrast to tax revenue, the central government does not have to share revenue from contributions with subnational governments. The central government's relative share of revenue has increased because it has strategically raised revenue from contributions more than from taxes. Table 9.1 reveals the federal government's increasing reliance on contributions.

---

[184] Originally, Cardoso proposed that the FSE be funded by "de-linking" 15 percent of all federal revenue, but he ultimately proposed that the FSE be funded from 20 percent of all federal revenue because he was unable to include the full amount of revenue from cutting transfers to subnational governments (*FSP* 2/1/94, p. A-6).

[185] Note this does not calculate the final percentage of total spending because it does not include intergovernmental transfers.

[186] An example of a "contribution" is the "Provisionary Contribution on Financial Operations" (CPMF), charged on financial transactions.

TABLE 9.1 *Evolution of Composition of Federal Revenue in Brazil*

Year	Taxes	Contributions	Other
1985	89.8	0.0	10.2
1990	72.2	27.2	0.7
1995	62.6	36.6	0.9
2000	54.4	45.5	0.2

Source: Brasil, Ministério de Fazenda, Secretaria da Receita Federal (2000a, 2001a).

Although revenue from contributions increased in relative importance, revenue from taxes also increased in absolute terms during the Cardoso administration. For example, personal income tax revenue increased from 2.83 percent to 3.95 percent of GDP from 1994 to 2000 due to the tax rate increase as well as "bracket creep" that resulted in greater numbers of Brazilians having to pay personal income taxes (Brasil, Ministério da Fazenda, Secretaria da Receita Federal 2001b). As a result, income tax revenue rose far beyond the 5.6 percent tax hike after 1994, increasing transfers and thus minimizing the impact of the FSE on subnational governments' coffers. Table 9.2 shows the increases in transfers through the two "Participation Funds."

Overall, constitutionally mandated transfers to states increased by 106 percent from 1994 to 2000 in real terms, and from the federal government to municipalities by 107 percent (Ministério da Fazenda, Secretaria do Tesouro Nacional 2001c and 2001d). During this same period, real GDP growth was only 17 percent.[187] In short, during the 1990s the central government increased its relative share of revenue mostly because it increased the amount of money that it took out of the hands of Brazil's citizens through the euphemistically named "contributions," not because the FSE decreased transfers to municipal and state governments.

The Nature of the FSE and Subnational Influence

Governors, mayors, and their ambassadors in Congress never liked to cite these figures, nor were they satisfied with the central government's assumption of subnational debts. Instead, they often complained that the FSE (hereafter referred to as "the Fund" because its name has changed twice) reduced their revenue. They used this claim as a negotiating tool, and each time the Fund required extension they have succeeded in extracting additional concessions from the President. The way the fund was implemented encourages

---

[187] Values were corrected to December 31, 2000 prices using the IPC-FIPE (Souza 2001). GDP data can be found at www.ipeadata.gov.br.

TABLE 9.2 *Growth of FPE and FPM Transfers – 1994–2000*
(values as of 12/31/00)

	Transfers of States	Transfers to Municipalities
1994	R$5,928,072,322	R$6,203,796,389
2000	R$12,182,458,536	R$12,816,400,876

Source: Calculated from Brasil, Ministério da Fazenda, Secretaria do Tesouro Nacional (2001c, 2001d).

this and reflects the degree to which the success of the Real Plan is a function of negotiations between the central and subnational governments, not simply an imposition.

The Real Plan is unlike previous economic reform programs in a crucial way: by discarding the strategy of exclusively relying on presidential decrees and instead employing a mix of decrees and constitutional amendments, the President involved the legislature to a much greater degree in the process of economic stabilization. Obtaining legislative support for a constitutional amendment in Brazil is difficult enough as it is; presidents must negotiate and provide side-payments or concessions in order to win their passage. However, the constitutional amendment that gave life to the Fund allows legislators to extract even greater concessions from the President than they otherwise might.

When we observe legislative approval of a constitutional amendment in a given country, we typically think that politicians have chosen to *permanently* alter a fundamental political arrangement. However, the constitutional amendment that enacted the Fund is different: it contains a "sunset provision," and has already expired and been renewed three times (in 1995, 1997, and 1999). It is set to expire again in 2003. This helps explain why Congress initially accepted the Fund: it was not and is not a permanent reform of intergovernmental fiscal relations. The sunset provision implies not only that the central government has not permanently reversed fiscal decentralization, but also that the president has had to periodically return to the table to renegotiate passage of essentially the same bill. This has given states and municipalities repeated opportunities to force the president to cede his hard line on fiscal matters and offer benefits in exchange for the Fund's renewal. This in turn implies that the president has had to cede more than if the amendment had been permanent.

In what follows, I provide details on the negotiations of the Fund's extensions to illustrate how subnational interests have extracted concessions from the executive branch. Although these concessions have not gone so far as to destroy the foundations of the Real Plan, they have made the government's belt-tightening efforts more difficult, and illustrate that the president has not simply imposed losses on subnational governments.

From its enactment, opposition parties criticized the Fund for shifting revenue from social spending to paying off the national debt (e.g., Partido dos Trabalhadores 2000). This has had no effect on the government's strategy, but criticism from other quarters has. As the Fund's first expiration date neared in late 1995, Cardoso requested a four-year extension, arguing that the work of economic stabilization was not complete. Congress approved only an eighteen-month extension (*GM* 6/17/97, p. A-13), meaning that the Fund would require renegotiation again just before the next elections. As the 1998 elections neared, mayors, governors, and their supporters in Congress suddenly became far less willing to believe the government's claim that the Fund required yet another extension, and complained that the Fund reduced revenue transfers to subnational governments (*GM* 4/2/97, p. A-10; *O Paraná* 4/8/97, p. A-8; *OESP* 5/9/97, p. A-6). Even Cardoso's allies attacked the Fund for cutting subnational government revenue (*FSP* 4/4/97, p. A-6; *OESP* 5/25/97, p. A-3).

President Cardoso's initial reaction was to threaten to cut deputies' budget amendments and to claim that states and municipalities had won real gains in central-government transfers (*FSP* 5/16/97, p. A-6; *FSP* 5/13/97, p. A-6; *FSP* 7/9/97, p. A-4). However, neither the threat nor the argument had much effect, as mayors held anti-Fund meetings and traveled en masse to Brasilia to directly pressure deputies (*OESP* 6/16/97, p. A-4; *OESP* 6/10/97, p. A-4; *OESP* 6/20/97, p. A-7). This pressure forced the government to exclude from the FSE extension proposal the revenue from the 1994 income tax increases, which meant that transfers to municipalities would increase (*FSP* 6/10/97, p. A-4; *OESP* 6/25/97, p. A-4; *Jornal de Brasilia* 7/9/97, p. A-3; *GM* 7/1/97 p. A-11; *Correio Braziliense* 7/16/97, p. A-11; *GM* 7/3/97 p. A-10; *GM* 7/11/97 p. A-9; *GM* 7/16/97, p. A-8; *FSP* 7/13/97, p. A-5; *FSP* 7/17/97, p. A-4).

States also pressured for compensation. The government responded that debt relief of R$103 billion (at the time) was sufficient (*GM* 7/14/97, p. A-11; *O Globo* 6/27/97, p. A-10), but this argument fell on deaf ears and the government was forced to promise that R$600 million from an Inter-American Development bank loan would fund public-works projects in the states (*OESP* 7/15/97, p. A-6). The government still had to get the extension through the Senate, where the lobbying of states and municipalities continued and again proved successful. Although the text of the proposal went unchanged, the government agreed to additional side payments for states that were losing revenue due to a law exempting exports from the main state tax (the "Kandir Law," see the following text), to reschedule municipal debts with the national social security and unemployment systems, to reimburse municipalities for pension contributions for personnel who were being encouraged to retire, and to increase the number of municipalities covered under federal-government poverty assistance programs (*OESP* 9/27/97, p. A-11; *FSP* 11/6/97, p. A-4). With these deals in hand, Congress finally approved the Fund extension, giving the president only two more years (until December 31, 1999). In short, in 1997 the government's own supporters in Congress altered both the length of the proposed Fund extension as well as the terms of the president's initial proposal, to the advantage of states and municipalities.

A similar dynamic recurred in 1999. Cardoso initially stated that he considered the Fund's third renewal "nonnegotiable," and some in the government even suggested that Congress approve a permanent extension. Yet soon states and municipalities began lobbying Congress, and even governors ostensibly allied with Cardoso indicated that they would orient their state's delegations to vote against the Fund if the government insisted on renewing it without alterations. The opposition grew so intense that Cardoso not only did not present the proposal for a permanent extension but feared that the Fund would not be extended at all (*Jornal de Brasilia* 5/7/99, p. A-10; *OESP* 4/19/99, p. A-6; *Jornal de Brasilia* 5/11/99, p. A-2; *JB* 3/9/99, p. A-3; *FSP* 7/9/99, p. A-4). Cardoso instead proposed an extension through 2007 and agreed to remove all aspects of the Fund that reduced transfers to subnational governments (*Jornal de Brasilia* 5/7/99, p. A-10). This would therefore increase transfers, principally to states, by about R$3.2 billion, and it implied that after January 1, 2000 the Fund would no longer affect transfers to subnational governments in any way.

Some states also obtained the federalization of their debts with federal social security funds in exchange for supporting the proposed extension of the Fund (*FSP* 8/14/99, p. A-13), and Cardoso was forced to accept a four-year renewal, not seven. However, these concessions still proved insufficient when the time to vote arrived. A first attempt to vote the extension simply failed, as the government's own supporters left the plenary and impeded a quorum (*FSP* 12/9/99, p. A-15). The government planned a second attempt the following week but did not call for a vote even though 473 of the 513 deputies were present, because it "feared defeat" (*FSP* 12/15/99, p. A-7). The same thing happened the next day. Ultimately the president negotiated additional concessions and called an extraordinary legislative session the following month to approve the Fund extension. The concessions included additional reimbursements for lost revenue from the Kandir Law, an expansion of the pool of revenue that the federal government divides with states, and another extension of state debt payments. Without any irony, the Chamber of Deputies' daily newspaper noted that the agreement to finally approve the Fund extension was signed "between the federal government and the governors" (*Jornal da Câmara* 2[328], pp. 1–2).

The Real Plan in Perspective

The Real Plan was the Cardoso administration's clearest success story. It corralled inflation and gave the central government flexibility to generate budget surpluses. Its consequences also put states in a relatively weaker position, allowing the central government to negotiate tighter fiscal and financial controls over subnational governments. However, we must also take into account the present and future costs of these gains, and the negotiated nature of the central government's gains. The central government assumed a huge portion of subnational governments' debts, trading off the increased budgetary flexibility of the Fund for a heavier debt burden that will limit its own budgetary flexibility far into the future. And although the government has no guarantee that Congress will continue to extend the Fund's life, the national debt will live on until paid off.

More generally, the central government never achieved its most-preferred outcome, *permanently* reversing the fiscal decentralization of the 1980s. This would have been a true alteration of the institutions of Brazilian federalism. However, deputies and senators refused such a reversal, and in fact used the Fund's sunset provision to repeatedly extract concessions to benefit states and municipalities. With each renegotiation they successfully reduced states' and municipalities' contributions to the Fund, so that presently they contribute nothing. These concessions illustrate how even when the central government was in a relatively advantageous position and even where the central government most demanded political autonomy, subnational interests limited the central government's capacity to permanently alter federal relationships.

FEDERALISM AND THE FAILURE OF FISCAL REFORM

The second major area of contention in intergovernmental relations during the Cardoso administration was fiscal reform. Fiscal reform can mean many different things. In Brazil, for a variety of reasons the effort has come to focus on improving the "quality" of taxation, to reduce the so-called *Custo Brasil* or "Brazil Cost." Some of the objectives of fiscal reform include eliminating "cumulative" taxes (charged at each stage of the production or consumption process without discounting previously charged taxes), spreading the tax base more broadly, reducing the number of taxes, generating incentives to increase tax collection, eliminating state governments' propensity to grant tax exemptions, and changing the way that production and consumption are taxed (Affonso and Silva 1995; Rezende 1996; Afonso et al. 1998; F. Bezerra 1999; Lima 1999).

Across-the-board support for some kind of fiscal reform appeared to exist at the start of Cardoso's administration. Economists agreed that reform would improve efficiency and attract investment (e.g., Afonso and Melo 2000). As Finance Minister, Cardoso stated that Brazil desperately needed fiscal reform; on the campaign trail, he affirmed that fiscal reform would be a priority for his administration, and in office he often repeated that statement (*Veja* 1/31/01, p. 42–3). Azevedo and Melo (1997, 81) report that over sixty fiscal reform proposals circulated in the legislature during the 1990s, indicating legislative interest. Brazil's powerful business peak associations also heavily lobbied both the executive and legislative branches for fiscal reform (Confederação Nacional de Indústria 1999a, 1999b, 2000), although specific proposals diverge across business sectors (M. Melo 2001).

In an attempt to follow through on his campaign promise, Cardoso presented a fiscal reform proposal to Congress seven months after taking office.[188] The proposal suggested exempting exports, capital investments, and agroindustry from taxes; extinguishing some taxes and fusing others; and unifying the administration of the main state tax (the ICMS), which would simplify taxation of consumption and eliminate states' race-to-the-bottom competition for industry by renouncing tax revenues, known as the "fiscal war." However, even though it seems that ideas and interests coincided, and in contrast to other reform proposals that eventually passed, broad fiscal reform proposals literally went nowhere during Cardoso's two terms.[189] Two factors explain this policy inertia: a general fear of the unknown, and the impact of federalism on the preferences and strategies of members of both the executive and legislative branches.

The Failure of Fiscal Reform: Actors' Common Interest in the Status Quo

The fear of the unknown has contributed to the failure of fiscal reform. The key political question for fiscal reform in Brazil is how to create a more efficient system that does not reduce overall revenue and does not alter the distribution of revenue between levels of government (Lima 1999). Yet any fiscal reform, especially in a country with a complex system like Brazil's, involves a high degree of uncertainty about future revenue flows. Consequently, although all actors may in principle favor reform, they also fear a loss of revenue. For example, despite repeatedly stating that fiscal reform was a high priority, Cardoso's highest priority has always been to maintain the *Plano Real*, which required yearly budget surpluses. Because tax revenue increased during the *Plano Real*, the government thus instinctively favored the status quo.[190] Similarly, given the difficulty subnational governments face meeting their own budgetary obligations, state and municipal representatives were reluctant to believe the central government's economic models that showed

---

[188] Constitutional Amendment Proposal 175.

[189] In an interview, Brazil's Secretary of Federal Revenue pointed out that several important changes have been introduced, despite the absence of comprehensive reform: corporate income taxation was simplified and rural land taxation was changed to encourage owners to declare a fair market value of their properties. However, he agreed that reform of consumption taxes had not advanced and that much more could be done. Interview with Everardo Maciel.

[190] Interviews with Everardo Maciel, Mussa Demes, Antônio Kandir, Germano Rigotto, and Gastão Viana.

no revenue losses from proposed reforms.[191] Even the economists behind the government's original proposal admitted that "one cannot continue to feed the illusion that a broad fiscal reform can be accomplished without provoking gains and losses for some [federal] entities. It is not possible to improve the quality of taxation without altering the status quo" (Afonso et al. 1998, 7). The central government never offered a proposal that credibly assured subnational governments that they would not lose revenue from fiscal reform. Thus, inertia favored the status quo.

The Failure of Fiscal Reform: The Perspective from the Executive Branch

All institutional actors fear the unknown future. However, this is insufficient to understand why consensus on a "least harmful" reform has been impossible to reach, if all actors also believe that reform would bring economic growth and thus revenue gains for everyone. A more important factor is that the central government never expended the political resources necessary to pass its own proposal. Cardoso never resolved the clear differences of opinion within his own administration about either the content or the desirability of fiscal reform (M. Melo 2000), and as a result the government did not have an obvious "policy advocate" to organize congressional support for reform (Azevedo and Melo 1997). This contributed to a lack of clarity in the executive's position, which is a recipe for inactivity in a system that depends so intensely on executive leadership.

The failure to resolve intraadministration conflicts is a symptom of the true problem: the president never expended the resources to resolve these conflicts (or to convince a reluctant Congress) because the government's need to maintain high levels of revenue combined with the impact of federal institutions set his government's strategy against fiscal reform.[192] Every broad reform proposal involves reduction or elimination of the so-called "contributions" because of their alleged economic inefficiency.[193] However, the government needed the revenue from contributions to generate budget surpluses. Contributions could be transformed into taxes, but if this path were taken the government would confront a fundamental principle of Brazilian federalism, set in the 1988 constitution: tax revenue must be shared with states and municipalities.

The president has chosen to expand the use of contributions, not rein them in, in order to generate revenue that does not have to be divided

---

[191] Interview with Pedro Novais.

[192] Interviews with Everardo Maciel, Sérgio Miranda, Mussa Demes, Germano Rigotto, Lúcio Alcântara, Raúl Velloso, Antônio Kandir, Clóvis Panzarini, Jefferson Peres, Gastão Viana, Maria Emília Coimbra, and Antônio Carlos Pojo do Rêgo.

[193] In an interview, Everardo Maciel disputed the economic inefficiency of contributions. Moreover, from his perspective contributions are extremely efficient because they are harder to avoid paying and easy to administer.

with subnational governments. This in turn has generated large budget surpluses.[194] The *rapporteur* of the Chamber of Deputies' Special Committee on
Fiscal Reform fingered the executive branch's refusal to allow modifications
to contributions as the "principal point of opposition" to broad tax reform
(CNI 1999a, 62). Opposition parties hold a similar view: an advisor to the
PT stated that "the federal government has boycotted attempts to negotiate
fiscal reform . . . why would they want to change anything, as long as the they
have the PIS, COFINS, and CPMF [contributions]?"[195]

The constitutional rules that allow the government to reap all revenue
from contributions but force it to share tax revenue put the government
between a rock and a hard place regarding fiscal reform. Cardoso chose to
avoid what from his perspective is the worst outcome of Brazil's revenue-
distribution system, sharing of tax revenue, and chose to stick with what
is from his perspective a less-worse system that permits Brazil to meet its
international obligations and maintain its macroeconomic program, even if
that system is relatively economically inefficient. A desire to avoid the effects
of federal revenue-sharing institutions, imposed by the decentralizing efforts
of subnational interests in the 1988 constitution, forced this strategic choice.

Failure of Fiscal Reform: the Perspective from Subnational Governments

The failure of fiscal reform cannot be laid solely at the feet of the executive
branch. After literally hundreds of hours of hearings, meetings, negotiation,
and debates, the Chamber of Deputies' Special Fiscal Reform Committee
reached near consensus and passed a reform proposal in 1999 (see CNI
1999a). Yet that proposal never came up for a plenary vote, partly because
of executive-branch opposition, but also because of the way in which federalism complicates any efforts to get subnational governments – and thus
their representatives in Congress – to support any fiscal reform proposal.
The proposal that the government originally submitted in 1995 contained
several reforms that would have dramatically altered intergovernmental political and fiscal relations, both between states and between states and the
central government. Although the Chamber Special Committee altered some
of the more centralizing aspects of the executive branch's proposal, its leaders
were unable to assuage the fears of those who defend subnational governments' interests. Consequently, mayors and especially governors continued
to oppose fiscal reform, and their influence has contributed to the proposal's
failure to advance. From states' perspectives, the two most problematic issues were the proposals to exempt exports from the ICMS tax and alter the

---

[194] One might thus ask why Congress doesn't simply eliminate contributions and decentralize
more revenue to states and municipalities. This would require an equally difficult constitutional amendment to pass, and without executive leadership such an attempt would die a
quick death.

[195] Interview with Maria Emília Coimbra.

ICMS' general structure and principles. An exploration of these two proposals illustrates how subnational interests impede broad fiscal reform.

Exempting exports from the ICMS makes Brazilian products more competitive on the world market, but negatively affects state government revenue (especially states that depend on taxing export industries). After submitting its initial proposal, the government realized that exempting exports from the ICMS would not require a constitutional amendment. Thus, the government perceived that a separate bill on this subject alone might pass through Congress more easily (Azevedo and Melo 1997). The president therefore coordinated the "extraction" of this issue from the constitutional reform proposal. The resulting bill (nicknamed the "Kandir Law" after the deputy who wrote it) passed both houses of Congress in September 1996 by large margins. However, this apparent central-government victory (and victory for export industries) had a cost: the export exemption would not have passed if the government had not promised to compensate states for their revenue losses.

The Kandir Law has given the central government headaches from the moment it was promulgated. Soon after the bill went into effect, states complained that their revenue had decreased more than the economic models had predicted, and they began pressuring the central government for additional compensation (Kandir 2001; *FSP* 8/27/97, p. A-8). In 1996 and 1997 the federal government reimbursed states for R$1.6 billion in lost revenue from the Kandir Law, but governors continued to complain that their losses exceeded the compensation (*GM* 1/28/98, p. A-6; *OESP* 1/30/98, p. A-6; *FSP* 2/21/99, p. A-5; *FSP* 2/26/99, p. A-7; *JB* 3/9/99, p. A-3). In March of 1999 the governors successfully extracted additional compensation (*FSP* 3/10/99, p. A-4), even though by that time one analyst had concluded that the central government had covered all of states' revenue losses (Nassif 2000). By the close of the 2000 fiscal year the central government had reimbursed states almost R$9 billion (in 2000 prices) for their losses (calculated from Brasil, Ministério da Fazenda, Secretaria do Tesouro Nacional 2001e and 2001f).

Governors also gained other forms of indirect compensation for supporting the Kandir Law. They cajoled the central government into assuming a portion of their debts (*FSP* 9/13/96, p. B-4), and obtained a reduction in their debt payments to the central government. This latter form of compensation involved a series of accounting tricks. State debt payments to the central government are calculated as a percentage of state revenue. To end states' opposition to the Kandir Law, the central government agreed to exclude revenue that is tied to education expenses from state governments' accounting of current revenue, permitting states to reduce their monthly debt payments to the central government. Governors also won a limit on the total percentage of state revenue going to pay debts to the central government, which reduced some states' payments by up to 80 percent (*GM* 3/10/99, p. B-1;

O Globo 3/19/99, p. A-4; *FSP* 3/20/99, p. A-8). In the end a reform that helps Brazilian exporters has cost the central government a great deal.

The Kandir Law can be seen as a small advance in terms of fiscal reform. It fulfills one demand of one part of the business community. Yet the states' reactions to the implementation of this reform of one element of Brazil's highly complex tax system illustrate the difficulties of overcoming subnational governments' opposition to broader fiscal reform, as well as the potential costs of such a reform. These difficulties become even more acute in the case of the proposal to alter the structure and principles of the ICMS. The ICMS is a form of value-added tax, and is the main source of state-government revenue apart from transfers from the federal government.[196] Simplifying greatly, there are two crucial aspects of the ICMS that states oppose changing. First, states can set their own ICMS rates (up to a certain point and depending on the product).[197] Second, even though the ICMS is technically a value-added tax, it is charged at the point of production, not consumption, which has a particular impact on interstate transactions.[198] For both issues, the key point is that states can set their ICMS rate at zero if they wish, for individual firms or for products.

Governors' ability to manipulate the ICMS rate combined with the fact that the tax is charged at the point of production makes the ICMS an important tool to attempt to attract firms that want to invest where tax rates are lowest. In the 1990s, governors have conducted bidding wars to win new industrial investment, particularly from large multinational corporations (See e.g., *Veja* 8/11/99, pp. 36–9). This interstate conflict has come to be known as the *guerra fiscal* or "fiscal war," a race-to-the-bottom game where states willingly sacrifice future revenue to win immediate investment. Brazil desperately needs industrial investment, but its governments ought not to be renouncing tax revenue given the country's infrastructural and other needs. However, the incentives to renounce are strong: exempting firms from the ICMS has become one of states' most important industrial policy tools in an age of privatization and deregulation. By attracting new industrial development through tax exemptions, state governments can claim credit for bringing hundreds or even thousands of well-paying jobs.

The fiscal war most hurts the states that depend on the ICMS for a substantial portion of their revenue. In effect the war mainly affects São Paulo, where much of Brazil's industrial base has historically been concentrated (São Paulo, with about 20 percent of the country's population, typically

---

[196] ICMS revenue varies based on the level of economic activity in each state. São Paulo generates nearly all its revenue from the ICMS, while poorer states rely much more heavily on federal-government transfers.

[197] The details of the ICMS rates are too complex to go into here. One analyst has written that there are "more or less" five rates within each state, plus the interstate rate, which can also vary (Lima 1999, 22).

[198] On interstate transactions, the two states involved share the ICMS charges.

accounts for about 40 percent of all ICMS revenue in Brazil [Lemgruber Viol 2001, 45]). States that want to attract investment away from São Paulo have strong incentives to maintain the fiscal war. The example of the Ford auto plant that the state of Bahia nabbed illustrates the problem.

Because the ICMS is charged at the point of production, if Ford manufactures a car in São Paulo and sells that car to an auto dealer in São Paulo, the ICMS charged on that transaction goes to the state of São Paulo. Likewise, when the dealer then sells the car to a consumer in São Paulo, the ICMS on the dealer's markup (the value added) goes to the state of São Paulo. Yet if Ford assembles a car in Bahia, the consumers in and the government of Bahia pay a relatively low cost, *because very few of the cars manufactured in Bahia will be purchased in Bahia.* Most cars will be "exported" to São Paulo or the other states in the South and Southeast regions. When Ford makes a car in Bahia and sells it to a dealer in São Paulo, the São Paulo dealer pays a price that includes the ICMS charged in Bahia. But Bahia has given Ford a tax exemption, so the state government then returns the ICMS to Ford.[199] Thus, because Bahia has a tiny proportion of the national car market, its consumers are not the ones subsidizing the tax exemption. This clarifies the incentives to engage in the fiscal war: when a state attracts a firm through an ICMS exemption, consumers in Brazil's other states finance much of the subsidy.

Politicians and economists condemn the incentives that lead to this kind of behavior, but battles in the fiscal war nevertheless increased in frequency during the 1990s. This is curious as well as unfortunate, because the fiscal war is entirely illegal. States began conceding tax exemptions in the 1960s (L. Oliveira 2000; Lemgruber Viol 2001). To end this behavior Congress passed a law in 1975 (Complementary Law 24/75) that requires any state that wishes to concede a tax exemption to obtain unanimous approval in the council of state finance secretaries (CONFAZ). Needless to say, the law has been wholly ignored, and in the early 1990s alone the fiscal war cost state governments an estimated U.S.\$9 billion in lost revenue (Abrucio 1998, 233).

Fiscal reform proposals presented during the Cardoso administration have suggested several mechanisms to end the fiscal war. Congress could pass a law prohibiting all states from renouncing any ICMS revenue, could change the ICMS so that it is charged at the point of consumption rather than the point of production, or it could nationalize the ICMS by creating some form of uniform value-added tax. Yet when the government's 1995 proposal suggested eliminating one federal tax in exchange for unifying the ICMS rate across states, sharing administration of the ICMS between the states and the national government, and charging at the point of consumption

---

[199] Even if a tax exemption is granted, the law requires the ICMS to first go to the state, which then rebates the tax to the firm in question.

instead of production (Azevedo and Melo 1997, 85), governors, state finance secretaries, and members of Congress widely attacked the proposal (M. Melo 1998, 15).[200]

Governors like the fiscal war because any governor that wins direct investment who is not the governor of São Paulo probably considers the investment a clear political victory, with minimal economic costs for his or her state. As one of São Paulo state's chief tax authorities argued,

> Other states want to continue the fiscal war ... taxing at the point of production is what the poor states have to attract investment. Since they have no industry to tax, they offer tax breaks for taxes that they're not generating in the first place. Thus there's no direct cost to these states, it's just foregone revenue.[201]

Governors oppose the loss of political autonomy that would accompany the proposed ICMS reforms, and use their considerable influence to sway members of Congress to favor the status quo.[202] The President of the Chamber Special Tax Reform Committee affirmed that the issue of state autonomy unites deputies against changes in the ICMS structure: "Even if the governor and deputy are not from the same party, the deputy will vote with the governor on these matters."[203] This means that opposition is widespread: one congressional advisor stated flatly that because of opposition from governors, "the problem with any fiscal reform is that the government's own support base opposes it."[204] In the end, states' resistance to *any* change in the ICMS provides the greatest source of opposition from subnational governments to fiscal reform (See *JB* 4/26/99, p. A-4; *OESP* 7/15/99, p. A-6; *JB* 7/24/99, p. A-2).

The Last Attempts at Fiscal Reform under President Cardoso

For five years the Chamber Special Committee worked on revisions to the President's proposal, but the executive branch never provided leadership and the committee failed to overcome the resistance of the states and municipalities to deep changes in the tax system. In an attempt to reinitiate negotiations, in late May 2000 the government sent new proposals to the Chamber leadership, but this proposal made no headway because it offered little that was

---

[200] The government's initial proposal also suggested fusing a municipal-level service tax with a new ICMS. Mayors and municipal finance secretaries immediately lobbied against this idea for the same reason that states oppose changing the ICMS: a smaller-scale "fiscal war" exists at the municipal level. The central government retreated on this item. The Chamber Special Committee's proposal included a similar change, and the same interests continued to oppose it. See *OESP* 8/14/99, p. A-5.

[201] Interview with Clóvis Panzarini.   [202] Interview with Everardo Maciel.

[203] Interview with Germano Rigotto.   [204] Interview with Maria Emília Coimbra.

new and because deputies and senators refused to believe the government sincerely desired to alter the revenue system at a time when central-government revenue was on the rise (*FSP* 5/28/00, p. A-5; *OESP* 5/30/01, p. A-2; *OESP* 5/31/01, p. A-4; *OESP* 6/8/00, p. A-11; *OESP* 7/7/00, p. A-6; *FSP* 7/15/00, p. A-14). Similarly, in June 2001 the government announced a final attempt at a "mini" fiscal reform, admitting that it would leave the attempt to pass a broad reform to the next president (Salomon 2001). Cardoso announced that he would concentrate on extending the life of the "Provisionary" Financial Transactions Contribution (CPMF) until 2004 and on federalizing the ICMS (*FSP* 6/19/01, p. A-7; *FSP* 6/24/01, p. A-11; *OESP* 6/19/01, p. A-7; *OESP* 6/28/01, p. A-4). The limited scope of the proposals disappointed the business community as well as members of Congress who had worked to build consensus for reform (*OESP* 6/30/01, p. A-4 and A-5; *OESP* 6/29/01, p. A-2; *FSP* 6/30/01, p. A-4; *FSP* 6/29/01, p. A-4).

Opposition to the proposed ICMS unification surged immediately. Governors and state secretaries of finance mobilized against the proposal (*OESP* 6/25/01, p. A-5; *OESP* 6/30/01, p. A-4), and congressional opposition quickly emerged. The government thus spent little energy pushing its proposal, and Cardoso soon announced that he would focus on extending the CPMF, a "reform" that contradicts the proposals the president had articulated on the campaign trail.

Brazil needs to overcome the perception that its political institutions encourage economic inefficiency, in order to generate long-term investment and increase the competitiveness of its products. Fiscal reform might help in this regard. However, despite the President's repeated statements, the work of well-intentioned members of Congress and heavy business lobbying, fiscal reform of the type initially advocated failed to advance. Generalized uncertainty about the impact of any potential reform strongly favored the status quo, but this would be true in any country. Thus, the impact of Brazil's federal institutions proves more critical to explaining the failure of fiscal reform. Revenue-sharing rules that state and municipal interests inscribed in the 1988 constitution reduce the executive's interest in broad reform, and state governments fear the loss of political autonomy that would come with reform of the ICMS. Indeed, fiscal reform appeared much less likely at the end of Cardoso's administration than it did at the beginning: the central government's increased reliance on "contributions" over the 1990s makes it less and less interested in reform, and the elimination of other mechanisms of industrial policy (through privatization of state-government banks and other corporations as well as the limitations on debt levels) means that states are even more reluctant to relinquish the power to use tax exemptions as an industrial policy tool. In sum, horizontal predatory federalism continues unabated and may have actually increased in intensity during the Cardoso administration.

THE "FISCAL RESPONSIBILITY LAW"

The most recent attempt to control vertical predatory federalism in Brazil is the "Fiscal Responsibility Law" (FRL).[205] The FRL aims to eliminate the perception that states and municipalities enjoy soft budget constraints: it sets strict debt limits for all levels of government and expressly prohibits the central government from refinancing subnational debt. The FRL also requires all subnational governments to publish an accounting of revenue and expenditures, and it outlines penalties for public officials who violate the law. In essence, the FRL attempts to legislate fiscal prudence (Mendes 1999; Afonso and Melo 2000; Cavalcanti and Quadros 2000; Kopits et al. 2000; Miranda 2001).[206]

The FRL had broad support within the executive branch, and although it appears to impose severe restrictions on subnational policy autonomy, state governors generally favored the bill (the fact that it only took a year to get through Congress indicates the relatively low degree of opposition).[207] Governors did not object to the FRL because the central government had already resolved their debt issues by 1998 and because the law clarifies the conditions under which governors may dismiss employees and/or reduce public-employees' salaries (*JB* 3/9/99, p. A-3). As explained previously, with the advent of the *Plano Real* and the subsequent end of inflation, governors no longer prefer to use the state government as an employment program and are far more reluctant to give pay raises, because doing so leaves them without resources to invest in pork-barrel projects. The FRL thus provides a useful excuse to explain their change in tactics.

The FRL is a major step forward in terms of strengthening hard budget constraints in Brazil. The main question surrounding its implementation is whether its regulations will "stick" in the long run. An examination of the law reveals several serious flaws that generate some doubt. This is of course an exercise in crystal-ball gazing, but I bring these points to the fore because the FRL is so rigid and detailed that it will be extremely difficult for executive-branch officials to fully comply with it. The FRL also expresses an extremely narrow (and pre-Keynesian) vision of what constitutes "good government," namely the absence of deficit spending. More generally, the idea that the FRL "seeks to develop a new fiscal culture" (Tavares et al. 1999, 24) runs counter to Brazilian history by attempting to legislate changes in behavioral norms. It remains to be seen whether the FRL can break with this history of laws passed that are ultimately ignored because the political elite lack incentives to obey, despite potentially harsh penalties. In

---

[205] *Lei Complementar* N° 101, of May 4, 2000.
[206] The FRL supersedes the "Lei Camata," which regulated personnel expenditures at the subnational level, as well as Senate Resolutions 49 and 78, which regulated subnational finances.
[207] Interview with Pedro Novais.

this regard, several potential problems with and loopholes in the FRL merit attention:

1) Despite a tremendous effort on the part of the central government to educate subnational officials, many of Brazil's municipalities still lack the technical capacity to fulfill the bill's administrative requirements for budget planning and transparency. In the law's first year, 25.2 percent of Brazil's municipalities did not send in the required paperwork (Brasil, Ministério da Fazenda, Secretaria do Tesouro Nacional 2001a, 2001b). And because the evaluation of the municipalities' accounts takes time, at the time of this writing there is no way to assess whether the accounts of the remaining 75 percent are entirely "in order" or not. Moreover, I am assuming that the municipalities that failed to send in the paperwork all did so for technical reasons, although this may not be the case: as one deputy stated, "Mayors just won't know how to comply, or will claim not to know how to."[208] Whether for technical or political reasons, the failure to send in the required paperwork may lead to political problems, with selective application of the FRL's rules and punishments (Mendes 1999; Cavalcanti and Quadros 2000; Kopits et al. 2000).[209]

2) If Brazil's economy slows down, pressure will increase to revisit the issue of subnational debt and debt refinancing. In June of 2001, just two weeks after President Cardoso had announced the possibility of rolling blackouts due to an energy crisis, and thus before the economic impact of any blackouts could be observed, several state governments signaled a desire to once again refinance their debts when the energy crisis forced them to alter their revenue forecasts (*FSP* 6/21/01, p. B-12). This is just the tip of the iceberg. If a deep economic crisis emerges and tax revenues decline such pressures will spread. The law does provide escape clauses to modify debt levels or repayment periods in crisis situations, but the sections of the bill that permit debt-payment extensions or debt-level increases are vague and thus subject to political manipulation (W. Oliveira 2000, 20).[210]

---

[208] Interview with Gastão Vieira.

[209] Moreover, a good portion of existing municipal debt was not part of the agreement. This will create pressures for "clarification" of the Law (Cavalcanti and Quadros 2000, p. 31).

[210] Article 30, paragraph 6 states that the president can request a change in subnational debt levels if Brazil's economic situation becomes "unstable" or if exchange rate or monetary policies are "altered." Article 66 contains other loopholes: the length of debt repayment terms can be doubled if national, regional, or state GDP growth is less than 1 percent in the previous four quarters; debt repayment terms can be extended by up to one year if the Senate "recognizes" a "drastic" change in monetary or exchange-rate policy; or, if a public calamity is declared (either at state or municipal level), then all the terms for debt repayment as well as the limits on personnel expenditures are invalid, for the duration of the calamity.

3) Similarly, a huge loophole exists in the FRL that the central government has attempted to hide. In principle, the FRL prohibits any
   spending increase if an equal tax increase is also not proposed. However, Article 17, paragraph 6 of the FRL states that this does not
   hold in the case of raises for federal public servants as per Article 37,
   paragraph 10 of the federal constitution. Article 37, paragraph 10 resulted from the administrative reform constitutional amendment that
   passed in 1998 (*Emenda Constitucional* #19). It states that federal-
   government employees' salaries must be adjusted every year, on the
   same date, without reference to the inflation rate. In April of 2001,
   the Supreme Court ordered the executive branch to comply with this
   rule (government employees had not received a raise since Cardoso
   took office), and to make the raise retroactive to 1999, the year that
   the administrative reform amendment took effect. The government
   estimated that such a raise would ruin its effort to run a budget
   surplus (*Correio Braziliense* 8/10/01, p. 20), and attempted to claim
   that a raise would contradict the FRL (See e.g., *FSP* 8/10/01, p. A-5).
   However, this is technically not true. More importantly, if and when
   federal-government employees receive a raise, state- and municipal-
   government officials will find themselves under pressure to grant similar raises (see e.g., *OESP* 8/20/01, p. A-4; *OESP* 8/22/01, p. A-5).
   This may increase the pressure on Congress for "relief" from the FRL's
   restrictions in the future.[211]
4) The procedure for changing subnational debt levels, one of the bill's
   centerpieces, has *not* been depoliticized. Under the FRL, to change debt
   levels the president sends a request to the Senate, which approves or
   rejects the request (Article 30). The difference between the FRL and the
   previous system is that the Senate had greater independence to determine subnational debt levels, whereas now the President has agenda
   control. However, this implies that subnational debt levels depend
   on the state of executive-legislative relations, which are a function
   of a number of political factors. For example, if the president needs
   Senate support to gain approval for some unrelated proposal, he might
   have to log roll and concede on subnational debt. The Senate might
   also find it politically expedient to use its prerogatives to manipulate how subnational governments calculate current and/or estimated
   future revenue, allowing for either increased debt levels or lower
   payments.[212]
5) By setting one uniform rule for fiscal policy across Brazil, the FRL as-
   sumes that such uniformity is adequate across Brazil's vast and varied

---

[211] Interviews with Eduardo Graeff and Raúl Velloso.
[212] Interview with Cosentino Tavares. The Chamber of Deputies has a long history of over-
   estimating federal government revenue in order to include more pork-barrel projects in the
   budget (Serra 1994).

territory. The same rules assume that exogenous economic shocks will affect each and every state and municipality similarly, which is highly unrealistic (Kopits et al. 2000). The FRL essentially prohibits state governments from engaging in countercyclical spending due to a regional slowdown. To take examples from the commodities market, if a sugar glut hits one year, tax revenue in several states will be hard hit while others will be largely unaffected. If the next year soybeans are in surplus, different states may experience a slowdown. As written, the law does not allow for potential regional or local necessities to be addressed independently of national dictates.[213] This has been likened to a straightjacket, with the possible implication that "As has been common in Brazil, this means that soon everyone will ignore it, which will make everyone an outlaw, which will mean that no one will be punished."[214]

6) Enforcement of the law will generate tremendous political problems, even under normal conditions.[215] Article 59 of the bill states that the state and national legislatures; the state and national Courts of Accounts (*Tribunais de Contas*); and the *Ministério Público* will oversee the compliance with the law's rules. This suggests that enforcement of the FRL is a function of the agility, capacity, political independence, and objectivity of these same agencies. It is true that the *Ministério Público* has made great strides in recent years, but there is no guarantee that it will have the resources to oversee the executive, legislative, and judicial branches in 27 states and over 5,500 municipalities. As for the other agencies, as Brazil's Attorney General (one of the bill's main authors) recognized,[216] they are notoriously slow; lack administrative and technical capacity; and are highly politicized, especially at the state and municipal level (see Abrucio 1998; Mendes 1999).

This exploration of problems with the FRL has been an exercise in futurology, which for political scientists is always dangerous. Still, given the attention the FRL has received, we ought to explore whether it contributes to ending vertical predatory federalism in Brazil without creating other problems at the same time. The FRL is a step in the right direction toward eliminating soft budget constraints, but the distance between the legal rules and the political culture is still great. At all levels of government there are already indications that politicians are searching for ways to skirt the law's rules (Miranda 2001). More importantly, despite the central government's strenuous efforts to publicize the law, and despite the changes due to the end of inflation, it is by no means obvious that Brazilian voters care any more about deficit spending in particular now than they did before the Real, or that they understand the complex relationship between deficit spending and

---

[213] Interview with Clóvis Panzarini.   [214] Interviews with Yoshiako Nakano.
[215] Interviews with Clóvis Panzarini, Weder de Oliveira, Gastão Vieira, and Sérgio Miranda.
[216] Interview with Gilmar Mendes.

inflation. Consequently, Brazilian politicians still lack *electoral* incentives to engage in fiscally responsible behavior. If Brazilian voters were fiscal conservatives, there would be little need to legislate fiscal responsibility (this merits research).

When voters not only do not hold politicians to account for deficit spending but in some cases even encourage profligacy, only an effort to legislate fiscal prudence remains.[217] As a result, a change in political or economic circumstances will be the law's true test.[218] Brazil has had too many examples of laws passed with good intentions that have failed to be enforced. Without there being some electoral punishment for violating the spirit of that law, it is unclear that the political will exists to punish violations of the letter of the law. To continue the provocation: will *Lei Complementar* 101, the Fiscal Responsibility Law, have as much lasting power as did *Lei Complementar* 24, which "ended" the fiscal war in 1975?[219] The passage of the FRL reflects a conjunction of political and economic circumstances, but Brazilian history teaches us to remain skeptical about whether behavior will follow the law if circumstances change.

EVALUATING THE EVOLUTION OF FEDERALISM UNDER CARDOSO

The emerging debate about the relationship between political institutions and democratic governability in Brazil is rooted in differing perceptions of Brazil's postauthoritarian experience. Some scholars see volatility, fragmentation, veto players, and thus potential instability, while others see emerging coherence, regularization of patterns of competition, and thus governability (Palermo 2000). These perceptions are partly a function of the period analyzed: for example, it is easier to accept a characterization of pre-1994 as wracked by political crises, a relatively weak presidency, and party-system fragmentation, while after 1994 a stronger and more coherent executive branch has organized broad legislative support. However, one should never suppose that the power and legitimacy of today's leader will transfer to tomorrow's leader, and ultimately I side with those who see Brazilian institutions as obstacles. In particular, the relationship between federalism,

---

[217] Or, as one budget expert affirmed, "The government's marketing of the Law is more important than the Law's rules themselves. After all, the central government doesn't really comply with the law, it can't really." Interview with Weder de Oliveira.

[218] Interviews with Raúl Velloso, Robison Gonçalves de Castro, Clóvis Panzarini, Weder de Oliveira, Gastão Vieira, and Sérgio Miranda.

[219] The FRL, if complied with, will have the biggest impact on the states and cities that contributed most to the subnational debt crisis, that is the richer states and municipalities in the South and Southeast regions. By nationalizing the issue of subnational debt, and requiring congressional action to modify the tight regulations, the FRL thus increases the veto power of the poorer states over the autonomous policy proposals and goals of the wealthier states, which can no longer choose to use debt as a policy tool if they wish.

the party system, and the president's ability to generate legislative support remains problematic.

Without a shadow of a doubt, the Real Plan heralded important political and economic changes. The political consequences of the plan provided the central government with unprecedented leverage over subnational governments, forcing a resolution of the subnational debt issue and creating propitious conditions for the privatization and/or restructuring of state banks and the passage of the FRL. For some, these and other policy reforms have permanently eliminated the political incentives that encouraged subnational governments to take advantage of the central government, and generally increased the degree of political centralization in Brazil (e.g., Afonso and Melo 2000, 19).[220] This argument implies that the Cardoso administration's policies produced deep and lasting changes in the nature of Brazilian federalism. I agree that the pre- and post-1994 periods differ in important ways, and that Cardoso's policies have attenuated some of the worst aspects of vertical predatory federalism. However, I suggest that Cardoso's emphasis on controlling fiscal profligacy at the subnational level has not fundamentally changed the political dynamics of Brazilian federalism. Confronting a highly legitimate, broadly supported president under relatively stable economic conditions, subnational interests *still* played a key role in shaping national politics. This suggests that federalism remains an important potential obstacle for future administrations.

Four points support this conclusion. First, as shown in this chapter, even a strong president like Cardoso could not unilaterally impose his most-preferred course of action. Policy output instead resulted from negotiations between the central and subnational governments. Subnational interests altered important aspects of the president's agenda and forced Cardoso to abandon key intergovernmental reform proposals. For example, as Garman et al. (2001) explained, Congress refused to accept the executive's initial proposal for resolving the state bank crisis, and ultimately forced the government to pay a much higher price for a solution. This was also true of the *Fundo Social de Emergência*, pension reform, administrative reform, fiscal reform, and other policies not discussed here (Abrucio and Ferreira Costa 1998; A. Souza 1999).

Second, forcing subnational governments to privatize banks or adjust their accounts reveals only one column of the accounting ledger. When evaluating the balance of intergovernmental relations during this period, we cannot simply count subnational "losses" without also counting the political and economic cost for each central government "gain." The Kandir Law provides a clear example: the ICMS exemption makes Brazilian exporters more competitive, but to benefit industry the central government has had to come

---

[220] The political consequences of recent changes in education and health funding also merit investigation.

up with billions of Reais to reimburse subnational governments for their lost revenue. More generally, to encourage states to conform to its vision of the requirements for economic stabilization, the central government has assumed the lion's share of the costs of reform. The bottom line includes both the billions of dollars in direct subsidies and the assumption of subnational debts, both of which have contributed to the rise in Brazil's national debt from 30.4 percent of GDP in 1994 to 49.3 percent in 2000 (OESP 6/30/01, p. B-4). This is the policy straightjacket of the Real Plan: the government could not maintain confidence in the Real without assuming subnational debt, but the subsequent increase in the national debt undermines both the principles of the Real Plan and Brazil's long-term macroeconomic health (Giambiagi 2000). The increase in Brazil's national debt imposes a heavy burden on the central government that will restrict its policy mobility far into the future.

Third, Cardoso's ability to shape the agenda was the fruit of contextual factors that may not recur. If not for the palpable threat of a Lula victory in 1994, Cardoso might not have been able to construct a broad political coalition and garner the political support for the Real Plan in the first place. The stable economy also made him an ideal candidate for reelection in 1998, and economic growth boosted tax revenue and helped keep government accounts in the black. Such conditions will be difficult to replicate given Brazil's still-fragmented party system and the country's continuing exposure to the vicissitudes of the international economy.

Even given these extremely favorable political conditions, perhaps better conditions than any other democratically elected Brazilian president, congressional resistance still forced Cardoso to offer substantial concessions to pass many of his most important proposals. In presidential systems this is normal, but I raise the point to highlight that future presidents may not enjoy such broad support, and that therefore executive-legislative relations might be more problematic. For example, future presidential elections might not resemble 1994 or 1998 but rather 1989, where the government had no strong candidate and the field was highly fragmented. Given the strength of gubernatorial coattails even in 1994 and 1998 (Chapter 5), a president elected with a less-solid base of support may encounter problems Cardoso never faced. Indeed, the pillars of Brazil's fiscal health stand on bills that have sunset provisions: the *Desvinculação da Receita da União*, which began its life as the *Fundo Social de Emergência*, and the *Contribuição Provisória sobre Movimentação Financeira*, the contribution on financial transactions. A president with less political authority or legitimacy may have greater difficulty winning congressional support for extending these provisions, jeopardizing many of the gains Cardoso has achieved.

The last contextual factor compares the situation state governments faced during the mid-1990s relative to what they might face in the future. State governments' moment of deepest crisis came at the start of the Cardoso administration. Somewhat ironically, the very success of Cardoso's efforts to cleanse subnational finances implies that states are unlikely to be at such a political disadvantage again. (And even in their moment of weakness governors and their ambassadors in Congress forced Cardoso to assume the lion's share of the costs for restructuring state finances, shaped negotiations over the Real Plan, and vetoed several reform proposals.)

Fourth – and most importantly for our analysis of the evolution of intergovernmental relations – despite subnational governments' relative weakness at the onset of the Cardoso administration, recent reforms have not reshaped the fundamental elements of Brazilian federalism. There are three core facets of Brazilian federalism: the constitutionally established resource base of subnational governments; the political power of state governors; and the organization of the traditional political elite and their articulation of subnational interests in the national Congress (Mainwaring and Samuels 1997). None of these have suffered dramatic alterations. As noted, the Real Plan was not a permanent fiscal reform; ultrapresidentialism still characterizes the institutions of state government (Abrucio 2001); and finally, electoral processes and political careers remain driven by subnational dynamics.[221]

As Abrucio (1998) has argued, the "Gordian knot" of Brazilian federalism, and thus the root of its predatory nature, is the president's need to obtain support for his proposals in the legislature. Brazilian parties appear to give the president cohesive support on the floor of the legislature (Figueiredo and Limongi 2000a). Yet appearances may be deceiving, because roll-call votes are taken only *after* the president has negotiated away contentious points or distributed whatever political goods deputies had demanded to approve the proposal. A more fundamental political question is the degree to which legislators obstruct or modify the president's proposals at earlier stages of the process, away from the president's or their party leaders' preferences.

What determines the degree of initial support? In any country, legislators may support party leaders or presidents from the start because they agree with the proposal. Or, if they don't support the proposal on principle, they might nevertheless indicate support if the president or party leaders can constrain or induce cohesive behavior. In Brazil, can the president or party leaders use "carrots" or "sticks" to encourage or force deputies to toe the line? The answer is *no*. The reason is that neither the president nor

---

[221] Privatization of state-owned firms occurred at both the state and national levels, taking substantial "political currency" out of circulation at both levels because jobs could no longer be handed out to political cronies. It is thus not clear whether privatization has strengthened or weakened one level of government over the other. For example, privatization means that the central government gained regulatory power while losing a form of currency that it could use in negotiations with Congress and subnational governments. The aspect that is considered "more important" for politics depends on one's point of view as well as the object of investigation. In any case, privatization has apparently not implied a redefinition of the fault lines of Brazilian electoral politics or of executive-legislative relations at either the national or subnational level.

national party leaders determine incumbents' career trajectories, because political careers are not directed at rising through the ranks of a national party or building up seniority in the national legislature. Brazilian presidents possess weak partisan powers (Mainwaring and Shugart 1997), and Brazilian national party leaders lack the tools to "whip" their back-benchers, or even to get them to show up for votes (Mainwaring 1999; Ames 2000). Party switching continues unabated (C. Melo 2000);[222] state-based political elites and not national partisan organizations continue to determine nomination for deputy elections; and deputy campaigns continue to be conducted in statewide districts with minimal input from national party organizations. Threats to use the stick sound hollow when incumbents can discount the future role of those who wield the stick. If deputies' career prospects depended on appeasing national party leaders (because, for example, these leaders controlled access to ministerial positions) they would have stronger incentives to toe the line. Likewise, if access to the pork-barrel were more important to deputies' careers, deputies would be less reluctant to miss important votes or indicate initial opposition to presidential proposals.

The implication is clear: the source of the resilience of Brazilian federalism resides in the absence of the president's and national parties' resources to constrain or induce legislators' career goals. The Brazilian president does possess strong institutional powers (Shugart and Carey 1992; Power 1998; Figueiredo and Limongi 2000a), but traditional political elites remain fundamentally organized at the state level, not the national level (Hagopian 1996); subnational actors and processes do influence incumbents' careers (Abrucio 1998); elections for federal deputy largely follow state-based dynamics, not national politics (Chapter 5); and deputies' own career goals generate strong incentives to advance the interests of both state and municipal governments within the national congress (chapters 1–4). In this way, federalism affects the initial calculations Brazilian presidents make when assessing the degree of legislative support for their proposals.[223] Federalism complicates the president's agenda because the forces that affect and direct Brazilian legislators' careers remain rooted at the subnational, not the national level.

What would it take to truly remake Brazil's federal contract? Political reforms to unravel the Gordian knot of Brazilian federalism would have to alter the forces that shape and direct Brazilian politicians' careers, by reducing the influence of subnational forces, by making state and local politics less attractive, or by increasing the attractiveness and importance of national

---

[222] As of August 2, 2001, about two-thirds of the way through the 1999–2002 legislature, 145 *titulares* and *suplentes* (25.4 percent of the total) had changed parties a total of 216 times, somewhat ahead of the previous legislature's pace.

[223] These proposals may be intimately related to intergovernmental relations (as I have focused on here), or may be part of a complex logroll where presidential support for subnational governments' claims is exchanged for legislative support for a presidential proposal in an area unrelated to federalism.

parties in incumbents' careers. However, little if any change in these directions occurred during the Cardoso administration. Such reforms would have to alter the resilient basis of elite political organization and socialization in Brazil, which is unlikely in so short a period. They would also have to circumscribe the state-based nature of political representation, which is also highly unlikely. Finally, reforms would also have to encourage the substantial strengthening of national party organizations. (The impact of changes in the rules regarding electoral alliances imposed by the TSE in early 2002 remain unknown at this time.)

Unfortunately, Cardoso opted to downplay "political" reform, and only pushed one important political-institutional reform during his eight years in office: a constitutional amendment permitting executive-office holders to run for reelection. This allowed Cardoso to clear his own path to victory in 1998, but it has had a potentially unintended impact at the subnational level: the ability to run for reelection reinforces incumbents' dominance of the political scene, which tends to scare off potentially viable challengers, thus reducing the level of political competition (Abrucio and Samuels 1997). In this way, the one political reform on which Cardoso expended substantial resources works to *increase* the power of the governors in state politics, and consequently in national politics.

The Cardoso administration's demonstrated ability to respond to Brazil's national and subnational fiscal crises does not signify the consolidation of a new federal pact (Abrucio and Ferreira Costa 1998; Abrucio 2000; Kugelmas 2001; Garman et al. 2001). History should teach us a lesson about the resilience of Brazilian federalism. Like the aftermath of both the *Estado Novo* and the 1964–85 military regime, federalism will continue to shape the contours of Brazilian politics long after whatever changes the Cardoso administration introduced have become history. On balance, Cardoso has given the central government needed coherence, but his administration has not changed the fundamental importance of subnational government in Brazil and thus of federalism in Brazilian national politics. His policies did not alter the structure of political power within states, did not reshape politicians' career incentives and the forces that shape their careers, did not alter the predatory nature of interstate competition, and most importantly, none of the changes introduced are set in stone. Thus, federalism and subnational interests will continue to play an extraordinarily prominent role in Brazilian national politics.

Conclusion

This book began with two questions: "What is the structure of political careers in Brazil?" and "What are some of the observable consequences of political ambition in Brazil?" These questions are at the heart of the theory of political ambition, namely, that individual politicians are motivated by the desire for office, and that they will act strategically to achieve their career goals. This notion is a useful simplification of reality, a heuristic device that provides insight into Brazilian politicians' behavior as well as into other far-ranging questions.

The first section of the book answered the first question, providing empirical evidence to support the notion that Brazilian federal deputies are not primarily motivated by a desire for a long-term legislative career, but rather that their ambitions are directed at positions outside the Chamber, particularly in the executive branch of subnational government. Having described the structure of political careers in Brazil, Section 2 demonstrated how state-level political dynamics affect elections to the national legislature, revealing the pressures on federal deputies to "represent" their state's interests while in Congress. In the third section of the book, I attempted to answer the second question and illustrate the consequences of the combination of federalism and ambition in Brazil. I showed that the reelection assumption cannot explain Brazilian deputies' famous pork-barreling behavior, and how an explanation that relies on extralegislative ambition and pressures from subnational governments, particularly states, provides a better explanation. I also showed how ambition and federalism help understand the process of fiscal decentralization as well as Congress' reaction to many of President Fernando Henrique Cardoso's most important attempts at political reform. These findings should encourage additional research into the consequences of political ambition and facilitate interpretation of other policy processes in Brazil.

This research also has several general implications. First, my approach supports the use of rational-choice methods to analyze politics outside the

United States, but with the important caveat that the assumptions about politicians' behavior that "work" for the United States may not apply outside the United States. I agree that one can assume that office-seeking motivates individual politicians, yet the offices that politicians seek in different countries might differ significantly, and these differences will have observable consequences in terms of legislative behavior and electoral and policy processes. For comparativists interested in exploring how the "electoral connection" works in Latin America or elsewhere, the lesson here is that while the method can travel across national boundaries, the particular motivational assumption that we adopt may not. Substantial research justifies the use of rational-choice tools to explore a wide range of topics in the United States. To develop more appropriate assumptions and thus support the applicability of rational-choice methods outside the United States, scholars ought to focus on the structure of political careers.

Second, my research, undertaken after ten years of democracy in Brazil, points to the ever-increasing importance of legislative institutions and executive-legislative relations in new democracies. As numerous scholars have done for the United States, I have demonstrated that politicians' career motivations in Brazil have significant consequences for the structure of the division of labor within the legislature and on the nature of executive-legislative relations. The same is no doubt the case in other countries, but the actors and interests that shape these relationships no doubt also differ. For example, in Argentina and Russia, recent research (e.g., Jones 1997 on Argentina; Treisman 1999 on Russia) demonstrates that provincial interests play a powerful role in national elections and policy making. On the other hand, in Mexico, Chile, or Venezuela (prior to 1999), national party organizations probably affect policy processes a great deal more.

Some of the questions my research generates include "How do politicians' different career incentives play out in terms of the legislature's relations with the president?" "What institutions or actors affect executive-legislative relations *through* the legislature?" and "How can the interrelationship between political ambition and political institutions account for the variation in executive-legislative relations observed across countries?" Many new democracies are still undergoing political transitions of some sort. For example, subnational elections and actors are gaining importance in Mexico. To what extent do politicians' emerging career interests at the subnational level drive these national transformations? How do federal dynamics affect the prospects for democratic consolidation? While out of necessity my research focused on only one country, future research ought to attempt to derive more substantial comparative conclusions.

Third, my conclusions have important implications regarding the effects of different political career structures and institutional configurations on both the process and output of democratic representation. I have not explored this question in great depth, but the "Mayhewian" model of a U.S.

House member implies a very distinct kind of "electoral connection" between voter and representative. Of course, the "electoral connection" in the United States may be unique for any number of reasons having to do with the particulars of U.S. history, as the electoral connection in other countries might also differ for similar reasons. Regardless, my research helps to identify some of the key factors that might account for such differences in the "efficiency" or "representativeness" of democratic government or democratic accountability or responsiveness, and in a different way than the existing literature suggests. Where politicians aim to spend a considerable portion of their career in the national legislature, they will most likely take a *relatively* greater interest in national policy making, instead of focusing purely on localistic or regional concerns. In the United States, representatives combine membership in a national party with representation of local interests. Both national partisan membership and the "personal vote" are important. In Brazil, on the other hand, while the leftist parties may be exceptions, for the vast majority of congressional deputies national partisan images are relatively unimportant, and few politicians see a career in the legislature as a way to influence policy.

The reason for this is not simply that Brazilian culture and history preclude strong parties or a strong legislature, but that Brazilian culture and history have shaped the political opportunity structure so that contemporary Brazilian politicians favor state and municipal interests while serving as national legislators. In particular, because of Brazil's history of comparatively strong federalism, state-based interests will continue to play a crucial role in shaping electoral and policy processes. This will also continue to contribute to the fragility of national partisan attachments at both the elite and mass levels in Brazil.

As a final thought I should address the question of just how "path dependent" or "sticky" the structure of political careers is in Brazil. While it is true that Brazil's history of strong federalism and a relatively weak legislature probably limits the extent to which the country might come to resemble a unitary system or a system like the United States with greater balance between the executive and legislative branches of government, we still should ask whether Brazil is fated to have comparatively weak national parties, presidential candidates with weak coattails, and a legislature full of politicians more interested in seeking an extralegislative position than a career in the legislature and in defending the interests of their states and municipalities rather than defending coherent national platforms.

In this regard, two recent institutional changes may be important. First, executive-level office holders (presidents, governors, and mayors) can now run for reelection for one consecutive term. The 1998 elections were the first time in Brazilian history that all incumbent executives could stand for reelection. Many were reelected, and the mere presence of the incumbent in the race transformed the nature of electoral politics. Reelection has already shaped all politicians' strategies, and may also affect deputies' career paths. Given incumbents tend to make naturally strong candidates for re-election, some deputies may refrain from running for the statehouse or for mayor and instead might decide to run for deputy again. Even if the rates at which incumbents *win* reelection remains relatively low, this ought to increase slightly the average length of a congressional career in Brazil. In the long run, this might mean that some deputies would become more interested in a legislative career, which in turn could transform the internal structure of the Chamber, shape executive-legislative relations, or even change the nature of Brazil's national political parties. However, it took decades of the evolution of political careers in the United States for the "textbook" House to emerge after World War II. Similar changes, if they occur at all in Brazil, will likewise only emerge in the long run.

Second, elections for president; governor; senator; and federal and state deputies are now all held concurrently. In the 1945–64 period this was not the case, nor was it the case prior to 1994 for the postauthoritarian period. Scholars such as Shugart (1995) have shown how a country's electoral cycle can affect its party system. In the United States, scholars have long argued that the concurrence of presidential and legislative elections has structured national partisan competition. As I demonstrated in Chapter 5, such links are extremely tenuous in Brazil, while the connection between gubernatorial and legislative elections is strong. The effect of presidential elections on legislative elections in the United States took some decades to emerge. Thus, as with potential changes in the structure of political careers, it may also take decades before the concurrence of presidential and legislative elections results in strong presidential coattails in Brazil.

These two institutional changes must also be weighed against the broader and more profound decentralization process that began in the early 1980s. Decentralization strengthened subnational governments considerably at the expense of the central government, and increased the attractiveness of positions in subnational government. All the empirical evidence I gathered indicates that as Brazil redemocratized, a centrifugal dynamic characterized the nature of political ambition in Brazil, as subnational politics and extralegislative positions gained importance in politicians' careers. Despite any recent reforms, federalism will continue to shape political ambition and thus will continue to shape executive-legislative relations in Brazil far into the future.

Appendix 1

Coding of Political Positions by Level of Government

1. The following positions were coded as "national level" (the order is random):
   (a.) Ambassador to the United Nations or another country
   (b.) Chief of Staff to the President
   (c.) Official in the Bank of Brazil in the Federal District
   (d.) Minister of State (Health, Foreign Relations, Education, etc.)
   (e.) Interim President
   (f.) Interim Prime Minister (Brazil briefly had a parliamentary system in 1963)
   (g.) Judge, *Tribunal Federal de Recursos* (an Appeals Court)
   (h.) Monetary council member
   (i.) Minister, *Tribunal de Contas da União* (spending oversight organization)
   (j.) Minister, *Supremo Tribunal Federal* (Supreme Court Justice)
   (k.) Director or President, NOVACAP (Parastatal that organized the construction of Brasília)
   (l.) Minister, *Tribunal de Contas do Estado* of a state not the deputy's home state (usually the DF)
   (m.) Minister, *Tribunal Regional de Trabalho* (Labor Court; not the deputy's home state)
   (n.) Mayor of the Federal District (before Brasilia had a governor, it had an appointed mayor)
   (o.) President
   (p.) National Revenue Service delegate in the Federal District
   (q.) *Caixa Econômica Federal* (government-owned savings and loan) official
   (r.) National Economic Council member
   (s.) Judge, state not the deputy's home state
   (t.) Special advisor to the President
   (u.) Secretary of State in the Federal District

(v.) Vice-President of Brazil

(w.) Executive Council member, National Industrial Council

2. The following positions were coded as "state level" (the order is random):

(a.) Governor

(b.) Vice-Governor

(c.) Chief of Staff to the Governor

(d.) Minister or Counselor (the position title depends on the state), *Tribunal de Contas do Estado*

(e.) Minister or Counselor, *Tribunal de Contas dos Municípios do Estado* (These organizations oversee municipal spending decisions. However, governors nominate the ministers, and tend to use them to politically intimidate mayors. Thus, it is a state-level position.)

(f.) State deputy

(g.) Bank of Brazil official, deputy's home state

(h.) Director, state-government supply company

(i.) Director, state-government social assistance organization

(j.) Senator

(k.) Interventor (a nominated governor)

(l.) State-government–owned bank director (e.g., BANESPA, BERON, BANERJ)

(m.) Judge, deputy's home state

(n.) Director, state-government–owned parastatal (e.g., electric company, telephone company)

(o.) State Secretary (Education, Health, Security, etc.)

3. The following positions were coded as "municipal level" (the order is random):

(a.) Mayor

(b.) Vice-Mayor

(c.) Municipal Secretary (Education, Culture, etc.)

Appendix 2

List of Interviews

I list interviewees in alphabetical order by first name. Not all interviewees are cited in the book – some provided only background information. I include the following information: name, partisan affiliation (if applicable), state of origin, political position held at the time of the interview, any other essential information, followed by the date and place of the interview. Some interviewees may have changed partisan affiliation during their career.

1. Abraham Lincoln Ferreira Cardoso, legislative aide to the PMDB leadership. Brasília, June 25, 1997; June 6, 1999; and June 7, 2000.
2. Adhemar de Barros Filho (PPB-SP) served six terms as federal deputy and as Secretary of Administration of the state of São Paulo. He also served as a member of Subcommittee on Taxes, Participation, and Distribution of Revenue, of the Committee on the Tax System, Budget, and Finances (TPDR/TBF) (the subcommittee that prepared the portion of the constitution that regulated the division of revenues and expenditures across levels of government in Brazil) of the 1987–8 Constitutional Convention. São Paulo, February 28, 1997.
3. Adilor Guglielme, city council member from Iraçá, Santa Catarina. Florianópolis, April 22, 1997.
4. Aglas Watson Barrera, staff economist for a São Paulo state government planning agency. São Paulo, July 16, 1997.
5. Airton Sandoval (PMDB-SP) served four terms as federal deputy. São Paulo, January 13, 1997.
6. Alberto Goldman (PSDB-SP) has served five terms as federal deputy, and has served as Secretary of Government of the state of Sao Paulo, and as Minister of Labor. He was also the Secretary of Administration for the State of São Paulo during the Constitutional Convention. In that capacity he acted as the liaison between the state government and the state's congressional delegation. São Paulo, November 10, 1996.

7. Aldo Fagundes (PMDB-RS) served four terms as federal deputy and is currently a judge in the Superior Military Tribunal. Brasília, June 6, 1997.
8. Alexandre Pelegi de Abreu, legislative aide to State Deputy Sidney Beraldo (PSDB-SP). São Paulo, September 25, 1996.
9. André Franco Montoro (PSDB-SP) served as senator and governor of the state of São Paulo, and also served two terms as federal deputy. São Paulo, March 17, 1997.
10. Antônio Carlos Pojo do Rêgo, Congressional Liaison for the Ministry of Planning. Brasília, June 13, 1997.
11. Antônio Delfim Netto (PPB-SP) served as Minister of Finance (1967–74), Minister of Agriculture (1979), and Minister of Planning (1979–85). He has also served as federal deputy since 1987. São Paulo, November 18, 1996.
12. Antônio Kandir (PSDB-SP) was first elected deputy in 1994, and was reelected in 1998. He also served as Minister of Planning (1996–8) and Secretary of Political Economy of the Ministry of Finance (1990–1). Brasília, August 7, 2001.
13. Armando Monteiro Neto (PMDB-PE) has been president of the National Industrial Council and the Pernambuco State Industrial Federation, and has served one term as federal deputy. Brasília, June 15, 2000.
14. Athos Pereira, chief of the PT leadership office in the Chamber of Deputies. Brasília, June 10, 1997 and June 6, 1999.
15. Carlos Estevam Martins (PMDB-SP) served as Secretary of Administration and of Education of the state of São Paulo. São Paulo, March 13, 1997.
16. Carmen Ruvira, aide to the PFL-SC statehouse leadership. Florianópolis, April 24, 1997.
17. Catalina Silvério, technical staff, Secretary of Education. São Paulo, September 24, 1996.
18. César Souza (PFL-SC) served one term as federal deputy and then was elected state deputy. Florianópolis, April 23, 1997.
19. Claudiano Manoel de Albuquerque, Coordinator-General of Financial Programming for the Ministry of Finance. Brasilia, June 20, 1997.
20. Clóvis Panzarini, Coordinator of Fiscal Administration for the State of São Paulo. Advised the São Paulo delegation on fiscal issues during the Constitutional Convention. São Paulo, November 4, 1996; July 28, 1999; and June 21, 2000.
21. Dielai C. Pereira, legislative aide to the PMDB leadership and candidate for federal deputy from Rio de Janeiro. Brasília, June 3, 1997.
22. Dyana Isabel Azeredo Dias, legal staff, Secretary of Transportation, Government of the Federal District of Brasília. June 24, 1997.

23. Eduardo Graeff, Special Advisor to President Fernando Henrique Cardoso. Brasília, August 7, 2001.
24. Eloy Galotti Peixoto, aide to the president of the Legislative Assembly of Santa Catarina. Florianópolis, April 22, 1997.
25. Eugênio Greggianin, Chief of Staff of the Congressional Budget Committee. Brasília, June 9, 1997.
26. Everardo Maciel, Secretary of the Federal Revenue Service. Brasília, August 8, 2001.
27. Francisco Küster (PSDB-SC), state deputy and President of the Santa Catarina legislative assembly. Florianópolis, April 23, 1997.
28. Frederico Mazzuquelli, São Paulo Secretary of Planning (1987–90) and Secretary of Finance (1991–4). São Paulo, October 18, 1996.
29. Gastão Viana (PMDB-MA), has served as federal deputy and Secretary of Finance of Maranhão. Brasília, June 1, 2000.
30. Germano Rigotto (PMDB-RS) has served several terms as federal deputy. He was the author of a major fiscal reform proposal in 2000. Brasília, June 6, 2000.
31. Gerson Camata (PMDB-ES). Governor of Espírito Santo from 1983–6, was senator during the Constitutional Convention. Brasília, June 11, 1997.
32. Getúlio Hanashiro (PPB-SP) was *suplente* for federal deputy, served two terms as state deputy, and also served as Municipal Secretary of Transportation of the city of São Paulo. São Paulo, October 30, 1996.
33. Gilmar Mendes Ferreira, Attorney General of Brazil. Brasília, August 15, 2001.
34. Gonzaga Mota (PMDB-CE) has served as governor and federal deputy from the state of Ceará. Brasília, June 11, 1997.
35. Ivo Wanderlinde (PMDB-SC). Member of the finances committee in the Constitutional Convention. President of a parastatal in Santa Catarina. Florianópolis, April 24, 1997.
36. Jacques Wagner (PT-BA) has served three terms as federal deputy. Brasília, June 20, 1997 and June 6, 2000.
37. Jarbas Passarinho (PPB-PA) served as governor and senator from the state of Pará, and Minister of Justice under President Collor. Brasília, June 13, 1997.
38. Jefferson Peres (PDT-AM), city council member from Manaus and then senator from the state of Amazonas. Brasília, June 6, 2000.
39. João Henrique (PMDB-PI) has served three terms as federal deputy. He also served as Secretary of Education, and as Secretary of Government of the state of Piauí. Brasília, June 3, 1997.
40. João Ricardo Motta is a legislative analyst specializing in fiscal policy in the Chamber of Deputies. Brasília, August 6, 2001.

41. José A. Pinotti (PMDB-SP) served one term as federal deputy. He also served as Secretary of Education and Secretary of Health of the state of São Paulo. São Paulo, January 10, 1997.
42. José Genoíno (PT-SP) has served as federal deputy since 1983. Brasília, July 8, 1999.
43. José Luis Guimarães, Municipal Secretary of Education, Assis, São Paulo, November 17, 1996.
44. José Maria Eymael (PDC-SP), served two terms as federal deputy, and was a member of the TBDR/TBF committee during the Constitutional Convention. São Paulo, December 3, 1996.
45. José Santilli Sobrinho (PSDB-SP) served several terms as federal deputy and twice as mayor of Assis, São Paulo. Assis, November 17 and 18, 1996.
46. José Vaz Bergalo, the PSDB's Chamber Leadership's advisor on budgetary matters. Brasília, June 5, 1997.
47. Lidia Quinan (PMDB-GO) has served two terms as federal deputy. Brasília, June 12, 1997.
48. Lúcio Alcântara (PSDB-CE), senator from the state of Ceará. Brasília, August 14, 2001.
49. Luiz Gonzaga Belluzo served as Secretary of Political Economy in the Ministry of Finance, and as Secretary of Science and Technology and Secretary of Foreign Relations of the state of São Paulo. São Paulo, April 16, 1997.
50. Luiz Tacca, Adjunct Secretary of the National Treasury. Brasília, June 20, 1997.
51. Marcelo Caracas Linhares (PDS-CE) served four terms as federal deputy, as well as Secretary of Planning of the state of Ceará. Fortaleza, February 7, 1997.
52. Maria Emília Coimbra, advisor to the PT Leadership in the Chamber of Deputies for Economic and Tax Policy. Brasília, May 31, 2000.
53. Maria José de Macedo, Coordinator of Regional Programming for the Secretary of Planning and Economy, State of São Paulo. São Paulo, October 22, 1996.
54. Maria Liz Roarelli, coordinator of a group within the National Treasury that oversees the execution of the federal budget *convênios* that distribute money to the states and municipalities. Brasília, June 3, 1997.
55. Milton Mendes (PT-SC) served one term as federal deputy. Brasília, June 20, 1997.
56. Mussa de Jesus Demes (PFL-PI) has served several terms as federal deputy as well as secretary of finance of the states of Ceará and Piauí. Brasília, June 16, 2001.
57. Onofre Quinan (PMDB-GO) was senator from the state of Goiás, and also served as vice-governor of his home state. Brasília, June 10, 1997.

58. Orestes Quércia (PMDB-SP). Senator, Vice-Governor, and Governor of São Paulo (1987–90). La Jolla, California, September 23, 1997.
59. Oswaldo Maldonado Sanches, member of the technical staff of the Congressional Budget Committee. Brasília, June 9, 1997.
60. Paulo Lustosa (PMDB-CE), federal deputy. Brasília, June 7, 1997.
61. Pedro Novais (PMDB-MA), federal deputy. Brasília, June 6, 2000.
62. Plínio de Arruda Sampaio served one term as federal deputy (PT-SP). São Paulo, November 5, 1996.
63. Raúl Velloso, economist. Has worked in various positions in the federal government, was part of the team that elaborated the FSE in 1993–4. Brasília, June 1, 2000 and August 8, 2001.
64. Ricardo Varsano, economist at IPEA-Rio de Janeiro, advised the Ministry of Finance prior and during the Constitutional Convention. Rio de Janeiro, January 23, 1997.
65. Rita Maciel, technical staff of the Congressional Budget Committee. Brasília, June 9, 1997.
66. Robison Gonçalves de Castro has served as director of the Senate's budget committee staff. Brasília, August 8, 2001.
67. Rosilene Gomes da Silva, Legislative Aide to Deputies Milton Mendes and Luci Choinacki (PT-SC). Brasília, June 23, 1997.
68. Salatiel Gomes dos Santos, Coordinator of Internal Control, Superior Electoral Tribunal. Brasília, June 17, 1997.
69. Sandro Scodro (PMDB-GO) served two terms as federal deputy. Brasília, June 11, 1997.
70. Sérgio Miranda (PCdoB-MG) has served two terms as federal deputy. Brasília, June 13, 2000 and August 15, 2001.
71. Sílvio Pessoa (PMDB-PE) has served as state secretary twice and as vice-mayor of Recife. He was serving as federal deputy at the time of the interview (as first suplente). Brasília, June 5, 1997.
72. Thereza Lobo, Economist (CEPP-Rio de Janeiro), advised the Ministry of Finance prior to and during the Constitutional Convention. Rio de Janeiro, January 24, 1997.
73. Tião Viana (PT-AC), senator from the state of Acre. Brasília, June 16, 2000.
74. Valéria Alves de Sousa, Coordinator of Internal Control for the TRE-SP, responsible for overseeing candidates' submission of campaign donation records, for the São Paulo Regional Electoral Tribunal. São Paulo, September 23, 1996.
75. Vigílio Guimarães (PT-MG) has served two terms as federal deputy, and was serving as city council member in Belo Horizonte at the time of the interview. Member of the finances committee during the Constitutional Convention. Belo Horizonte, December 27, 1996.

76. Waldeck Ornellas (PFL-BA) served two terms as federal deputy, as Secretary of Planning, and as senator from the state of Bahia, and has served as Minister of Social Welfare. Brasília, June 16, 1997.
77. Weder de Oliveira, technical staff of the Chamber Budget Committee. Brasília, August 16, 2001.
78. Yeda Crusius (PSDB-RS) served as Minister of Planning under President Franco, ran for mayor of Porto Alegre, and has served two terms as federal deputy. Brasília, June 12, 1997.
79. Yoshiako Nakano served as Secretary of Finance of the state of São Paulo from 1995 to 2000. São Paulo, July 4, 2001.

References

BOOKS AND ARTICLES

Abramson, P. R., John Aldrich, and David Rohde. 1995. *Change and Continuity in the 1992 Elections*. Washington, DC: CQ Press.

Abranches, Sérgio H. Hudson de. 1988. "Presidencialismo de Coalizão: O Dilema Institucional Brasileiro." *Dados* (1):5–33.

Abranches, Sérgio H. Hudson de. 1993. "Strangers in a Common Land: Executive/Legislative Relations in Brazil." In Siegfried Marks, ed., *Political Constraints on Brazil's Economic Development*. New Brunswick: Transaction Publishers.

Abrucio, Fernando. 1996. "Jogos federativos: o modelo predatório brasileiro." Unpublished manuscript. São Paulo: CEDEC.

Abrucio, Fernando. 1998. *Os Barões da Federação: O Poder dos Governadores no Brasil Pós-Autoritário*. São Paulo: Editora Hucitec/Departamento de Ciência Política da USP.

Abrucio, Fernando. 2000. "Os Laços Federativos Brasileiros: Avanços, Obstáculos e Dilemas no Processo de Coordenação Intergovernamental." Unpublished Ph.D. thesis, Universidade de São Paulo.

Abrucio, Fernando. 2001. "A reconstrução das funções governamentais no federalismo brasileiro." In Hofmeister and Carneiro, eds., 2001.

Abrucio, Fernando and David Samuels. 1997. "Efeitos da reeleição no sistema político." *O Estado de São Paulo*, July 20.

Abrucio, Fernando and Valeriano M. F. Costa. 1998. *Reforma do Estado e o Contexto Federativo Brasileiro*. Pesquisas #12, São Paulo: Kondrad Adenauer Stiftung.

Afonso, José Roberto R. Fernando Rezende, and Ricardo Varsano. 1998. "Reforma Tributária no Plano Constitucional: uma Proposta para o Debate." Texto para discussão #606. Rio de Janeiro: IPEA.

Afonso, José Roberto R. and Luiz de Mello. 2000. "Brazil: An Evolving Federation." Presented at the IMF/FAD Seminar on decentralization, Washington D.C.

Affonso, Rui. 1994. "A Crise da Federação no Brasil." *Ensaios FEE* 15(2):321–37.

Affonso, Rui. 1998. "Coordenação ou Recentralização: O Federalismo Brasileiro na Encruzilhada." Presented at the twenty-first meeting of the Latin American Studies Association, Chicago.

Affonso, Rui and Pedro L. B. Silva, eds. 1995. *Reforma Tributária e Federação.* São Paulo: FUNDAP/Editora da UNESP.

Ames, Barry. 1987. *Political Survival: Politicians and Public Policy in Latin America.* Berkeley: University of California Press.

Ames, Barry. 1994. "The Reverse Coattails Effect: Local Party Organization in the 1989 Brazilian Presidential Election." *American Political Science Review* 88(1): 95–111.

Ames, Barry. 1995a. "Electoral Strategy Under Open-List Proportional Representation." *American Journal of Political Science* 39(2):406–33.

Ames, Barry. 1995b. "Electoral Rules, Constituency Pressures, and Pork Barrel: Bases of Voting in the Brazilian Congress." *The Journal of Politics* 57(2):324–43.

Ames, Barry. 2001. *The Deadlock of Democracy in Brazil.* Ann Arbor: University of Michigan Press.

Ames, Barry and David Nixon. 1993. "Understanding New Legislatures? Observations and Evidence from the Brazilian Congress." Paper presented at the 1993 APSA meeting, Washington, D.C.

Amorim Neto, Octávio. 1995. "Cabinet Formation and Party Politics in Brazil." Paper prepared for the 1995 meeting of the Latin American Studies Association, Washington D.C.

Amorim Neto, Octávio and Gary W. Cox. 1997. "Electoral Institutions, Cleavage Structures, and the Number of Parties." *American Journal of Political Science* 41(1):149–74.

Andrade, Régis de Castro (1998). *O Processo de Governo no Município e no Estado: Análise a Partir do caso de São Paulo.* São Paulo: EDUSP.

Araújo, Genésio, ed. 1984. *Personalidades do Piauí.* Teresina, São Paulo: COMEPI.

Arbix, Glauco. 2000. "Guerra Fiscal e Competição Intermunicipal por Novos Investimentos no Setor Automotivo Brasileiro." *Dados – Revista de Ciências Sociais* 43(1):5–43.

Arnold, R. Douglas. 1990. *The Logic of Congressional Action.* New Haven: Yale University Press.

Arretche, Marta. 2000. *Estado Federativo e Políticas Sociais: Determinantes da Descentralização.* Rio de Janeiro: Revan; São Paulo: FAPESP.

Ascher, William. 1989. "Risk, Politics, and Tax Reform." In Malcolm Gillis, ed., *Tax Reform in Developing Countries.* Durham: Duke University Press.

Atkinson, Michael M. and David C. Docherty. 1992. "Moving Right Along: The Roots of Amateurism in the Canadian House of Commons." *Canadian Journal of Political Science* 25(2):295–318.

Avelino Filho, George. 1994. "Clientelismo e Política no Brasil: Revisitando Velhos Problemas." *Novos Estudos CEBRAP* 38:225–40.

Azevedo, Sérgio de and Marcus A. Melo. 1997. "A Política da Reforma Tributária: Federalismo e Mudança Constitucional." *Revista Brasileira de Ciências Sociais* 12:75–99.

Barrera, Aglas W. 1994. "Aspectos Federativos das Relações Intergovernamentais: Brasil 1988–92." In Projeto "Balanço e Perspectivas do Federalismo Fiscal no Brasil," vol. 7, Tomo 2. São Paulo: FUNDAP.

Bastos, Cláudio. 1994. *Dicionário Histórico e Geográfico do Estado do Piauí.* Teresina: Fundação Cultural Monsenhor Chaves.

Beck, Paul Allen. 1996. *Party Politics in America* (8th ed.). New York: Longman.

Beloch, Israel and Abreu, Alzira Alves de (coordinators). 1983. *Dicionário Histórico-Biográfico Brasileiro 1930–83* (4 vols.). Rio de Janeiro: Fundação Getúlio Vargas/Forense Universitária/FINEP.

Bernardes, Franco César. 1996. "Democracia Concentrada: Estrutura do Processo Decisório da Câmara dos Deputados." Unpublished M.A. thesis, IUPERJ.

Bernardo, Paulo. 1997. "Fundo de Estabilização Fiscal." Brasília: Gabinete do Deputado Paulo Bernardo.

Bezerra, Fernando. 1999. "Roteiro seguido pelo Presidente da CNI, Senador Fernando Bezerra, na reunião da CESP que examina a PEC n:175/95, no dia 04/05/99." Mimeo, office of Senator Fernando Bezerra.

Bezerra, Marcos Octávio. 1999. *Em Nome das 'Bases': Política, Favor e Dependência Pessoal.* Rio de Janeiro: Relume Dumará.

Bianco, William T. and Charles H. Stewart III. 1996. "Careerism and Career Ladders in the Early Days: New Hypotheses and New Data." Paper presented at the 1996 meeting of the American Political Science Association, San Francisco.

Bickers, Kenneth and Robert Stein. 1994. "Universalism and the Electoral Connection: A Test and Some Doubts." *Political Research Quarterly* 47:295–317.

Black, Gordon. 1972. "A Theory of Political Ambition: Career Choices and the Role of Structural Incentives." *American Political Science Review.* 66(1):144–59.

Bonfim, Antúlio N. and Anwar Shah. 1991. "Macroeconomic Management and the Division of Powers in Brazil." World Bank Working Paper in Public Economics #WPS567.

Born, Richard. 1984. "Reassessing the Decline of Presidential Coattails: US House Elections from 1952–1980." *The Journal of Politics* 46(1):60–79.

Brady, David, Kara Buckley, and Douglas Rivers, 1999. "The Roots of Careerism in the House of Representatives." *Legislative Studies Quarterly* 24(4):489–510.

Bremaeker, François E. J. de. 1995. "Perfil das Receitas Tributárias dos Municípios Brasileiros." Série Estudos Especiais #7. Rio de Janeiro: Instituto Brasileiro de Administração Municipal.

Buckley, Kara. n.d. "The Rewards of Pork: Particularized Spending and the Electoral Connection, 1870–1930." Unpublished manuscript, Stanford University.

Cain, Bruce, John Ferejohn, and Morris Fiorina. 1987. *The Personal Vote.* Cambridge, MA: Harvard University Press.

Camargo, Aspásia. 1993. "La Federación Sometida: Nacionalismo Desarrollista e Inestabilidad Democrática." In Marcello Carmagnani, ed., *Federalismos Latinoamericanos: México/Brasil/Argentina.* México City: Fondo de Cultura Económica/El Colegio de México.

Cammack, Paul. 1982. "Clientelism and Military Government in Brazil." In Christopher Clapham, ed., *Private Patronage and Public Power: Clientelism in the Modern State.* London: Frances Pinter.

Campbell, James E. 1986b. "Presidential Coattails and Midterm Losses in State Legislative Elections." *The American Political Science Review* 80(1):45–63.

Campbell, James E. and Joe A. Summers. 1990. "Presidential Coattails in Senate Elections." *The American Political Science Review* 84(2):513–24.

Campello de Souza, Maria do Carmo. 1987. "O Processo Político-Partidário na Primeira República." In Carlos Guilherme Mota, ed., *Brasil em Perspectiva* (16th ed.). São Paulo: Bertrand Brasil.

Campello de Souza, Maria do Carmo. 1994. "Aspectos políticos-institucionais do federalismo (1930–1964)." Unpublished manuscript, São Paulo.

Carey, John M. 1994. "Term Limits and Legislative Representation." Ph.D. diss. in political science, University of California at San Diego.

Carey, John M. 1996. *Term Limits and Legislative Representation.* Cambridge: Cambridge University Press.

Carey, John. 2002. "Electoral Reform and the Chilean Legislative System." In Scott Morgenstern and Benito Nacif, eds., *Legislatures and Democracy in Latin America.* New York: Cambridge University Press.

Carey, John and Gina Y. Reinhardt. 2001. "Coalition Brokers or Breakers? Governors and Legislative Voting in Brazil." Unpublished manuscript, Washington University at St. Louis.

Carey, John M. and Matthew S. Shugart. 1995. "Incentives to Cultivate a Personal Vote." *Electoral Studies* 14(4):417–35.

Carvalho, José Murilo de. 1993. "Federalismo y Centralización en el Imperio Brasileño: Historia y Argumento." In Marcello Carmagnani, ed., *Federalismos Latinoamericanos: México/Brasil/Argentina.* Mexico City: El Colegio de México/ Fondo de Cultura Económica.

Cavalcanti, Carlos E. G. and Waldemir Luiz de Quadros. 2000. "Economia do Setor Público." *Indicadores DIESP* 77:28–31 (March/April 2000).

Confederação Nacional de Indústria. 1998. *Cartilha da Reforma Tributária.* Brasília: CNI.

Confederação Nacional de Indústria. 1999a. *Reforma Tributária: Relatório Final da Comissão Especial da Câmara dos Deputados.* Brasília: CNI.

Confederação Nacional de Indústria. 1999b. "Desta vez sai." *CNI: Indústria e Produtividade* 32(313):26–38 (June).

Confederação Nacional de Indústria. 1999c. *Reforma Tributária Já. Pronunciamentos, Fernando Bezerra.* Brasília: CNI.

Confederação Nacional de Indústria. 2000. *Agenda Legislativa da Indústria.* Brasília: CNI.

Coppedge, Michael. 1994. *Strong Parties and Lame Ducks: Presidential Partyarchy and Factionalism in Venezuela.* Stanford: Stanford University Press.

Coutinho, Luciano Galvão. 1982. "Evolução da Administração Descentralizada em São Paulo." *Cadernos FUNDAP* 2(3):54–74.

Couto, Cláudio Gonçalves. 1997. "A Agenda Constituinte e a Difícil Governabilidade." *Lua Nova* 39:33–52.

Couto, Cláudio G. and Fernando L. Abrucio. 1995. "Governando a Cidade? A Força e Fraqueza da Câmara Municipal." *São Paulo em Perspectiva* 9(2):57–65.

Cox, Gary W. 1987. *The Efficient Secret.* New York: Cambridge University Press.

Cox, Gary W. 1997. *Making Votes Count: Strategic Coordination in the World's Electoral Systems.* Cambridge: Cambridge University Press.

Cox, Gary W. and Mathew D. McCubbins. 1993. *Legislative Leviathan: Party Government in the House.* Berkeley: University of California Press.

Crisp, Brian. 1999. *Democratic Institutional Design: The Powers and Incentives of Venezuelan Politicians and Interest Groups.* Stanford: Stanford University Press.

Dallari, Dalmo de Abreu. 1977. *O Pequeno Exército Paulista.* São Paulo: Editora Perspectiva.

Departamento Intersindical de Assessoria Parlamentar. 1988. *Quem foi Quem na Constituinte*. São Paulo: Cortez/Oboré.

Departamento Intersindical de Assessoria Parlamentar. 1992. *Boletim do DIAP*. No. 8. Brasília: Departamento Intersindical de Assessoria Parlamentar.

Departamento Intersindical de Assessoria Parlamentar. 2000. *Prefeitáveis 2000: Radiografia dos Deputados e Senadores Candidatos*. Série Atuação Parlamentar – Ano 1. Brasília: Departamento Intersindical de Assessoria Parlamentar.

Desposato, Scott. n.d. "Parties for Rent? Careerism, Ideology, and Party Switching in the Brazilian Chamber of Deputies." Unpublished paper, University of California at Los Angeles.

Dillinger, William and Steven B. Webb. 1999. "Fiscal Management in Federal Democracies: Argentina and Brazil." Policy Research Working Paper No. 2121, World Bank, Washington, DC.

Dimenstein, Gilberto, and Josias de Souza. 1994. *A História Real: Trama de uma Sucessão*. São Paulo: Editora Ática/Folha de São Paulo.

Diógenes, Glória Maria dos Santos. 1989. *As Eleições de 1954 e 1958 no Ceará: Os Partidos e Suas Lideranças*. Fortaleza: Edições UFC/Stylus.

Eaton, Kent. n.d. "The link between political and fiscal decentralization in Latin America." In Montero and Samuels, eds., forthcoming.

Epstein, David, David Brady, Sadafumi Kawato, and Sharyn O'Halloran. 1997. "A Comparative Approach to Legislative Organization: Careerism and Seniority in the United States and Japan." *American Journal of Political Science* 41(3): 965–98.

Fausto, Boris. 1987. "A Revolução de 1930." In Carlos Guilherme Mota, ed., *Brasil em Perspectiva* (16th ed.). São Paulo: Bertrand Brasil.

Ferejohn, John and Randall Calvert. 1984. "Presidential Coattails in Historical Perspective." *American Journal of Political Science* 28(1):127–46.

Figueiredo, Argelina and Fernando Limongi. 1994. "Mudança Constitucional, Desempenho do Legislativo e Consolidação Institucional." Paper presented at the XVIII Annual ANPOCS Meeting, Caxambú, Minas Gerais.

Figueiredo, Argelina and Fernando Limongi. 1996. "Congresso Nacional: Organização, Processo Legislativo e Produção Legal." *Cadernos de Pesquisa CEBRAP 5*.

Figueiredo, Argelina and Fernando Limongi. 1999. *Executivo e Legislativo na Nova Ordem Constitucional*. Rio de Janeiro: Editora da FGV.

Figueiredo, Argelina and Fernando Limongi. 2000a. "Presidential Power, Legislative Organization, and Party Behavior in Brazil." *Comparative Politics* (January): 151–70.

Figueiredo, Argelina and Fernando Limongi. 2000b. "Executivo e Legislativo na Formulação e Execução do Orçamento Federal." Paper presented at the second meeting of the Brazilian Political Science Association, São Paulo.

Figueiredo, Marcus. 1994. "Competição Eleitoral: Eleições Casadas, Resultados Solteiros." *Monitor Público* 2:21–7.

Filgueiras, Luiz. 2000. *História do Plano Real*. São Paulo: Boitempo Editorial.

Fiorina, Morris. 1977. *Congress: The Keystone of the Washington Establishment*. New Haven: Yale University Press.

Fleischer, David V., 1976. "Thirty Years of Legislative Recruitment in Brazil." Center of Brazilian Studies (Washington, D.C.) Occasional Papers Series No. 5.

Fleischer, David. V. 1981. "O Pluripartidismo no Brasil: Dimensões Sócio-Econômicas e Regionais do Recrutamento Político no Brasil, 1946–67." *Revista de Ciência Política* 24:49–75.

Fleischer, David V. 1990. "The Constituent Assembly and the Transformation Strategy: Attempts to Shift Political Power from the Presidency to the Congress." In Lawrence Graham and Robert Wilson, eds., *The Political Economy of Brazil: Public Policies in an Era of Transition*. Austin: University of Texas Press.

Freire, Aldenor Nunes. n.d. Eleições Municipais 1982. Fortaleza: N.P.

Fundação Getúlio Vargas (FGV), CPDOC. n.d. "Gabinete Civil da Presidência da República: Ministros-Chefes." Rio de Janeiro: FGV-CPDOC.

Garman, Christopher, Christiane Kerches da Silva Leite, and Moisés da Silva Marques. 2001. "Impactos das relações Banco Central versus bancos estaduais no arranjo federativo pós-1994: análise à luz do caso BANESPA." *Revista de Economia Política* 21(1):40–61.

Geddes, Barbara. 1994. *Politician's Dilemma: Building State Capacity in Latin America*. Berkeley: University of California Press.

Geddes, Barbara. 1995. "The Politics of Economic Liberalization." *Latin American Research Review* 30(2):195–214.

Geddes, Barbara and Artur Ribeiro Neto. 1992. "Institutional Sources of Corruption in Brazil." *Third World Quarterly* 13(4):641–61.

Giambiagi, Fábio. 2000. "A Política Fiscal depois de 2002: Algumas Simulações." *Revista do BNDES* 7(14):3–28.

Gierzynski, Anthony and David Breaux. 1993. "Money and the Party Vote in State House Elections." *Legislative Studies Quarterly* 18(4):515–33.

Gilmour, John B. and Paul Rothstein. 1996. "A Dynamic Model of Loss, Retirement, and Tenure in the US House of Representatives." *The Journal of Politics* 58(1):54–68.

Goés Consultores Associados. 1999. "Coligações Estaduais 1998." Unpublished document.

Gonçalves, Roberto John. 1995. "O Poder Oligárquico na Transição para o Neoliberalismo: Conservação, Mudança ou Metamorfose na Elite Política Piauiense de 1930 a 1994?" Unpublished manuscript, Universidade de São Paulo.

Gonçalves, Wilson Carvalho. 1992. *Dicionário Histórico-Biográfico Piauiense*. Teresina: Gráfica e Editora Junior.

Graham, Lawrence. 1990. *The State and Policy Outcomes in Latin America*. New York: Praeger.

Graham, Richard. 1990. *Patronage and Politics in 19th-Century Brazil*. Stanford: Stanford University Press.

Greggianin, Eugênio. 1997. "O Poder Legislativo e o Processo Orçamentário." Presented at the Conference "O Poder Legislativo e o Processo Orçamentário." Brasília: Câmara dos Deputados, Assessoria de Orçamento e Fiscalização Financeira.

Hagopian, Frances. 1996. *Traditional Politics and Regime Change in Brazil*. Cambridge: Cambridge University Press.

Hayama, Akira. 1992. "Incumbency Advantage in Japanese Elections." *Electoral Studies* 11(1):46–57.

Herrick, Rebekah and David L. Nixon. 1996. "Is There Life After Congress? Patterns and Determinants of Post-Congressional Careers." *Legislative Studies Quarterly* 21(4):489–99.

Hibbing, John R. 1998. "Legislative Careers: Why and How We Should Study Them." Paper prepared for the Shambaugh Conference on Comparative Legislative Research, Iowa City.

Hofmeister, Wilhelm, and José Mário Brasiliense Carneiro, eds. 2001. *Federalismo na Alemanha e no Brasil*. São Paulo: Konrad Adenauer Stiftung.

Instituto de Estudos Socio-Culturais. 1993a. *Informativo INESC*. Vol. 8(41).

Instituto de Estudos Socio-Culturais. 1993b. *Informativo INESC*. Vol. 7(32).

Instituto de Estudos Socio-Culturais. 1994. *Informativo INESC*. First semester 1994.

Instituto de Estudos Socio-Culturais. 1999. *Informativo INESC*. First semester 1998.

Jacobson, Gary. 1992. *The Politics of Congressional Elections* (3rd ed.). New York: HarperCollins.

Jones, Mark P. 1995. *Electoral Laws and the Survival of Presidential Democracies*. Notre Dame: University of Notre Dame Press.

Jones, Mark P. 1997. "Federalism and the Number of Parties in Argentine Congressional Elections." *The Journal of Politics* 59(2):538–49.

Jones, Mark. 2002. "Federalism and Party Discipline in the Argentine Congress." In Scott Morgenstern and Benito Nacif, eds., *Legislatures and Democracy in Latin America*. New York: Cambridge University Press.

Kandir, Antonio. 2001. "Breve nota sobre processos politico-legislativos em favor das reformas tributária e de mercado de capitais no Brasil." Paper presented at the Forum on Social Equity, Santiago de Chile, March 16–17.

Katz, Jonathan and Brian Sala. 1996. "Careerism, Committee Assignments, and the Electoral Connection." *American Political Science Review* 90:21–33.

Kernell, Samuel. 1977. "Toward Understanding 19th Century Congressional Careers: Ambition, Competition, and Rotation." *American Journal of Political Science* 21(4):669–93.

Kernell, Samuel. n.d. (a). "The Emergence of the Modern Political Career Structure in America." Unpublished manuscript, University of California, San Diego.

Kernell, Samuel. n.d. (b). "Ambition and Politics: An Exploratory Study of the Political Careers of 19th Century Congressmen." Unpublished manuscript, University of California, San Diego.

Kiewiet, D. Roderick and Mathew D. McCubbins. 1991. *The Logic of Delegation: Congressional Parties and the Appropriations Process*. Chicago: University of Chicago Press.

Kingstone, Peter, and Timothy Power, eds. 2000. *Democratic Brazil: Actors, Institutions, and Processes*. Pittsburgh: University of Pittsburgh Press.

Kopits, George, Juan Pablo Jiménez, and Alvaro Manoel. 2000. "Responsabilidad fiscal a nivel subnacional: Argentina y Brasil." Presented at the XII Seminario Regional de Política Fiscal, CEPAL, Santiago de Chile, 24 al 26 de enero del 2000.

Kugelmas, Eduardo. 1985. "Políticas Públicas na Administração Paulista: 1946–77." *Cadernos FUNDAP* 5(9):30–45.

Kugelmas, Eduardo. 2001. "A evolução recente do regime federativo no Brasil." In Hofmeister and Carneiro, eds., 2001.

Kugelmas, Eduardo, Brasílio Sallum Jr., and Eduardo Graeff. 1989. "Conflito federativo e transição política." *São Paulo em Perspectiva* 3:95–102.

Kugelmas, Eduardo and Lourdes Sola. n.d. "Recentralização/Descentralização – A Dinâmica do Regime Federativo no Brasil dos Anos 90." Unpublished manuscript.

Laakso, Markku and Rein Taagepera. 1979. "Effective Number of Parties: A Measure with Applicability to West Europe." *Comparative Political Studies* 12:3–27.

Langston, Joy. 1995. "Sobrevivir y prosperar: una búsqueda de las causas de las facciones políticas intrarrégimen en México." *Política y Gobierno* 2(2):243–77.

Lavareda, Antônio. 1991. *A Democracia nas Urnas: O Processo Partidário-Eleitoral Brasileiro.* Rio de Janeiro: IUPERJ/Rio Fundo Editora.

Leeds, Anthony, 1965. "Brazilian Careers and Social Structure: A Case History and a Model." In Dwight Heath and Richard Adams, eds., *Contemporary Cultures and Societies of Latin America.* New York: Random House.

Leme, Heládio J. de C. 1992. "O Federalismo na Constituição de 1988: Representação Política e a Distribuição de Recursos Tributários." Unpublished Master's thesis, Universidade Estadual de Campinas.

Lemenhe, Maria Auxiliadora. 1996. *Família, Poder, e Tradição: O(caso) dos Coronéis.* São Paulo: Annablume/Edições UFC.

Lemgruber Viol, Andréa. 2001. "O Fenômeno da Competição Tributária: Aspectos Teóricos e uma Análise do Caso Brasileiro." Brasília: Secretaria do Tesouro Nacional. Downloaded from www.stn.fazenda.gov.br.

Lenzi, Carlos Alberto Silveira. 1983. *Partidos e Políticos de Santa Catarina.* Florianópolis: Editora da UFSC.

Levin, J. 1991. "Measuring the Role of Subnational Governments." IMF Working Paper. Washington, DC: International Monetary Fund.

Levine, Martin D. and Mark S. Hyde. 1977. "Incumbency and the Theory of Political Ambition: A Rational-Choice Model." *Journal of Politics* 39:959–83.

Levine, Robert M. 1970. *The Vargas Regime: The Critical Years, 1934–38.* New York: Columbia University Press.

Levitt, S. and Snyder, J. 1997. The Impact of Federal Spending on House Election Outcomes. *Journal of Political Economy* 105(1):30–53.

Lijphart, Arend. 1990. "The Political Consequences of Electoral Laws, 1945–85." *American Political Science Review.* 84:481–96.

Lijphart, Arend. 1994. *Electoral Systems and Party Systems: A Study of Twenty-Seven Democracies, 1945–1990.* Oxford: Oxford University Press.

Lima, Edilberto Carlos Pontes. 1999. "Reforma tributária no Brasil: entre o ideal e o possível." Texto para discussão 666. Brasília: IPEA.

Lima Jr., Olavo Brasil de. 1983. *Partidos Políticos Brasileiros: A Experiência Federal e Regional: 1945–64.* Rio de Janeiro: Graal.

Lima Jr., Olavo Brasil de, ed. 1997. *O Sistema Partidário Brasileiro.* Rio de Janeiro: Fundação Getúlio Vargas.

Linz, Juan and Alfred Stepan. 1996. *Problems of Democratic Consolidation and Transition.* Baltimore: Johns Hopkins University Press.

Longo, Carlos Alberto. 1991. "O Processo Orçamentário no Brasil." *Revista de Economia Política* 11(2):78–91.

Love, Joseph L. 1980. *São Paulo in the Brazilian Federation, 1889–1937.* Stanford: Stanford University Press.

Love, Joseph L. 1993. "Federalismo y Regionalismo en Brasil, 1889–1937." In Marcello Carmagnani, ed., *Federalismos Latinoamericanos: México/Brasil/Argentina.* México City: Fondo de Cultura Económica/El Colegio de México.

Loyola, Maria, Andréa. 1980. *Os Sindicatos e o PTB: Estudo de um Caso em Minas Gerais*. Petrópolis: Editora Vozes/CEBRAP.

Mahar, Dennis J. 1971. "The Failures of Revenue Sharing in Brazil and Some Recent Developments." *Bulletin for International Fiscal Documentation* 25(3):71–9.

Mahar, Dennis J. and Fernando Rezende. 1975. "The Growth and Pattern of Public Expenditure in Brazil, 1920–1969." *Public Finance Quarterly* 3(4):380–99.

Mainwaring, Scott. 1995. "Brazil: Weak Parties, Feckless Democracy." In Scott Mainwaring and Timothy Scully, eds., *Building Democratic Institutions: Parties and Party Systems in Latin America*. Stanford: Stanford University Press.

Mainwaring, Scott. 1997. "Multipartism, Robust Federalism, and Presidentialism in Brazil." In Scott Mainwaring and Matthew Shugart, eds., *Presidentialism and Democracy in Latin America*. Cambridge: Cambridge University Press.

Mainwaring, Scott. 1999. *Party Systems in the Third Wave of Democratization: the Case of Brazil*. Stanford: Stanford University Press.

Mainwaring, Scott and David Samuels. 1997. "Federalism and Democracy in Brazil." Paper prepared for the Conference on Democracy and Federalism, Oxford University.

Mainwaring, Scott and Matthew S. Shugart. 1997. "Conclusion: Presidentialism and the Party System." In Mainwaring and Shugart, eds., *Presidentialism and Democracy in Latin America*. Cambridge: Cambridge University Press.

Mayhew, David. 1974. *Congress: The Electoral Connection*. New Haven: Yale University Press.

McCormick, Richard P. 1982. *The Presidential Game: Origins of American Politics*. New York: Oxford University Press.

Medeiros, Antônio Carlos de. 1986. "Politics and Intergovernmental Relations in Brazil, 1964–82." Ph.D. diss., London School of Economics. London: Garland Publishing.

Melhém, Célia Soibelmann. 1998. *Política de Botinas Amarelas: O MDB-PMDB Paulista de 1965 a 1988*. São Paulo: Editora Hucitec/Departamento de Ciência Política da USP.

Melo, Carlos Ranulfo Felix de. 2000. "Partidos e Migração Partidária na Câmara dos Deputados." *DADOS: Revista de Ciências Sociais* 43(2):207–39.

Melo, Marcus A. 1996. "O Jogo das Regras: A Política da Reforma Constitucional, 1993–96." Paper presented at the twentieth meeting of the ANPOCS, Caxambú, Minas Gerais.

Melo, Marcus A. 1998. "When Institutions Matter: The Politics of Administrative, Social Security, and Tax Reforms in Brazil." Presented at the twenty-first meeting of the Latin American Studies Association, Chicago.

Melo, Marcus A. 2000. "Institutional Obstacles to Market Reforms? The Politics of Tax Reform in Brazil." Presented at the twenty-second meeting of the Latin American Studies Association, Miami.

Melo, Marcus A. 2001. "Promessas In(críveis), Multidimensionalidade e aversão ao risco na reforma tributária." Chapter 5 from *O Jogo das Regras: As Reformas Constitucionais no Brasil*. Rio de Janeiro: Editora Revan.

Mendes, Marcos. 1999. "Lei de Responsabilidade Fiscal: Análise e Alternativas." Unpublished paper, Instituto Fernand Braudel de Economia Mundial.

Miranda, Sérgio. 2001. *Verdades e Mentiras da Lei de Responsabilidade Fiscal*. Brasília: Centro de Documentação e Informação, Coordenação de Publicações.

Montero, Alfred. 2000. "Devolving Democracy? Political Decentralization and the New Brazilian Federalism." In Kingstone and Power, eds., 2000.

Montero, Alfred. 2001. "Competitive Federalism and Distributive Conflict in Democratic Brazil." Paper Presented at the Bildner Center Conference on Brazil, Columbia University.

Montero, Alfred and David Samuels, eds. n.d. *Decentralization and Democracy in Latin America*. Forthcoming, University of Notre Dame Press.

Morgenstern, Scott. 2002. "US Models and Latin American Legislatures." In Morgenstern and Benito Nacif, eds., *Legislatures and Democracy in Latin America*. New York: Cambridge University Press.

Motta, João Ricardo. 1998. "A prorrogação do FEF." *Correio Braziliense*, November 25.

Nassif, Luis. 2000. "Defesa da Lei Kandir." *Folha de São Paulo*, March 4.

Nicolau, Jairo M. 1994. "Breves Comentários sobre as eleições de 1994 e o Quadro Partidário." *Cadernos de Conjuntura IUPERJ* #50 (June), 15–19.

Nicolau, Jairo. 1996. *Multipartidarismo e Democracia: Um Estudo Sobre o Sistema Partidário Brasileiro, 1985–94*. Rio de Janeiro: Fundação Getúlio Vargas.

Nicolau, Jairo M. 1998. *Dados Eleitorais do Brasil (1982–96)*. Rio de Janeiro: Editora Revan/IUPERJ/UCAM.

Nogueira, Júlio César de A. 1995. "O Financiamento Público e Decentralização Fiscal no Brasil." Texto para Discussão #34. Rio de Janeiro: CEPP.

Novaes, Carlos Alberto Marques. 1994. "Dinâmica Institucional da Representação." *Novos Estudos CEBRAP* 38:99–147.

Nunes, Edson de Oliveira. 1978. "Legislativo, Política e Recrutamento de Elites no Brasil." *Dados* 17:53–78.

Nunes Leal, Victor. 1975[1949]. *Coronelismo, Enxada e Voto: o Município e o Regime Representativo no Brasil*. São Paulo: Editora Alfa-Omega.

O Estado de São Paulo. 1996. "Relação dos candidatos a cargos municipais." Computer file.

Oliveira, Fabrício Augusto de. 1986. "O Sistema Fiscal Brasileiro: Evolução e Crise (1965/1985). Texto para Discussão No. 9. São Paulo: IESP/FUNDAP.

Oliveira, Fabrício Augusto de. 1995a. *Autoritarismo e Crise Fiscal no Brasil (1964–84)*. São Paulo: Editora Hucitec.

Oliveira, Fabrício Augusto de. 1995b. *Crise, Reforma e Desordem do Sistema Tributário Nacional*. Campinas: Editora da UNICAMP.

Oliveira, Luiz Guilherme de. 2000. *Federalismo e Guerra Fiscal*. São Paulo: Edições Pulsar.

Oliveira, Wéder de. 2000. "Lei de Responsabilidade Fiscal: Principais Aspectos Concernentes aos Municípios – Avaliação Preliminar." Brasília: Câmara dos Deputados, Consultoria de Orçamento e Fiscalização Financeira.

O'Neill, Kathleen. n.d. "Decentralization in Bolivia: Electoral Incentives and Outcomes." In Montero and Samuels, eds., forthcoming.

Ordeshook, Peter. 1996. "Russia's Party System: Is Russian Federalism Viable?" *Post-Soviet Affairs* 12 (July–September):195–217.

Packenham, Robert. 1990[1970]. "Legislatures and Political Development." In Philip Norton, ed., *Legislatures*. Oxford: Oxford University Press.

Palermo, Vicente. 2000. "Como se Governa o Brasil? O Debate sobre Instituições Políticas e Gestão de Governo." *Dados* 43(3):521–57.

Pandolfi, Dulce, ed. 1999. *Repensando o Estado Novo*. Rio de Janeiro: FGV.

Partido dos Trabalhadores. 2000. "Nota sobre o Fundo de Estabilização Fiscal." http://www.pt.org.br/assessor/fef.htm. Accessed on April 24, 2000.

Patzelt, Werner J. 1998. "Legislative Recruitment and Retention in Western Europe: What do we know, and what should we investigate in the future?" Paper prepared for the Shambaugh Comparative Legislative Research Conference, Iowa City.

Payne, James L. 1968. *Patterns of Conflict in Colombia*. New Haven: Yale University Press.

Pereira, Carlos and Bernardo Mueller. 2000. "Uma Teoria da Preponderância do Executivo: O Sistema de Comissões no Legislativo Brasileiro." *Revista Brasileira de Ciências Sociais* 15(43):45–68.

Pereira, Carlos and Lúcio Rennó. 2000. "Local and National Political Dynamics in the Brazilian Congress Elections [sic]." XXIV Encontro Anual da ANPOCS, Petrópolis, October.

Piazza, Walter F., ed. 1994. *Dicionário Político Catarinense* (2nd ed.). Florianópolis: Assembléia Legislativa do Estado de Santa Catarina.

Pinheiro, Vinícius Carvalho. 1996. "Inflação, Poder e Processo Orçamentário no Brasil – 1989 a 1993." *Revista do Serviço Público* 120(1):141–65.

Polsby, Nelson. 1968. "The Institutionalization of the US House of Representatives." *American Political Science Review* 62:144–68.

Polsby, Nelson, Miriam Gallagher, and Barry Rundquist. 1969. "The Growth of the Seniority System in the US House of representatives." *American Political Science Review* 63:787–807.

Popkin, Samuel. 1990. *The Reasoning Voter*. Chicago: University of Chicago Press.

Power, Timothy. 1998. "The Pen is Mightier than the Congress: Presidential Decree Power in Brazil." In Matthew S. Shugart and John M. Carey, eds. *Executive Decree Authority*. New York: Cambridge University Press.

Power, Timothy. 2000. "Political Institutions in Democratic Brazil: Politics as a Permanent Constitutional Convention." In Peter Kingstone and Timothy Power, eds., *Democratic Brazil: Actors, Institutions, and Processes*. Pittsburgh: University of Pittsburgh Press.

Price, H. Douglas. 1971. "The Congressional Career Then and Now." In Nelson Polsby, ed., *Congressional Behavior*. New York: Random House.

Price, H. Douglas. 1975. "Congress and the Evolution of Legislative 'Professionalism'." In Norman J. Ornstein, ed., *Congress and Change*. New York: Praeger.

Price, H. Douglas. 1977. "Careers and Committees in the American Congress: The Problem of Structural Change." In William Aydelotte, ed., *The History of Parliamentary Behavior*. Princeton: Princeton University Press.

Rae, Douglas. 1971. *The Political Consequences of Electoral Laws* (rev. ed.). New Haven: Yale University Press.

Ramseyer, J. Mark and Frances Rosenbluth. 1993. *Japan's Political Marketplace*. Cambridge, MA: Harvard University Press.

Rezende, Fernando. 1995. "Federalismo Fiscal no Brasil." *Revista de Economia Política* 15(3):5–17.

Rezende, Fernando. 1996. "O Processo da Reforma Tributária." *Texto para Discussão* 420. Rio de Janeiro: IPEA.

Rezende, Fernando. 2001. "Compensações financeiras e desequilíbrios fiscais na federação brasileira." In Wilhelm Hofmeister and José Mário Brasiliense Carneiro, eds., *Federalismo na Alemanha e no Brasil*. São Paulo: Konrad Adenauer Stiftung.

Rigolon, Francisco and Fábio Giambiagi. 1998. "Renegociação das dívidas estaduais: um novo regime fiscal ou a repetição de uma antiga história?" Unpublished manuscript, BNDES.

Rohde, David. 1979. "Risk-Bearing and Progressive Ambition: The Case of the United States House of Representatives." *American Journal of Political Science* 23(February):1–23.

Rohde, David. 1991. *Parties and Leaders in the Postreform House*. Chicago: University of Chicago Press.

Sá, William Carvalho de. 1993. "Rearranjo Federativo, Revisão Constitucional, e os Interesses de Minas." Sub-Projeto II.3 – Os Interesses Regionais e a Revisão Constitucional, Instituto de Estudos do Setor Público (unpublished). São Paulo: IESP.

Sallum Jr., Brasílio. 1996. "Folio." (CD-ROM). São Paulo: CEDEC.

Salomon, Marta. 2001. "Ao successor, a ábobora." *FSP* (June 15):A-2.

Sampaio, Regina. 1982. *Adhemar de Barros e o PSP*. São Paulo: Global Editora.

Samuels, David. 1999. "Incentives to Cultivate a Party Vote in Candidate-Centric Electoral Systems: Evidence from Brazil." *Comparative Political Studies* 32(4):487–518.

Samuels, David. 2000a. "Reinventing Local Government? The Evolution of Brazil's Municipalities." In Peter Kingstone and Timothy Power, eds., *Democratic Brazil*. Pittsburgh: University of Pittsburgh Press.

Samuels, David. 2000b. "Ambition and Competition: Explaining Turnover in the Brazilian Chamber of Deputies." *Legislative Studies Quarterly* 25(3):481–97.

Samuels, David. 2001a. "Money, Elections and Democracy in Brazil." *Latin American Politics and Society* 43(2):27–48.

Samuels, David. 2001b. "Incumbents and Challengers on a Level Playing Field: Assessing the Impact of Campaign Finance in Brazil." *The Journal of Politics* 63(2):569–84.

Samuels, David. 2001c. "Does Money Matter? Campaign Finance in Newly Democratic Countries: Theory and Evidence from Brazil." *Comparative Politics* 34 (October).

Samuels, David and Fernando Abrucio. 2001. "The 'New' Politics of the Governors: Federalism and the Brazilian Transition to Democracy." *Publius: The Journal of Federalism* 30(2):43–61.

Sanches, Oswaldo Maldonado. 1993. "O Ciclo Orçamentário: uma Reavaliação à Luz da Constituição de 1988." *Revista de Administração Pública* 27(4):54–76.

Sanches, Oswaldo Maldonado. 1995. "Processo Orçamentário Federal: Problemas, Causas e Indicativos de Solução." *Revista de Administração Pública* 29(3):122–56.

Sanches, Oswaldo Maldonado. 1996. "A Participação do Poder Legislativo na Análise e Aprovação do Orçamento." *Revista de Informação Legislativa* 33(131):59–77.

Santos, André Marenco dos. 1995. "Nas fronteiras do campo político: raposas e outsiders no Congresso Nacional." Unpublished manuscript, Universidade Federal do Rio Grande do Sul.

Santos, Fabiano M. 1998. "Recruitment and Retention of Legislators in Brazil." *Legislative Studies Quarterly* 24(2).

Santos, Fabiano M. 1999. "Party Leaders and Committee Assignments in Brazil." Paper presented at the 1999 Annual Meeting of the American Political Science Association, Atlanta, September.

Santos, Luiz Alberto dos. 1996. "A Organização de Planos de Carreira no Serviço Público Federal – Evolução, Conceitos, Limites e Possibilidades." Unpublished Master's thesis, Universidade Nacional de Brasília.

Santos, Maria Helena de Castro, et al. 1997. "O jogo orçamentário da União: relações Executivo – Legislativo na terra do *pork-barrel.*" In Eli Diniz and Sérgio de Azevedo, eds., *Reforma do Estado e Democracia no Brasil.* Brasília: Editora da UnB/ENAP.

Santos, Milton. 1994. *A Urbanização Brasileira* (2nd ed.). São Paulo: Editora Hucitec.

Sautheir, Elir. 1993. *Santa Catarina: O Estado Político – 1993.* Florianópolis: Editora Papa-Livro.

Schlesinger, Joseph. 1966. *Ambition and Politics: Political Careers in the United States.* Chicago: Rand McNally.

Schlesinger, Joseph. 1991. *Political Parties and the Winning of Office.* Chicago: University of Chicago Press.

Schmitt, Rogério. 1999. "Migração Partidária e Reeleição na Câmara dos Deputados." *Novos Estudos CEBRAP* 54:127–46.

Schmitter, Phillippe. 1973. "The 'Portugalization' of Brazil?" In Alfred Stepan, ed., *Authoritarian Brazil: Origins, Policies, Future.* New Haven: Yale University Press.

Schwartzman, Simon. 1975. *São Paulo e o Estado Nacional.* São Paulo: DIFEL.

Selcher, Wayne. 1998. "The Politics of Decentralized Federalism, National Diversification, and Regionalism in Brazil." *Journal of Interamerican Studies and World Affairs* 40(4):25–50.

Serra, José. 1993. "As Vicissitudes do Orçamento." *Revista de Economia Política* 13(4):143–9.

Serra, José. 1994. *Orçamento no Brasil* (2nd ed.). São Paulo: Atual Editora.

Shugart, Matthew S. 1995. "The Electoral Cycle and Institutional Sources of Divided Presidential Government." *American Political Science Review* 89:327–43.

Shugart, Matthew S. and John M. Carey. 1992. *Presidents and Assemblies: Constitutional Design and Electoral Dynamics.* New York: Cambridge University Press.

Silva Fernandes, André Eduardo da e Nélio Lacerda Wanderlei. 2000. "A Questão da Guerra Fiscal: uma Breve Resenha." *Revista da Informação Legislativa* 37(148):5–20.

Skidmore, Thomas E. 1967. *Politics in Brazil, 1930–64: An Experiment in Democracy.* Oxford: Oxford University Press.

Smith, Peter H. 1979. *Labyrinths of Power: Political Recruitment in Twentieth-Century Mexico.* Princeton: Princeton University Press.

Soares, Gláucio A. D. 1973. *Sociedade e Política no Brasil.* São Paulo: DIFEL.

Sola, Lourdes. 1987. "O Golpe de 1937 e o Estado Novo." In Motta, ed., 1998.

Sonnewend, Paulo. 1975. "O Evolver das Secretarias de Estado na Administração Paulista, desde 1892 até 1974." *Administração Paulista* 26:49–61.

Sonnewend, Paulo. 1976. "O Evolver das Secretarias de Estado na Administração Paulista, desde 1892 até 1975." *Administração Paulista* 27:13–15.

Souza, Amaury de. 1999. "Cardoso and the Struggle for Reform in Brazil." *Journal of Democracy* 10(3):49–63.

Souza, Celina. 1994. "Political and Financial Decentralisation in Democratic Brazil." *Local Government Studies* 20(4):588–609.

Souza, Celina. 1996. "Redemocratization and Decentralisation in Brazil: The Strength of the Member States." *Development and Change* 27:529–55.

Souza, Paulo Cézar R. da. 2001. "Inflação Annual (em %)." From "Site dos Índices," http//:geocities.com/Paris/Rue/5045/INFLA1.HTM. Accessed on July 17, 2001.

Stepan, Alfred. 1997. "Towards a New Theory of Federalism and Democracy." Paper presented at the Conference on Democracy and Federalism, Oxford University.

Stepan, Alfred. 1999. "Para uma Nova Análise Comparativa do Federalismo e da Democracia: Federações que Restringem ou Ampliam o Poder do Demos." *Dados* 42(2):197–251.

Taagepera, Rein and Matthew S. Shugart. 1989. *Seats and Votes: The Effects and Determinants of Electoral Systems*. New Haven: Yale University Press.

Tavares, Martus, Álvaro Manoel, José Roberto Rodrigues Afonso, and Selene Peres Peres Nunes. 1999. "Principles and Rules in Public Finance: The Proposal of the Fiscal Repsonsibilities Law in Brazil." Revised version of a paper presented at CEPAL's XI Regional Seminar on Fiscal Policy, Brasília, January 1999.

Teixeira, Tomaz. 1983(?). *A Outra Face da Oligarquia do Piauí*. Teresina: N.P.

Tendler, Judith. 1996. *Good Government in the Tropics*. Baltimore: The Johns Hopkins University Press.

Treisman, Daniel. 1999. *After the Deluge: Regional Crises and Political Consolidation in Russia*. Ann Arbor: University of Michigan Press.

Tsebelis, George. 1990. *Nested Games: Rational Choice in Comparative Politics*. Berkeley: University of California Press.

Varsano, Ricardo. 1996. "A Evolução do Sistema Tributário Brasileiro ao Longo do Século: Anotações e Reflexões para Futuras Reformas." Texto para Discussão #405. Rio de Janeiro: IPEA.

Varsano, Ricardo. 1997. "A Evolução do Sistema Tributário Brasileiro ao Longo do Século: Anotações e Reflexões para Futuras Reformas." *Pesquisa e Planejamento Econômico* 27(1):1–46.

Velloso, Raúl. 1993. "Origens e dimensões da crise fiscal brasileira." *Estudos Econômicos* 23:17–34.

Verner, Joel. 1975. "The Structure of Public Careers of Brazilian Legislators, 1963–1970." *International Journal of Comparative Sociology*. 16(1–2):64–80.

Weingast, Barry. 1979. "A Rational Choice Perspective on Congressional Norms." *American Journal of Political Science* 23:245–64.

Weingast, Barry. 1995. "The Economic Role of Political Institutions: Market-Preserving Federalism and Economic Development." *Journal of Law, Economics, and Organization* 11:1–31.

Weldon, Jeffrey A. 1997. "The Political Sources of *Presidencialismo* in Mexico." In Scott Mainwaring and Matthew Soberg Shugart, eds. *Presidentialism and Democracy in Latin America*. New York: Cambridge University Press.

Werneck, Rogério. 1995. "Federalismo Fiscal e Política de Estabilização no Brasil." *Revista Brasileira de Economia*. 49(2):375–90.

Weyland, Kurt. 2000. "The Brazilian State in the New Democracy." In Kingstone and Power, eds., 2000.

Willis, Eliza, Stephan Haggard, and Christopher Garman. 1999. "The Politics of Decentralization in Latin America." *Latin American Research Review* 34(1):73–102.
Wirth, John D. 1970. *The Politics of Brazilian Development*. Stanford: Stanford University Press.
Wirth, John D. 1977. *Minas Gerais in the Brazilian Federation, 1889–1937*. Stanford: Stanford University Press.
Young, James Sterling. 1966. *The Washington Community 1800–1828*. New York: Columbia University Press.

GOVERNMENT AND RELATED DOCUMENTS

Brasil. 1987(?). 'Projetos de Constituição (Quadro Comparativo). Brasília: Gráfica do Senado Federal (?).
Brasil. Câmara dos Deputados. 1974–1994. *Anais da Câmara dos Deputados*. Brasília: Câmara dos Deputados.
Brasil. Câmara dos Deputados. 1979. *Deputados Brasileiros: Repertório Biográfico, 46ª Legislatura, 1979–83*. Brasília: Câmara dos Deputados.
Brasil. Câmara dos Deputados. 1981. *Deputados Brasileiros 1945–67*. Brasília: Câmara dos Deputados.
Brasil. Câmara dos Deputados. 1983. *Deputados Brasileiros: Repertório Biográfico, 47ª Legislatura, 1983–86*. Brasília: Câmara dos Deputados.
Brasil. Câmara dos Deputados. 1987. *Eleições de 15 de Novembro de 1986: Candidatos e Votos Obtidos*. Brasília: Centro de Documentação e Informação, Coordenaçao de Publicações, Câmara dos Deputados.
Brasil. Câmara dos Deputados. 1989. *Deputados Brasileiros: Repertório Biográfico, 48ª Legislatura, 1987–91*. Brasília: Câmara dos Deputados.
Brasil. Câmara dos Deputados. 1991. *Deputados Brasileiros: Repertório Biográfico, 49ª Legislatura, 1991–95*. Brasília: Câmara dos Deputados.
Brasil. Câmara dos Deputados. 1994. *Regimento Interno da Câmara dos Deputados*. 3rd ed. Brasília: Câmara dos Deputados/CDI/CP.
Brasil. Câmara dos Deputados. 1995. *Deputados Brasileiros: Repertório Biográfico, 50ª Legislatura, 1995–99*. Brasília: Câmara dos Deputados.
Brasil. Câmara dos Deputados. Secretaria-Geral da Mesa. 1987–2001. "Quadro de Titulares e Suplentes." Brasília: CD/SGM/NI.
Brasil. Câmara dos Deputados. Secretaria-Geral da Mesa. 1991–2001. "Mudanças de Partido." Brasília: CD/SGM/NI.
Brasil. Câmara dos Deputados. AOFF/CD. 1997. "Emendas ao Orçamento Aprovadas pelo Congresso Nacional." Unpublished report. Brasília: PRODASEN/AOFF/CD.
Brasil. Congresso Nacional. 1979. *Anais da Câmara dos Deputados*. Vol. 5, No. 16 (Supplement). Brasília: Congresso Nacional.
Brasil. Congresso Nacional. 1997. Comissão Mista de Planos, Orçamentos Públicos e Fiscalização. "Proposta Orçamentária da União para 1997: Reuniões Regionais." Brasília: Congresso Nacional.
Brasil. Congresso Nacional. 1998. "Sessão Conjunta de 22/5/98, Ano 53, No. 12." Brasília: Congresso Nacional.

Brasil. Congresso Nacional. 1999. "Acompanhamento da Execução Orçamentária da União – 1998." At www.camara.gov.br. Adobe Acrobat file.
Brasil. Congresso Nacional. 2000a. "Acompanhamento da Execução Orçamentária da União – 1999." At www.camara.gov.br. Adobe Acrobat file.
Brasil. Congresso Nacional. 2000b. "Emendas dos Parlamentares à Lei Orçamentária de 1998." Brasília: Comissão Mista do Orçamento. Microsoft Access file.
Brasil. Congresso Nacional. 2000c. "Emendas dos Parlamentares à Lei Orçamentária de 1999." Brasília: Comissão Mista do Orçamento. Microsoft Access file.
Brasil. Congresso Nacional. 2001a. "Emendas dos Parlamentares à Lei Orçamentária de 2000." Brasília: Comissão Mista do Orçamento. Microsoft Access file.
Brasil. Ministério da Administração Federal e Reforma do Estado. 1996. *Boletim Estatístico Mensal* 1(8). Brasília: MARE.
Brasil. Ministério da Fazenda, Secretaria da Receita Federal. 2000a. "Participação percentual no PIB (1985–1999)." Microsoft Excel file, download from www.receita.fazenda.gov.br.
Brasil. Ministério da Fazenda, Secretaria da Receita Federal. 2000b. "Transferências constitucionais das receitas líquidas." Microsoft Excel file, download from www.receita.fazenda.gov.br.
Brasil. Ministério da Fazenda, Secretaria da Receita Federal. 2000c. "Carga Fiscal 1999 – Arrecadação Tributária." Microsoft Excel file, download from www.receita.fazenda.gov.br.
Brasil. Ministério da Fazenda, Secretaria da Receita Federal. 2000d. "Quadro III – Arrecadação das Receitas Federais – Variação percentual (1995 a 1999 – preços de dezembro/99 – IGP-DI)". Microsoft Excel file, download from www.receita.fazenda.gov.br.
Brasil. Ministério da Fazenda, Secretaria da Receita Federal. 2000e. "Tabela 1 – Carga Tributária Bruta em Milhões de Moeda Corrente." Microsoft Excel file, download from www.receita.fazenda.gov.br.
Brasil. Ministério da Fazenda, Secretaria da Receita Federal. 2001a. "Carga Tributária do Brasil – 2000 (texto)." Download from www.receita.fazenda.gov.br.
Brasil. Ministério da Fazenda, Secretaria da Receita Federal. 2001b. "Carga Tributária do Brasil – 2000 (tabelas)." Microsoft Excel File. Download from www.receita.fazenda.gov.br.
Brasil. Ministério da Fazenda, Secretaria do Tesouro Nacional. 1997. "Transferências Negociadas a Estados e Municípios, Comparativo 1995 e 1996." Brasilia: MINFAZ/STN/CONED.
Brasil. Ministério da Fazenda, Secretaria do Tesouro Nacional. 2000. "Fundo de Participação dos Estados e Municípios – 1999." Microsoft Excel file, download from www.stn.fazenda.gov.br.
Brasil. Ministério da Fazenda, Secretaria do Tesouro Nacional. 2001a. "LRF: Municípios homologados." Microsoft Excel file, download from www.tesouro.fazenda.gov.br/contasmunicipais/default.htm.
Brasil. Ministério da Fazenda, Secretaria do Tesouro Nacional. 2001b. "LRF: Municípios pendentes." Microsoft Excel file, download from www.tesouro.fazenda.gov.br.
Brasil. Ministério da Fazenda, Secretaria do Tesouro Nacional. 2001c. "Fundo de Participação dos Estados 1991–2000." Microsoft Excel file, download from www.tesouro.fazenda.gov.br.

Brasil. Ministério da Fazenda, Secretaria do Tesouro Nacional. 2001d. "Fundo de Participação dos Municípios 1991–2000." Microsoft Excel file, download from www.tesouro.fazenda.gov.br.

Brasil. Ministério da Fazenda, Secretaria do Tesouro Nacional. 2001e. "Desoneração ICMS – LC87/96 – Estados." Microsoft Excel file, download from www.tesouro. fazenda.gov.br.

Brasil. Ministério da Fazenda, Secretaria do Tesouro Nacional. 2001f. "Desoneração ICMS – LC87/96 – Municípios." Microsoft Excel file, download from www. tesouro.fazenda.gov.br.

Brasil. Senado Federal. 1997. "Emendas às Leis Orçamentárias Anuais, 1992–97." Brasília: PRODASEN. Microsoft Access database.

Brasil. Senado Federal. 1991–99. Secretaria-Geral da Mesa. "Commissão Mista de Planos, Orçamentos Públicos e Fiscalização." (Committee membership rolls) Brasília: SF/SGM.

Brasil. Senado Federal. 2001. *Constituição da República Federativa do Brasil.* Brasília: Centro Gráfico do Senado Federal.

Brasil. Tribunal Superior Eleitoral. 1945–74, 1982. *Dados Estatísticos: Eleições Federais, Estaduais, e Municipais.* Vols. 1–14. Rio de Janeiro: Departamento de Imprensa Nacional.

Brasil. Tribunal Superior Eleitoral. 1978. "Relação dos Candidatos Eleitos e Não-Eleitos, Eleições Proporcionais de 1978." Brasília: Tribunal Superior Eleitoral (photocopied results).

Brasil. Tribunal Superior Eleitoral. 1986. No title. Mimeographed election returns for federal deputy from state Regional Electoral Tribunals. Brasília: TSE.

Brasil. Tribunal Superior Eleitoral. 1989. "Resultados da Eleição para Presidente da República" (computer file). Brasília: TSE.

Brasil. Tribunal Superior Eleitoral. 1990. "Resultados das Eleições de 1990" (computer file). Brasília: TSE.

Brasil. Tribunal Superior Eleitoral. 1991. "Eleições de 1990" (computer files). Brasília: Tribunal Superior Eleitoral.

Brasil. Tribunal Superior Eleitoral. 1993. "Eleições de 1992" (computer files). Brasília: Tribunal Superior Eleitoral.

Brasil. Tribunal Superior Eleitoral. 1995. "Resultados das Eleições de 1994" (computer files). Brasília: TSE.

Brasil. Tribunal Superior Eleitoral. 1997a. "Eleições de 1996" (computer files). Brasília: Tribunal Superior Eleitoral.

Brasil. Tribunal Superior Eleitoral. 1997b. "Relação dos Partidos Políticos." Coordenação de Recursos e Informações Processuais (computer files). Brasília: Tribunal Superior Eleitoral.

Brasil. Tribunal Superior Eleitoral. 1997c. Sistema de Controle de Recursos Arrecados – SISCRA (computer files). Brasília: TSE/SCI.

Brasil. Tribunal Superior Eleitoral. 1999. "Eleições de 1998" (computer files). Brasília: Tribunal Superior Eleitoral.

Brasil. Tribunal Superior Eleitoral. 2000. Financiadores de Campanha 1998 (computer files). Brasília: TSE/SCI.

Ceará. 1976. *Eleições Municipais 1976.* Fortaleza: Imprensa Oficial do Ceará.

Ceará. Tribunal de Contas dos Municípios. 1973. *Conselheiro de Contas dos Municípios.* Fortaleza: Tribunal de Contas dos Municípios-CE.

Ceará. Tribunal de Contas dos Municípios. 1977. *Revista do Conselho de Contas dos Municípios do Ceará.* Vol. 5. Fortaleza: Tribunal de Contas do Estado-CE.

Ceará. Tribunal de Contas dos Municípios. 1982. *Informativa Tribunal de Contas dos Municípios.* Vol. 1. Fortaleza: Tribunal de Contas dos Municípios-CE.

Ceará. Tribunal Regional Eleitoral. 1947–85. "Arquivo: Atas de Apuração das Eleições Municipais." Fortaleza: Tribunal Regional Eleitoral-CE.

Ceará. Tribunal Regional Eleitoral. 1982. "Eleição de 1982: Resultado Geral Estado do Ceará." Fortaleza: Tribunal Regional Eleitoral-CE.

Ceará. Tribunal Regional Eleitoral. 1982–97. Fichário: Membros dos Diretórios Municipais e Regionais. Fortaleza: Tribunal Regional Eleitoral-CE.

Ceará. Tribunal Regional Eleitoral. 1986. "Eleição de 1986: Classificação Final dos Candidatos por Partido." Fortaleza: Tribunal Regional Eleitoral-CE.

Ceará. Tribunal Regional Eleitoral. 1992. "Eleições Municipais" (computer file). Fortaleza: Tribunal Regional Eleitoral-CE.

Ceará. Tribunal Regional Eleitoral/Assembléia Legislativa do Ceará. 1988. *Eleições Municipais 1988.* Fortaleza: Tribunal Regional Eleitoral-CE/ALCE.

Ceará. Tribunal Regional Eleitoral/Assembléia Legislativa do Ceará. 1996. *Eleições Municipais 1996.* Fortaleza: Tribunal Regional Eleitoral-CE/ALCE.

Federal Elections Commission. 1998. "Candidate Expenditures for House and Senate Races, 1982–96." At www.fec.gov/press/canye96.htm.

Goiás. Tribunal de Contas do Estado. 1956. "Parecer Prévio Sobre as Contas do Governador do Estado." Goiânia: TCE-GO.

Goiás. Tribunal de Contas do Estado. 1967. *Regimento Interno do Tribunal de Contas do Estado.* Goiânia: TCE-GO.

Goiás. Tribunal Regional Eleitoral. 1972. "Arquivo: Atas de Apuração, Eleições de 1972." Goiânia: Tribunal Regional Eleitoral-GO.

Goiás. Tribunal Regional Eleitoral. 1982. "Arquivo: Atas de Apuração, Eleições de 1982." Goiânia: Tribunal Regional Eleitoral-GO.

Goiás. Tribunal Regional Eleitoral. 1982–97. Arquivo: Livros de Registro de Diretório de Partido. Goiânia: Tribunal Regional Eleitoral-GO.

Goiás. Tribunal Regional Eleitoral. 1988. "Arquivo: Atas de Apuração, Eleições de 1988." Goiânia: Tribunal Regional Eleitoral-GO.

Goiás. Tribunal Regional Eleitoral. n.d. "Relação de Prefeitos de Goiânia." Goiânia: Tribunal Regional Eleitoral-GO.

Inter-American Development Bank. 1997. "Brazil: Synthesis of State Finance Studies." Discussion paper, Regional Operations Department. Washington, DC: IDB.

International Monetary Fund. 1998. "Brazil: Recent Economic Developments." Unpublished manuscript. Washington, DC: IMF.

Minas Gerais. Tribunal Regional Eleitoral. 1966. "Eleições Municipais de 1966" (photocopied results). Belo Horizonte: Tribunal Regional Eleitoral-MG.

Minas Gerais. Tribunal Regional Eleitoral. 1970. "Eleições Municipais de 1970" (photocopied results). Belo Horizonte: Tribunal Regional Eleitoral-MG.

Minas Gerais. Tribunal Regional Eleitoral. 1972. "Eleições Municipais de 1972" (photocopied results). Belo Horizonte: Tribunal Regional Eleitoral-MG.

Minas Gerais. Tribunal Regional Eleitoral. 1976. "Eleições Municipais de 1976" (photocopied results). Belo Horizonte: Tribunal Regional Eleitoral-MG.

Minas Gerais. Tribunal Regional Eleitoral. 1982–97. Archive: Documentation Regarding Registries of State Party Directories. Belo Horizonte: Tribunal Regional Eleitoral-MG.

Minas Gerais. Tribunal Regional Eleitoral. 1997a. "Eleições de 1945" (computer file). Belo Horizonte: Tribunal Regional Eleitoral-MG.

Minas Gerais. Tribunal Regional Eleitoral. 1997b. "Eleições de 1947" (computer file). Belo Horizonte: Tribunal Regional Eleitoral-MG.

Minas Gerais. Tribunal Regional Eleitoral. 1997c. "Eleições de 1949" (computer file). Belo Horizonte: Tribunal Regional Eleitoral-MG.

Minas Gerais. Tribunal Regional Eleitoral. 1997d. "Eleições de 1950" (computer file). Belo Horizonte: Tribunal Regional Eleitoral-MG.

Minas Gerais. Tribunal Regional Eleitoral. 1997e. "Eleições de 1954" (computer file). Belo Horizonte: Tribunal Regional Eleitoral-MG.

Minas Gerais. Tribunal Regional Eleitoral. 1997f. "Eleições de 1958" (computer file). Belo Horizonte: Tribunal Regional Eleitoral-MG.

Minas Gerais. Tribunal Regional Eleitoral. 1997g. "Eleições de 1963" (computer file). Belo Horizonte: Tribunal Regional Eleitoral-MG.

Minas Gerais. Tribunal Regional Eleitoral. 1997h. "Eleições de 1982" (computer files). Belo Horizonte: Tribunal Regional Eleitoral-MG.

Minas Gerais. Tribunal Regional Eleitoral. 1997i. "Eleições de 1985" (computer file). Belo Horizonte: Tribunal Regional Eleitoral-MG.

Minas Gerais. Tribunal Regional Eleitoral. 1997j. "Eleições de 1986" (computer file). Belo Horizonte: Tribunal Regional Eleitoral-MG.

Minas Gerais. Tribunal Regional Eleitoral. 1997k. "Eleições de 1988" (computer files). Belo Horizonte: Tribunal Regional Eleitoral-MG.

Minas Gerais. Tribunal Regional Eleitoral. 1997l. "Eleições de 1990" (computer files). Belo Horizonte: Tribunal Regional Eleitoral-MG.

Minas Gerais. Tribunal Regional Eleitoral. 1997m. "Eleições de 1992" (computer files). Belo Horizonte: Tribunal Regional Eleitoral-MG.

Piauí. 1984. *Relação de Autoridades*. Teresina: COMEPI.

Piauí. Tribunal de Contas do Estado. 1946. *Regimento Interno*. Teresina: Imprensa Oficial.

Piauí. Tribunal de Contas do Estado. 1961. *Revista de Tribunal de Contas do Estado*. Teresina.

Piauí. Tribunal de Contas do Estado. 1995. *Revista de Tribunal de Contas do Estado*. Teresina.

Piauí. Tribunal Regional Eleitoral. 1997a. "Relação dos Partidos Políticos que Obtiveram Representação Parlamentar no Congresso Nacional nos Pleitos de 1982 a 1994." Teresina: Tribunal Regional Eleitoral-PI.

Piauí. Tribunal Regional Eleitoral. 1997b. "Relação dos Prefeitos e Vice-Prefeitos Eleitos no Estado do Piauí, 1970–1996." Teresina: Tribunal Regional Eleitoral-PI.

Santa Catarina. 1947. *Constituição do Estado de Santa Catarina*. Florianópolis: Imprensa Oficial.

Santa Catarina. Tribunal Regional Eleitoral. 1946–92. "Arquivo: Atas de Apuração, Eleições Municipais." Florianópolis: Tribunal Regional Eleitoral-SC.

Santa Catarina. Tribunal Regional Eleitoral. 1982–97. "Arquivo: Requerimentos: Pedidos de Registro de Diretórios Regionais." Florianópolis: Tribunal Regional Eleitoral-SC.

Santa Catarina. Tribunal Regional Eleitoral. 1990. "Eleições 1990 – Deputado Estadual, Resultado Final." Florianópolis: Tribunal Regional Eleitoral-SC.

Santa Catarina. Tribunal Regional Eleitoral. 1997. "Eleições Municipais de 1996" (computer files). Florianópolis: Tribunal Regional Eleitoral-SC.

São Paulo. Fundação do Desenvolvimento Administrativo. (various years). *Perfil da Administração Paulista.* São Paulo: FUNDAP/Secretaria da Administração e Modernização do Serviço Público.

São Paulo. Instituto de Economia do Setor Público. 1992. "As Finanças Públicas dos Estados durante o Período 1980–89." Projeto IESP/FUNDAP p0109: Estudo das Finanças de Estados e Municípios 1980–9. São Paulo: Instituto de Economia do Setor Público.

São Paulo. Instituto de Economia do Setor Público. 1993. "Os Interesses Regionais e a Revisão Constitucional" (Unpublished collection). São Paulo: IESP.

São Paulo. Tribunal de Contas do Estado. 1957–97. *Revista do Tribunal de Contas do Estado de São Paulo: Jurisprudência e Instruções.* Vols. 1–81. São Paulo: Tribunal de Contas do Estado-SP.

São Paulo. Tribunal Regional Eleitoral-SP. 1945–72. "Arquivo: Atas de Apuração, Eleições Municipais." São Paulo: Tribunal Regional Eleitoral-SP.

São Paulo. Tribunal Regional Eleitoral-SP. 1945–72. 1982–97. "Arquivo: Relação de Diretórios Municipais e Regionais." São Paulo: Tribunal Regional Eleitoral-SP.

São Paulo. Tribunal Regional Eleitoral/SEADE. 1996. "Eleições no Estado de São Paulo, 1974–94" (computer database). São Paulo: Tribunal Regional Eleitoral-SP/SEADE.

Universidade Federal de Minas Gerais/Assembléia Legislativa de Minas Gerais. 1994. *Dicionário Político-Biográfico de Minas Gerais.* Belo Horizonte: UFMG/ALMG.

Universidade Federal do Ceará. 1995. *O Nordeste nos Debates da Constituinte: Catálogo dos Depoimentos.* Fortaleza: UFC/BNB.

World Bank. 1997. *Decentralization in Latin America: Learning Through Experience.* Washington DC: World Bank.

NEWSPAPERS AND MAGAZINES

Correio Braziliense
Economist
Estado de Minas
Folha de São Paulo
Gazeta Mercantil
Istoé
Jornal de Brasília
Jornal do Brasil
Jornal da Câmara
New York Times
O Estado de São Paulo
O Globo
O Paraná
Veja

Author Index

Subject Index